*Charand-o Parand*

World Thought in Translation

A joint project of Yale University Press and the MacMillan Center for International and Area Studies at Yale University, World Thought in Translation makes important works of classical and contemporary political, philosophical, legal, and social thought from outside the Western tradition available to English-speaking scholars, students, and general readers. The translations are annotated and accompanied by critical introductions that orient readers to the background in which these texts were written, their initial reception, and their enduring influence within and beyond their own cultures. World Thought in Translation contributes to the study of religious and secular intellectual traditions across cultures and civilizations.

Series editors

Steven Angle
Karuna Mantena
Andrew March
Paulina Ochoa
Ian Shapiro

# Charand-o Parand

Revolutionary Satire from Iran, 1907–1909

Ali-Akbar Dehkhodā

Translated and with an introduction and notes
by Janet Afary and John R. Perry

Yale UNIVERSITY PRESS
New Haven and London

This publication was made possible in part by a grant from the Carnegie Corporation of New York. The statements made and views expressed are solely the responsibility of the authors.

Published with assistance from the Louis Stern Memorial Fund.

Yale University Press books may be purchased in quantity for educational, business, or promotional use. For information, please e-mail sales.press@yale .edu (U.S. office) or sales@yaleup.co.uk (U.K. office).

Set in Adobe Caslon Pro type by Newgen North America.
Printed in the United States of America.

Library of Congress Control Number: 2015951236
ISBN 978-0-300-19799-0 (cloth : alk. paper)

A catalogue record for this book is available from the British Library.

This paper meets the requirements of ANSI/NISO Z39.48–1992 (Permanence of Paper).

10 9 8 7 6 5 4 3 2 1

# Contents

# Acknowledgments

A grant in 2010 from the Farhang Foundation in Los Angeles enabled us to undertake this project. We offer our special thanks to Mark Amin, Ladan Behnia, Haleh Emrani, Shahzad Ghanbari, Ahmad Gramian, Fasha Mahjoor, Mehran Mavaddat, Houshang Pak, Ali Razi, and Shidan Taslimi from Farhang for their unwavering support and encouragement. A sabbatical leave from the University of California, Santa Barbara, in spring 2013 also supported Janet Afary's work on this project. Our research was conducted primarily in the Regenstein Library of the University of Chicago and in the University of California library system. Meryle Gaston at the UCSB library, David Hirsch at the Research Library of the University of California, Los Angeles, and Marlis Saleh at Regenstein Library were most helpful in obtaining and locating relevant books and journals.

Tracing both the numerous individuals mentioned in the essays and obscure incidents from more than a century ago sometimes proved daunting. Here Willem Floor and Hasan Javadi (whose publications alone were a gold mine) provided enthusiastic encouragement and timely help in person: their thorough reading of our draft translation identified many a missing link and veiled allusion. Javadi also kindly translated the Azeri poem in *Sur-e Esrāfil* no. 23 into English. Mehdi Sarreshtedari read and critiqued early drafts of the translation. Colleagues who responded helpfully to individual queries include Habib Borjian, Saeed Ghahremani, Susan G. Hauser, Ahmad Karimi-Hakkak, Judith Pfeiffer, and Thomas R. Ricks. When we reached absolute dead ends, we turned to Elham Malekzadeh in Tehran, who was invaluable in tracking down individual names. Rohangiz Karachi, Navid Yousefiar, Gisoo Jafari, and Milad Mohammadi were other helpful contacts in Tehran. Mir Yarfitz advised us on translating Persian idioms into US, rather than British, equivalents. Nikki Keddie alerted us to Yale University Press's new translation series for the publication of our project. Bijan Assadipour, the editor of *Daftar-e Honar,* most graciously provided us with an illustration of Dehkhodā that appears in *Daftar-e Honar* 19–20, no. 21 (Farvardin 1392 / March 2013). This special issue includes an unrivaled collection of Dehkhodā illustrations in print. The original painting that we have reproduced is part of the private collection of Hamid Reza Ahmadi, who gave us permission to reprint.

We owe a considerable debt of gratitude to Juliana Froggatt, our sensitive copy editor. At Yale we express our profound thanks to our series editor, Andrew March, and to executive editor William Frucht for their encouragement; to Mary Pasti, our patient production editor; and to Jaya Aninda Chatterjee for keeping us in touch. Not forgetting the anonymous readers for the press, who made a number of valuable suggestions at a critical juncture.

Janet Afary and John R. Perry

# Abbreviations and Other Conventions

*For full citations, see the bibliography.*

EIr     *Encyclopaedia Iranica*

IS      *Iranian Studies*

LHP    Edward Granville Browne, *A Literary History of Persia*

MD    Ali-Akbar Dehkhodā, *Maqālāt-e Dehkhodā*

RMM  *Revue du monde musulman*

SE     *Sur-e Esrāfil*

*SE* was published from May 1907 to March 1909. Its issues appeared in two series: "year 1," which actually spanned two calendar years (1907-8), even by the Persian solar and Islamic lunar reckoning, and "year 2," which was in 1909. Two of the first publications of Dehkhodā's *Charand-o Parand* as a separate work (in Saʻid Nafisi's anthology of 1951, and the Ketāb-e Jibi paperback of 1962) use the Persian term for "series" instead of "year," a practice adopted here. Series 1 comprised weekly issues numbered 1 to 32 (though *SE* skipped 9 and 10; see our headnote for no. 11). Series 2 comprised just three issues, each several weeks apart, numbered 1 to 3. In this book, references to particular *Charand-o Parand* columns cite the issue number of the *SE* in which they were published. Since almost all belong to series 1, we omit the series number for series 1 and add it just for series 2. In labeling the columns we give the series and issue number and the date of publication in the Gregorian calendar.

Editorials and articles in *SE* other than those under the heading *Charand-o Parand* are referred to by issue number, Persian title (if present), and page range.

Dates cited from the text or masthead of *SE* and contemporary periodicals are in the Islamic lunar (*Hejri-e qamari*) calendar and are followed (unless the month is named) by the abbreviation *Hq* and the Gregorian equivalent. Publication dates of Persian works in the bibliography (except *SE*) are in the Islamic solar or Iranian Shāhanshāhi calendar, followed by the Gregorian equivalent.

Transliteration of Persian names and terms (where there is no conventional English form) follows a common Persianist system, using *a, e, o* for the "short" vowels and *ā, i, u* for the "long" vowels and usually omitting initial *'ayn*. A few Arabic words and phrases used in an Arabic or general Islamic context are transcribed in accordance with the Arabist convention, with *a, i, u* for the short vowels and *ā, ī, ū* for the long vowels. Diacritics to distinguish Arabic consonants (on *d, h, s, t, z*) are not used, except in a very few cases where orthographic precision is essential to the meaning.

Unless otherwise indicated, all translations are ours. Headings and subheads within brackets have been supplied.

# Translators' Introduction

In the early years of the Iranian Constitutional Revolution (1906–11), Ali-Akbar Dehkhodā (1879–1956) published a series of satirical columns under the title *Charand-o Parand* for the social democratic newspaper *Sur-e Esrāfil*. The name *Sur-e Esrāfil* (henceforth *SE*) refers to the trumpet call of the archangel (Qur'an 18:99; the "last trump" of I Corinthians 15:52 and Handel's *Messiah*), to be sounded on the day of bodily resurrection, when all humans are to answer for their deeds in this world.

*SE* began publication on May 30, 1907, ten months after the August 1906 revolution. The eight- to ten-page weekly paper was issued on Thursdays (the day before the Friday weekend). As with

Portrait of Ali-Akbar Dehkhodā based on an old photograph. Artist: Ali Akbar Sanati, circa 1960, Tehran. Image courtesy of Bidjan Assadipour, editor of *Daftar-e Honar*, from vols. 19–20, no. 21 (Farvardin 1392 / March 2013), p. 3268. Reproduced courtesy of Hamid Reza Ahmadi.

other popular newspapers of the period, a few hours after it appeared, each issue was sold and resold and the contents shared by thousands of literate, semiliterate, and even illiterate citizens.[1] The masthead of the paper, "Liberty, Equality, and Fraternity," is an obvious reference to the 1789 French Revolution, though the paper's ideology was a mix of liberal, populist, and socialist positions.

The social democratic newspaper *Mollā Nasreddin*, which had begun publication in Tiflis (Tbilisi) a year earlier, had a significant influence on *SE*. However, the relationship soon became reciprocal as the two frequently had satirical exchanges on major issues of the time. Like *Mollā Nasreddin*, *SE* adopted an uncompromising anticolonialist position and routinely exposed the machinations of Western diplomats in Iran, specifically those of Russia and Great Britain. The paper was also critical of the new monarch, Mohammad-Ali Shah (r. 1907–9), who took the reins after the death of his father in January 1907 and immediately began a relentless battle against the new constitutional order. *SE*, which was heavily influenced by Enlightenment ideas and freely referenced icons of Western liberalism such as Jean-Jacques Rousseau, also dabbled in contemporary European discussions on social democracy. But the paper reserved by far its harshest criticisms for the clerical establishment, both the lowest-ranking members of the caste of mullas, who were blamed for propagating ignorance and superstition, and those belonging to the highest echelons (*mojtaheds*), such as Shaykh Fazlollāh Nuri, who had openly sided with the anticonstitutionalist faction.[2]

1. According to a visiting American diplomat, in 1907 Tehran had at least four dailies and thirty weeklies (W. P. Cresson, *Persia*, p. 113).

2. (Hajji) Shaykh Fazlollāh Nuri (1843–1909) is mentioned in a number of *Charand-o Parand* columns ("Telegram from Fars," *SE* no. 5; "Response,"

Despite their many common interests and similarities in tactics, *Mollā Nasreddin* and *SE* were quite different in several respects. From the outset, the Tbilisi paper was strikingly modern looking, with its cover and content in both Arabic and Latin scripts, and abounding in color and illustrations. It specialized in humorous cartoons, skillfully drawn and mostly in color, appealing to the illiterate as well as the educated public. Its Tehran counterpart was in black and white, written in uncompromising lines of Arabic script, with only the masthead offering a patch of calligraphy and illustration. Whereas *Mollā Nasreddin*, written in Turkish, the vernacular and/or literary medium of most of the Ottoman realms, the Caucasus, and Central Asia, became "the satirical journal for the whole Muslim East,"[3] *SE*, in Persian, was more restricted ter-

no. 6; "[Events at Tupkhāneh Square]," no. 20; "['Watch Out—Sayyid Ali!']," no. 21; "Condolence Addressed to *Mollā Nasreddin* on the Death of the Shaykh al-Eslām," no. 23; "The Year in Review," nos. 26 and 27; "'The Speech of Kings Is the King of Speeches,'" series 2, no. 1; "Political Economy," series 2, no. 2). He was born in Tehran and later studied in Najaf under the ranking mojtahed, Mirza Hasan Shirāzi, before returning to Tehran in 1883. See Vanessa Martin, "Shaikh Fazlallah Nuri." In the summer of 1906 Nuri briefly supported the constitutionalists, before turning against them when the aims of the new democratic movement became clearer. He was soon its most vociferous opponent, joined the new king, Mohammad-Ali Shah, and issued fatwas and wrote articles in his newspaper, *Lavāyeh-e Shaykh Fazlollāh Nuri* (see bibliography), accusing supporters of the movement of heresy and apostasy. When constitutionalist forces regained the capital in July 1909, Nuri was tried for the murder of several constitutionalists and found guilty. After receiving permission from some of the Najaf clerics and allowing the public to check, through open telegraph lines, with the highest-ranking clerics of Najaf to confirm that Nuri could indeed be executed for the crimes he had committed, the constitutionalists hanged Nuri in public. He was rehabilitated after the Islamic Revolution of 1979 and is considered one of the early martyrs of Islamism.

3. Dzh[ehangir] Dorri, *Persidskaia satiricheskaia proza*, p. 78.

ritorially. Persian was still widely read in Afghanistan, India, and Central Asia, but the journal's commitment to criticism of abuses specific to Shi'i Islam diminished its interest for most Muslims outside Qajar Iran and the South Caucasus. In Iran, its interest for all classes, sects, and religions was unprecedented. Crucially, the Russian rulers (since 1800) were nominally committed to supporting the modernist, liberal, and secularist aspirations of the *Mollā* and its readers, and though their suspicions of Pan-Turkist plots did lead them to censor or close the journal at times, it survived well into the Soviet period. In Iran, the vacillating Qajar establishment, resisting intermittent pressure from European diplomats to liberalize, soon clamped down and silenced the constitutionalists and their loudest voice.

*SE* initiated an epistemological debate on concepts such as knowledge (*'elm*) and freedom (*āzādi*). The paper routinely discussed tenets of social democracy, such as greater respect for the labor and dignity of workers and peasants. It called for the free distribution of crown and waqf (religious endowment) lands and the sale to the peasants who tilled it of land owned by major landowners. Dehkhodā and *SE*'s other writers called upon the Majlis deputies to set up a national bank that would facilitate such an agenda, by purchasing the land of major landlords and distributing it among the cultivators. The paper also called for an eight-hour workday, free education, and universal suffrage for both men and women.

By drawing parallels between Persian proverbs or folkloric witticisms and the contemporary situation, Dehkhodā broke with the ornate and abstruse style of Persian literature and discussed complicated political issues of the time in an easily accessible language. No one was excused. Not the despotic shah and the royal elite, who lived extravagant lifestyles ("[The Shah on the War-path]," *SE* no. 32), nor the clerics who labeled as blasphemy any reform or innovation in the law ("[Religion for the Elite, Religion for the Masses]," no. 14), nor the simple peasants and illiterate mothers who, despite a lot little better than slavery, perpetuated the superstitions and acquiesced in the injustices that reinforced their bondage ("Reply to Letter," no. 11; "Reply from the News-paper," no. 13).

Soon after its first publication, *SE*, with its *Charand-o Parand* columns, created a literary sensation because of its innovative style. *Revue du monde musulman* translated some of the articles into French and called it "the most literary, the best written, the best composed, and the most vehement of the newspapers that appear in Iran today."[4] Edward Granville Browne called *Charand-o Parand* "the best specimen of literary satire in Persian" and published his English translations of five extracts (from *SE* nos. 1, 2, 4, 17, and 24) in his *Literary History of Persia* and *Press and Poetry of Modern Persia*.[5] These accolades continued decades after the demise of the paper. Sorour Soroudi writes that classical Persian literature had provided few examples of social satire, and when it did, their scope was limited. In contrast, Dehkhodā's satirical columns "form a turning point in the literary history of Iran in both their content and style."[6] Likewise, Touraj Atabaki writes that *SE* was the first Iranian newspaper to understand the dual meaning of modernity,

4. *RMM* 3, p. 309. For excerpts and other comments in *RMM,* see vol. 3, pp. 209–11, 318–24; vol. 5, pp. 324–27; vol. 6, p. 339; vol. 7, pp. 362–64.

5. Browne, *Press and Poetry*, p. 116.

6. Sorour Soroudi, "Sur-e Esrāfil, 1907–08," p. 231. Rezā Barāheni expresses similar sentiments in "Tanz-e Dehkhodā," pp. 508–9, 517–19. See also Gholam Hoseyn Yousofi, "Dehkhodā's Place."

"self-determination of the individual and critical thinking."[7] Several critics have expressed the view that Dehkhodā's prose works form a bridge between journalism and the modern short story in Persian.[8]

## The Work and Its Title

The phrase *charand-o parand* has a range of meanings, from the neutral or condescending "(idle) chit-chat, prattle" to the skeptical, dismissive, or indignant "bull, balderdash, stuff and nonsense." Etymologically, it derives from the Persian participles for "grazing" and "flying"; Steingass's *Persian–English Dictionary* of 1892 glosses it only as "beasts and birds," which—coincidentally, or not?—brings to mind the English phrase "cock and bull" or the American "horsefeathers."

Browne's translation of the title, "charivari," boldly goes beyond dictionary synonyms to between-the-lines interpretation.[9] His word is originally the French expression (in US English, "shivaree") for a noisy folk ritual of late medieval to early modern times, in which a community expressed its disapproval of an inappropriate marriage or other social infraction with satirical songs and jests. *Le Charivari* was the apt title of a Paris satirical newspaper famous for its political cartoons (1832–1937), and the English humorous weekly *Punch* appeared in 1841 with the subtitle "The London Charivari." Dehkhodā, in one place where he explicitly connects

---

7. Touraj Atabaki, "Sur-e Esrāfil payāmāvar-e tajaddod."

8. Dorri, *Persidskaia satiricheskaia proza*, p. 192; Barāheni, "Tanz-e Dehkhodā," p. 508; Christophe Balaÿ and Michel Cuypers, *Nouvelle persane*.

9. Browne, *Press and Poetry*, p. 116; Browne, *LHP*, p. 469.

the Persian idiom with the title of his columns (just before quoting the text of the shah's letter to the clerics of Najaf), appeals to his readers to "judge whether I have ever in all my life written such balderdash or whether you have ever read the like"—implying that serious criticism underlies his own brand of chitchat, while the real *charand-o parand* is the illogical and tendentious verbiage of the shah ("'The Speech of Kings Is the King of Speeches,'" *SE*, year 2, no. 1). Quite consciously, *SE* and its impertinent "prattle" declared themselves the scions of a venerable line of middle-class troublemakers.

Primarily because of the popularity of the *Charand-o Parand* columns, *SE* became one of the best-known publications of the Constitutional Revolution and a harbinger of modern journalism in Iran. Below we briefly assess the historical period in which the newspaper appeared, the life and career of Dehkhodā, and the groundbreaking contributions of the *Charand-o Parand* essays. These have been reprinted several times in Tehran (see Dehkhodā, *Charand-o Parand* and *Maqālāt-e Dehhodā;* Mirza Ali Akbar Khan Dehkhodā with Mirza Jahāngir Khan Sur-e Esrāfil, *Sur-e Esrāfil,* facsimile edition), and we have benefited from these Persian editions, especially the notes by Mohammad Dabirsiāqi in the 1980 annotated edition of Dehkhodā's *Maqālāt* (articles and columns). However, the book in your hands is the first English translation of this series of columns in its entirety. Dabirsiāqi glosses many of the historical references and some generally well-known idioms (we have cited notes in only the first impression of his book [Faridun Elmi, 1358/1980]), but his apparatus omits many of the more obscure allusions and colloquialisms. Our work should be of interest to both Persian and non-Persian speakers, since we have attempted to explain the many ambiguities of the text, the puns, the allusions, and the myriad historical references that were aimed at an Iranian audience of more than a century ago and are often lost on the contemporary reader.

Cultural differences are of course the chief source of problems and misjudgments in a translation. And when cultural norms or shibboleths are themselves the target of satire, the translator (or the reader) is virtually predestined to lose, or at least blunt, the point of the barb. An instance here is the stock Persian phrase *din raft*, "religion has gone (away)," as repeated by Muslims at numerous junctures where conventional morality is flouted in the story told by the country boy Āzād Khan Kerendi in *SE* no. 6. At the time of the Constitutional Revolution, conservatives also used the expression to criticize the progressive views of their opponents. The English cultural equivalent of this universal grouse (and the real meaning of the Persian phrase, unknown to Āzād Khan)— that people are not as honest, kind, modest, reliable, and so on, as they used to be—would be "religion is dead" or (depending on context) "God has forsaken us." But neither of these translations will work in every case, for several reasons. First, the base meaning of *raft* is "went, has gone (away), disappeared": contextual connotations such as "died, is dead" or "(has) left, deserted (us)" will sometimes ring false. Then, uppermost in the context of the story is that religion (*din*) for Āzād Khan is a mysterious something that his sketchy schooling has taught him he must possess in order not to end up in hell. His naïve accounts of half-understood experiences as a waif astray in the city (into which Dehkhodā, of course, injects clues to corruption and scandals that were obvious to his readers) convince the boy that "religion" must be one of a succession of material, financial, or sexual advantages that he and others have missed out on. *Raft* in these cases cannot always reasonably connote "died" or "left (of its own volition)," and the mysterious "religion" cannot be glossed by the familiar term "God." In this dilemma, a quasi-literal rather than an idiomatic rendition of the lament seems the only workable one.

The historical hiatus mentioned above adds to the usual cultural challenges of translation. Dehkhodā's determination to write in the living language rather than the timeworn molds of classical Persian introduced into literary Persian a host of colloquial idioms. Spoken Persian has changed at least as much as colloquial English in the course of the past century, so that Dehkhodā's up-to-the-minute forms and meanings of 1907–9 are not always recognizable, or have subtly shifted in connotation, in the Persian of today. A parallel may be seen in his contemporary Edward Granville Browne's English translations of *Charand-o Parand* columns, one of which we have included untouched in our text (see *SE* no. 17). Browne's Edwardian "toil and moil,"[10] for instance, sounds quaint to modern ears, just as Dehkhodā's phrase *charand-o parand* is no longer the Persian idiom of choice (any more than are "twaddle" or "balderdash" in English) to dismiss someone's discourse as nonsensical, irrelevant, or deceptive.

Which is perhaps why this phrase—like other copulative compounds in Persian, traditionally pronounced as we transcribe it, with a connective -*o*, "and"—is nowadays often realized as *charand parand*, without a connective, and transcribed as such. In Perso-Arabic script the idiom was often written without an overt *vāv*, as *charand-parand* (cf. *goft-gu* for *goft-o gu*, "chat, gossip," and *jost-ju* for *jost-o ju*, "search, quest"). This is how the title is printed in *SE* and in Dabirsiāqi's edition. However, the calligraphed rubric in the

10. In his translation from *SE*, series 2, no. 2, in *LHP*, p. 482.

newspaper always has a small superscript *vāv* over the final letter of *charand* to indicate the pronunciation. In the Ketāb-e jibi edition of the essays, the title is spelled out in full, with overt *vāv*. This is also how the idiom is printed in Dehkhodā's own dictionary, the *Loghatnāmeh*, and in most other Persian dictionaries; in some (e.g., Abu'l-Hasan Najafi's two-volume *Farhang-e Fārsi-e 'āmmiyāneh*, from 1999) it is shown with both options, as *charand(-o) parand*. We have chosen to transcribe the connective.

As well as being a man of the people, Dehkhodā was a former diplomat, a future lexicographer, an intellectual with a classical and a Shi'i Islamic education, a poet and wordsmith, a polemicist, a journalist with a deadline: he varied his vocabulary, style, and literary register in accordance with the communicative imperatives of the moment. We have tried to maintain a comfortable modern English idiom, while keeping our ears attuned to the author's conscious modulations of voice.

## The Constitutional Revolution: Social Democracy and a New Public Sphere

The Russian Revolution of 1905 was followed by a surprising number of social movements and uprisings in the non-European world. India (1905–8), Turkey (1908), and China (1911–12) all witnessed revolutions that challenged imperialist incursions and called for a more democratic social order at home. Transcaucasia was home to hundreds of thousands of Turkish-speaking Shi'ites who regarded Iran as their cultural homeland even after the area became part of the Russian Empire at the beginning of the nineteenth century. Cities such as Baku and Tbilisi were home to large populations of Iranian immigrant workers and merchants who joined the revolutionary movement in Russia. Soon Iranian immigrants, with the help of local revolutionaries, formed a secret social democratic organization known as the Ferqeh-ye Ejtemāʻiyun-e Āmmiyun (Social-Democratic Party) in Baku. The Ferqeh subsequently played an important role in the Iranian Constitutional Revolution. Members of the organization maintained close links with Hemmat, a radical-democratic party organized by Transcaucasian revolutionaries of both Muslim and non-Muslim origins. Close ties were also maintained with the Baku and Tbilisi committees of the Russian Social-Democratic Workers Party (RSDWP). The Ferqeh had a hybrid ideology, a mixture of European socialism and indigenous Shiʻi Iranian ideas. It upheld liberalism and nationalism and maintained some religious beliefs but was critical of the conservative ulama (Muslim clerics). The Ferqeh advocated changes beyond limited political reforms and demanded the redistribution of land to peasants, reforms in child labor, modern schools and curricula for boys and girls, an eight-hour workday for factory employees, and other similar social democratic measures.[11]

A progressive educational movement also developed in Central Asia in roughly the same period. In the Turkish- and Persian-speaking khanates of Russian-ruled Central Asia, the educational reformers known as Jadids (from *nezām-e jadid*, "new system") introduced modern curricula and textbooks in Uzbek and Tajik Persian, earning the enmity of the ulama. After the Russian Revolution of 1917, the Bolsheviks mostly appropriated the Jadids' agenda while anathematizing them as "bourgeois nationalists." One of their number, Sadr al-Din Ayni (1878–1954; almost an exact con-

11. J. Afary, "Ferqa-ye Ejtemāʻiūn," in *EIr* (1998), also online (updated 2011).

temporary of Dehkhodā), survived co-optation into the Soviet Union and Stalin's purges to become the leading journalist, satirist, lexicographer, and all-round writer in the reformed vernacular Persian of the Tajik Soviet Socialist Republic. Unlike Dehkhodā, he had to stick strictly to social and anti-imperialist satire and scrupulously avoid criticism of a regime even more jealous of its power than that of Qajar Persia.[12]

In Iran, after more than a year of taking sanctuary (*bast*) and mounting protests in Tehran and Qom in 1905–6, supporters of a new constitutional order succeeded in gaining the country's first constitution and parliament. In August 1906 the ailing monarch Mozaffar al-Din Shah (r. 1896–1907) signed an unprecedented royal proclamation that allowed the formation of a national parliamentary assembly, known as the Majlis, and the drafting of a constitution.

Popular elections were soon held, and the Majlis opened on October 7, 1906. A limited male franchise brought about a parliament whose members were drawn from the Qajar elite; the ulama and theology students; nobles and notables, landowners, and smallholders; and merchants and guild members. Women were excluded from the electoral process, while property and language qualifications barred peasants, workers, and many non-Persian-speaking tribes and communities. Still, the heavy representation of trade guilds of Tehran and Tabriz and the contribution of liberal and social democratic deputies made the First Majlis one of the most respected political institutions of modern Iran.

The First Majlis accomplished a number of unprecedented feats during its short-lived existence. It ratified a modern constitution;

12. See Sadriddin Aini, introduction to *Sands of Oxus*, esp. pp. 1–3, 14–15.

set up executive, legislative, and judicial branches of the government; and substantially reduced the powers of the monarchy. The shah's directives now had to be countersigned by his ministers, and Majlis deputies gained the right to remove irresponsible ministers and government officials. The First Majlis also determined the state budget and allocated major expenses. These measures drastically curtailed the court budget and soon led to the permanent closing of the royal harem.

The national assembly also challenged the authority of the British and Russian governments in Iran. The new constitution decreed that all major foreign transactions had to be ratified by the national assembly. The era when European entrepreneurs and governments gained lucrative concessions in the country by slipping handsome payouts to the king and his cronies had come to an end.

Additionally, the Majlis tried to reduce the powers of the clerical establishment. At the start of the twentieth century, Iran was ruled by two sets of laws: shari'a religious law, which the Shi'i ulama controlled, and 'orf customary law, which the state administered. Clerics who initially supported the Constitutional Revolution in the summer of 1906 assumed that the new political order would reduce the powers of the king and reform 'orf law, leaving shari'a laws more or less intact. But liberal and social democratic deputies and journalists were determined to replace the binary legal system of Iran with a modern secular structure. Deputies such as Hasan Taqizādeh, who were influenced by liberalism and social democratic ideas from Russian-controlled Transcaucasia, spearheaded these radical reforms. The Ferqeh sent representatives to Iran to open branches of the association in various cities and implement a modified social democratic agenda. Many deputies and journalists, including Taqizādeh, Dehkhodā, and Mirza Jahāngir Khan (the founder and first editor of *SE*), were affiliated with the National Revolutionary Committee, the most important social democratic society in Tehran, which was connected to the Ferqeh in Baku.

The constitutionalists' agenda also included the creation of modern secular schools, the establishment of a Ministry of Education that would be independent of the clerics, the formation of a modern judiciary, and support for a free press. Some deputies backed greater educational rights for women, thus crossing the sacrosanct gender barrier which until then had denied women participation in the new public sphere.

In their fight against Mohammad-Ali Shah, constitutionalists relied on two new institutions of the revolution: local councils, known as *anjomans*—and in some cases their volunteer military force, known as *mojāhedin*—and radical newspapers. Indeed, many Majlis reforms could not have happened without the backing of the popular councils and the radical newspapers.

Starting in late 1906, provincial and other popular anjomans appeared in large and small cities and even in a few northern village communities. Some members of these local councils in the Iranian provinces of Azerbaijan and Gilan encouraged peasants to embark on rent and tax strikes. Urban women of Tehran and a few other cities also formed their own societies, schools, and orphanages. They sent petitions to newspapers and in a few instances wrote for leading newspapers of the time, including *SE* (despite continuing opposition from conservative government ministers and Majlis deputies: see "[Women's Education]," *SE* no. 31).

By 1907, provincial anjomans had become local administrative units in large cities and towns. Liberal and social democratic supporters of the constitutional movement played an influential role in promoting multiethnic participation in northern councils. Anjomans collected taxes, published newspapers, established modern elementary schools, and backed the liberal and radical constitutionalists in the Majlis. Occasionally they stood up to despotic governors, landowners, and clerics. In both Tabriz and Rasht, provincial anjomans expelled anticonstitutionalist clerics from the city.

For obvious reasons the royalist faction was adamantly opposed to the newly formed anjomans. Royalists formed their own anjoman and planted informers in progressive anjomans (see "News from the City [A Case of Indigestion]," *SE* no. 3).[13] Many Majlis deputies also feared the proliferation of the anjomans and the decentralized form of power that the Majlis had sanctioned. One year after the revolution, the Majlis denied requests from midsize and small towns and villages to form their own anjomans and ratified a law that limited the number of provincial and departmental anjomans, arguing that one or two provincial and departmental councils in a province were sufficient.[14]

As a social democrat, Dehkhodā maintained that the greatest guarantors of the Majlis were the anjomans and not the constitution, which could be trampled at any moment. "What an old stick-in-the-mud I am to be writing that until our ministers get their own offices properly 'organized' our constitution can be demolished by a puff of wind! What business have I to claim that

13. Two important anjomans with mixed membership were the Ādamiyat and Khedmat Anjomans.

14. Mansoureh Ettehadieh [Nezam Mafi], *Peydāyesh va tahavvol-e ahzāb*, pp. 152–53.

anyone who blocks our lawful anjomans and associations is aiming to have the Majlis suspended?" ("[Letter to Russian Diplomat Shāpshāl Khan]," *SE* no. 19).

A number of social democrats also called for a comprehensive program of land distribution. The Majlis revised the procedure for land revenue collection but did not implement a land distribution measure. Traditionally, members of the nobility, officers, and clerics were assigned land grants (known as *tiyul*) in the form of annual revenue from a village, in return for services to the court, similar to medieval European fiefs. To increase the state budget, the Majlis decreased the tiyul land allotments. Henceforth, the grantees would receive a fixed annual amount from the government, which would tax the villages directly, thus reducing the grantees' share and increasing state revenue. Although peasants did not benefit from the new arrangement, there was a considerable reduction in the income of the landlords and a parallel increase of two million tumans in the revenue of the state.[15] This reform antagonized the Qajar landed elite, who decided to support the royalist faction. It also alarmed the clerical establishment, since reforms in tiyul land grants could theoretically be extended to waqfs, charitable religious property endowments which were supervised by clerics and provided a substantial source of income for them. It was in response to this incident that Dehkhodā wrote, "These days, now that feudal land grants [*tiyul*] are overseen by the state and there is talk of monthly salaries and pensions, and the powers of some of the governors have been reduced, and some people have lost their

15. *Majlis* no. 103, April 22, 1908. *Majlis* was the first newspaper in Iran to report on the deliberations of the national assembly.

income, I'm hearing 'Religion has deserted us' yet again" ("Letter from the City [Looking for Religion]," *SE* no. 6).[16]

## The Style and Structure of *Charand-o Parand*

The demise of the convoluted and turgid style in which virtually all genres of postclassical Persian prose had come to be written by the late Qajar period is generally attributed to the influence of Mohammad-Ali Jamālzādeh's collection of short stories *Yeki bud, yeki nabud* (Once upon a time), published in Berlin in 1921.[17] Particularly striking in terms of language is the first story, "Fārsi shekar ast" (Persian is sugar-sweet), with its delicious mockery of both the Europeanized jargon of the *fokoli*[18] and the Arabicized argot of the *ākhund*: each of these disastrous results of a little learning and an inflated sense of privilege is implicitly contrasted with the simple Persian of a local youth and the linguistic integrity of the author, a returned expatriate who has not abandoned his Persian roots. Jamālzādeh clinches this indictment with the example of his other stories, written in a lively, educated colloquial Persian; an introduction that serves as a manifesto of a new literary style; and an appended glossary of colloquial idioms not found in dictionaries. The earliest of Jamālzādeh's successors to take up

16. Land reform was again a hot topic in the Majlis in spring 1907. For details see Janet Afary, "Peasant Rebellions of the Caspian."

17. See, e.g., H. K. Kamshad, *Modern Persian Prose Literature*, p. 58.

18. The type of the Frenchified nineteenth-century dandy who affected European dress and manners; see "[A Villager Goes to the City]," *SE* nos. 7–8, note 76.

the baton, Sādeq Hedāyat (1903–41), perfected the new colloquial style in his short stories.

Fourteen years before Jamālzādeh and two decades before Hedāyat, Ali-Akbar Dehkhodā was writing Persian prose in a conversational language of comparable clarity, in an even broader range of colloquial style, register, and lexical and orthographic variation, and with an infectious humor that brought him thousands of readers every week. Only because he was a journalist, not a literary writer, and his output was not literary fiction but satirical newspaper articles was he initially denied his due measure of acclaim as a pioneer of the new Persian prose. As noted above, British and French observers were enthusiastic exceptions when *Charand-o Parand* first appeared. More recent critics, including some in Iran, have made up for past neglect.[19]

The individual essays that, singly or by two, three, or more, make up a *Charand-o Parand* column depart from the conventions of classical prose essays or traditional fables in a striking and immediately obvious way. There is no introductory formula, such as "Know, O my son" or "I was told by . . ." or "Once there was, once there was not."[20] Each piece has its own format, whether it be letter(s), reminiscence, dialogue, complaint, poem, or pseudo-advertisement, –committee meeting, –scholarly paper, or -telegram. It may be preceded by a straightforward introduction or, more often, an initially puzzling, seemingly irrelevant

19. In addition to Barāheni and Soroudi (see note 6 above), mention should be made of Bozorg Alavi, *Geschichte und Entwicklung* (1964), p. 79; Christophe Balaÿ and Michel Cuypers, *Nouvelle persane* (1983), pp. 53–63; and Nahid Nosrat Mozaffari, "Iranian Modernist Project" (2010), pp. 210–11.

20. Cf. Balaÿ and Cuypers, *Nouvelle persane*, pp. 79–80.

prelude—or it may plunge in medias res, challenging the reader to catch up. Each one seems to have a different pace and mood and to come from a unique template.

Dehkhodā was the first Persian writer to signal the colloquial nature of his diction by transcription, spelling in accordance with pronunciation, as later writers of fiction perfected for dialogue.[21] Except for a few standard terms of colloquial address, such as *kablāy* (from *karbalā'i*, "pilgrim"), he uses the device sparingly, allowing the lexical register of his idioms to indicate familiar or uneducated speech. Occasional exceptions are made for angry or sarcastic address (even when not actually spoken, e.g., *pahlavun* and *junat* in "Personal Letter," *SE* no. 17) and deliberate misspelling to indicate a common solecism or misunderstanding (e.g., *'alam nashreh* for the Arabic *a-lam nashrah* in "Reply to Letter," *SE* no. 11).

Though he never claimed to be more than an occasional poet, Dehkhodā was a skilled versifier and incorporated satirical poems in *Charand-o Parand* (see *SE* nos. 4, 17, 20, 23, and 24). In this he was linking arms with dissident poets such as Abu'l-Qāsem 'Āref of Qazvin, who contributed to the constitutional uprising by composing popular songs called *tasnif*; the specimen in *SE* no. 4 is explicitly modeled on this genre. Often with satirical content, and in a tradition that antedated newspapers by decades, these could be learned even by the illiterate or copied as broadsheets and circulated, to be used (like modern union and protest songs) as marches and collective exhortations or challenges.[22] Curiously, although these five poems are each included within the *Charand-o*

21. Barāheni, "Tanz-e Dehkhodā," p. 521.
22. See Bozorg Alavi, *Geschichte und Entwicklung*, pp. 47–48.

*Parand* column of the relevant issue of *SE*, they are not reproduced in any of the published editions of *Charand-o Parand*.

Dehkhodā's originality is not confined to style; he was likewise an innovator in the nature of Persian satire. Hitherto, satire (*hajv*) as a literary genre, generally in verse, had consisted chiefly of personal vituperation and mockery, typically in revenge for a patron's failure to deliver the expected reward. It was simply the converse of *hamd*, "praise, encomium," and though frequently clever and witty was not obliged to preserve any semblance of veracity or reality in its demonization of the target or to venture into political or social criticism at large. Closer to the latter field was *hazl*, "lampoon, ridicule," a usually derogatory term for nonserious verse which might include realistic (though subjective) criticism but tended toward broad comedy spiced with sexual or scatological vocabulary and allusions. A notable exception and pioneer in extending these genres and their techniques to contemporary social and political satire in prose (interspersed with ribald verse) was Obeyd-e Zākāni, in his *Akhlāq al-Ashrāf* (The ethics of the aristocracy; 1340).[23] The modern type of precisely targeted social and political criticism exemplified in *Charand-o Parand*—sharpened by wit, humor, and fantasy but validated by a modicum of truth and reason—is of necessity called by a new term, *tanz*.[24]

Dehkhodā's use of colloquial speech and his accumulation of a variety of characters in the course of his serial essays permit him to construct theatrical scenarios, playing off contrasting types against

23. See Paul Sprachman's "Aklāq al-Ašrāf," in *EIr* (1984), also online (updated 2011).

24. See Hasan Javadi, *Satire in Persian Literature*, pp. 13–17; Barāheni, "Tanz-e Dehkhodā," p. 508.

each other in the social or political crises he illuminates. Typical of such dramas is the exchange with the nervous Mr. Fickle, whom Dehkhodā in his journalist persona repeatedly assures that, of course, he would never dream of publishing this or that government scandal, or the name of such-and-such an embezzler or bribe taker, in the newspaper—thereby alerting us, his readers, to actual instances ("[Hazards of Journalism]," *SE* no. 5; this device, in the form of a letter, was used by other journalists at this dangerous time).[25] Other examples are the debate among the author-editor and virtually the whole cast of his characters (Messrs. Fickle, Meddler, and Gadfly, the peasant Owyār-qoli, the Kurdish youth Āzād Khan, and Mulla Inek-Ali), in a staff meeting of an independent newspaper, on whether or not to accept a gift of expensive carpets from a provincial governor (*SE* no. 15); and the argument (again in the journal's office) over the shaykh's translation of a recently received letter in Arabic (*SE* no. 16). This parody incidentally anticipates Jamālzādeh's mockery of the cleric's Arabicized diction in "Persian Is Sugar-Sweet"—though Dehkhodā's is the more scathing, since his shaykh cannot turn real Arabic into comprehensible Persian.[26]

Apart from dramatic dialogue, *Charand-o Parand* pieces often take the form of letters that the author supposedly receives and his replies, and direct personal commentary or critique (both serious and humorous). The language scholar perforce intervenes to skewer fatuous verbiage (*SE*, year 2, no. 1) or clichés (*SE* no. 21); or he may use a catchphrase as a leitmotif to link a succession of complaints (*SE* nos. 12, 19, 21, and 24). Only rarely does he show off his erudi-

25. See Javadi, *Satire in Persian Literature*, pp. 154–55.
26. Cf. Balaÿ and Cuypers, *Nouvelle persane*, p. 87.

tion in set pieces (see the five consecutive idioms conventionally evoked to avert a misfortune in "[Letter to the Russian Diplomat Shāpshāl Khan]," *SE* no. 19). Occasionally he will compromise his scholarship to invoke, tongue in cheek, a false etymology or grammatical analogy in order to make a point (*SE*, year 2, no. 1).

A related technique used to good effect by Dehkhodā and other constitutional-era satirists is that of extended false analogy, called in Persian *goriz-zadan*: a proverb, common saying, or truism is applied incongruously to a current social or political situation, leading to a *reductio ad absurdum* that emphasizes the iniquity of present conditions.[27] Examples in *Charand-o Parand* are the "novel" treatment for opium addiction by graduated withdrawal, equated with the landlords' adulteration of the peasants' grain (*SE* no. 1); the explanation for a whole series of murders and assorted unjust and irrational acts—that the person responsible *hers-esh dar-āmad*, "lost his or her temper" (*SE* no. 12); and a disquisition on incompatible foods and incompatible social classes ("Six Place Settings and No Food," *SE* no. 25).

One device that Dehkhodā deploys to suddenly introduce an otherwise eccentric topic or argument is a parody of the style of Qajar chronicles, those dynastic histories (such as *Montazem-e Nāseri* and *Fārsnāmeh-ye Nāseri*) that record events in strict chronological order, year by year. In the two *sālnāmeh* episodes ("The Year in Review," *SE* nos. 26 and 27 ) his solemn recital of the doings of the mighty in Iran, interspersed with odd items of news from abroad (suffragettes; an international balloon race), is punctuated by odder, at times hilarious, domestic episodes. An Iranian civil servant misses his old Oxford college chum Lord Curzon

27. Javadi, *Satire in Persian Literature*, p. 155.

(now the viceroy of India) and petitions a personified Government for leave to go and see him—in vain; so persistent and importunate is he that the exasperated Government throws him bodily out of the office (no. 26). A Sufi devotee floats up into heaven, sees a spring of pure water beneath his feet . . . and is rudely awakened by his companion to find himself in the *khānqāh*,[28] peeing in his pants (no. 27).

It would seem that Dehkhodā intended to round off his farrago of fact, fiction, and fun by writing a serious fictional story, perhaps to neutralize the journalistic stigma. Issues 27 and 28 of *SE* (late April and early May of 1908) carry the first two episodes of "Qandarun"—here translated as "Gum [The Story of Hajji Abbās]"—which follows the rise of a poor but shrewd rural youth to urban respectability as a hypocritical mulla. The tale promises to have more similarities than just the name of its antihero to Sādeq Hedāyat's satirical novella *Hājji Āghā* (1945);[29] however, the advertised continuation never appeared.

## Ali-Akbar Dehkhodā: Diplomat, Radical Journalist, and Scholar

In 1906 Dehkhodā was one of the most gifted and sophisticated young intellectuals of Iranian society, fluent in Turkish and French and with a training that prepared him for either a clerical position or a lucrative post in the diplomatic corps.

28. A place of gathering for a Sufi brotherhood.
29. See Kamshad, *Modern Persian Prose Literature*, pp. 192–98.

He was born in 1879 in Tehran to a family of small landowners who hailed from the province of Qazvin, ninety-four miles northwest of Tehran.[30] His surname, *deh-khodā*, "lord of the village," refers to this background. In rural Qazvin the term was often applied to one of the farmers who was charged with overseeing the distribution of water to the fields.[31]

There is little information about his parents. The father, Khan Baba Khan, was married twice, first to his uncle's widow, with whom he had no children, and then to Dehkhodā's mother.[32] When Ali-Akbar was nine or ten years old, his father passed away, leaving behind three sons and a daughter. When the *vakil* ("trustee, attorney," the executor of the family estate) also died, the family was cheated out of its considerable assets, leaving the members in penury in a modest house near the Tehran bazaar. Several of the stories and allusions in *Charand-o Parand* columns refer to dishonest vakils—a term that was also used for parliamentary deputies—reflecting this bitter early experience of Dehkhodā's life (see, e.g., *SE* no. 22).

Dehkhodā began his early education with Shaykh Gholām-Hoseyn Borujerdi, who took young Dehkhodā under his wing for a decade and taught him Arabic morphology (*sarf*) and Islamic jurisprudence (*osul al-feqh*), theology (*kalām*), and philosophy

30. In compiling this biography, we have relied on the short autobiographical essay that appears in Dabirsiāqi's preface to D-S ("Sarāghāz," pp. iv–xxxi), as well as Dehkhodā, *Nāmeh'hā-ye siyāsi-e Dehkhodā*; and Fereydun Ādamiyat, *Ideolozhi-e Nehzat-e Mashrutiyat-e Irān*, pp. 273–81.

31. Dorri, *Persidskaia satiricheskaia proza*, p. 36. This important functionary was known in medieval times as *mir-āb*, "water lord."

32. Nahid Nosrat Mozaffari, "Crafting Constitutionalism," p. 73.

(*hekmat*). This extensive religious education, which could have led to his becoming a respectable cleric, instead served him remarkably well as a journalist. As a satirist he was able to lambast the clerical establishment, its books, and its rituals with the sharp insight of an insider who was well versed in such matters.

Borujerdi's cubicle was in the school of the most respected Tehran mojtahed, Hajji Shaykh Hādi Najmābādi. Najmābādi, who was known as a freethinker with Azali Bābi sympathies,[33] had a reputation for scrupulous honesty and was appointed the administrator of the endowment to build the Vaziri Hospital in 1898 (see "A Cure for Addiction," *SE* no. 1). Dehkhodā's family lived near Najmābādi, and Dehkhodā's father had been an admirer of the great mojtahed, making it possible for the young Dehkhodā to attend the circle of his students and colleagues and benefit from their discussions. Najmābādi was a mojtahed of the first rank whose religious tolerance was exemplary by the standards of the time: E. G. Browne writes that he was a mentor to a number of constitutionalists. Poor and rich alike visited him, including Mozaffar al-Din Shah himself, and considered him "absolutely incorruptible." From Najmābādi, Dehkhodā learned to be tolerant of diverse views, including those of non-Muslims, and to challenge superstitious beliefs. Every afternoon Najmābādi sat outside his

33. In the 1860s the Bābi religion (an offshoot of Shi'ism) split in two. A majority followed Bahāullāh, who claimed to be the new messiah of Bābism; they were henceforth known as Bahā'is. A minority continued to follow Bahāullāh's half-brother Sobh-e Azal and became known as Azalis or Azali Bābis. For the early history of Bābism see Abbas Amanat, *Resurrection and Renewal*; for the role of Azali Bābis in the Constitutional Revolution see Mangol Bayat, *Iran's First Revolution*; and for the less known participation of the Bahā'is see Juan R. I. Cole, *Modernity and the Millennium*.

house and accepted visitors, "people of all classes and all faiths, statesmen and scholars, princes and poets, Sunnís, Shí'ís, Bábís, Armenians, Jews, 'Alí-Iláhís, etc., with all of whom he discussed all sorts of topics with the utmost freedom. Though a *mujtahid*, he was at heart a free-thinker, and used to cast doubts into men's minds and destroy their belief in popular superstitions, and he was instrumental in 'awakening' a large proportion of those who afterwards became the champions of Persia's liberties."[34]

Dehkhodā credited his early education to these three devoted individuals: his beloved mother, Borujerdi, and Najmābādi. "More or less, all I have is due to these three exceptional persons. Few people get to benefit from three such simultaneous gifts."[35] After completing his basic education, he enrolled at the newly established School of Political Science, where he quickly distinguished himself academically. He studied French and modern sciences such as political science, international law, history, and geography. Upon graduation, he was employed at the Ministry of Foreign Affairs, and around 1903 he accompanied Ambassador Mo'āven al-Dowleh Ghaffāri to the Balkans as a junior diplomat (see *SE* no. 12).

Dehkhodā spent two years in Europe, mostly in Vienna and Bucharest. There he improved his knowledge of French, furthered his understanding of European culture and civilization, and became acquainted with the tenets of liberalism and social democracy. Vienna was the center of one of the oldest and largest social

34. Edward Granville Browne, *Persian Revolution*, p. 406.
35. *MD*, p. vi. The preface to *MD* ("Sarāghāz," pp. iv–xxxi), by its editor, Dabirsiāqi, contains a detailed account of Dehkhodā's life and works. There is also an unrivaled display of pictures of Dehkhodā and his associates in *Daftar-e Honar* 19–20, no. 21 (Farvardin 1392 / March 2013).

democratic parties of Europe. The Social Democratic Party of Romania had recently split, into the National Labor Party and the Marxist Socialist Union of Romania. Dehkhodā was thus exposed to various debates within leftist and social democratic groups. This background turned him into one of the most sophisticated young men of his time in Iran, equally well versed in Islamic jurisprudence, knowledgeable about current political and economic issues, and aware of the latest radical discourses in European circles.

Yet when he returned to Tehran in 1905, in the early stages of the Constitutional Revolution, instead of a more prominent diplomatic post he sought employment from Hajji Mohammad Hasan Amin al-Zarb, a successful entrepreneur and industrialist and an early supporter of the revolution (see "From Semnān [A Silent Parliamentary Deputy]," *SE* no. 23). Perhaps by this time Dehkhodā's radical politics had dissuaded him from becoming a state-appointed diplomat. His new job was to translate for a Belgian engineer who was building a road in the northeastern province of Khorasan (see "[Hazards of Journalism]," *SE* no. 5). In 1906, with the revolution in full force, Dehkhodā joined the circle of dissident intellectuals who formed secret societies. He campaigned for a new social democratic order and became a member of the secret Ferqeh and the Revolutionary Committee. In the spring of 1906, Mirza Jahāngir Khan, the paper's founder and managing editor, invited Dehkhodā to join the board of the soon-to-be published *SE*. Mirza Jahāngir Khan was a graduate of Dār al-Fonun, the first modern institution of higher learning in Iran. Earlier he had Azali Bābi sympathies, but like many others he had gravitated toward social democracy and joined the Ferqeh by this period.

The paper began publication at the Tarbiat Library, a progressive bookstore in Tehran founded by Sayyid Hasan Taqizādeh and his friends. Taqizādeh, the best-known social democratic deputy of the Majlis, remained a strong backer of the paper. Mirza Jahāngir Khan wrote some of the articles, while functioning as managing editor, and Mirza Qāsem Tabrizi became the primary financial backer. Dehkhodā published an article in the first issue under the pen name Dakhow (or Dekhow), which is a vernacular form of *Dehkhodā* and in the dialect of Qazvin denotes an artless simpleton. A local folkloric figure with this name stars in a cycle of numbskull tales (portraying him occasionally as a wise fool or faux naïf), some of which have recognizable analogues in the humorous anecdotes of the Qazvini poet Obeyd-e Zākāni (ca. 1280–1370) or those about that universal eastern Islamic jokester Mollā Nasr al-Din.[36] The nickname thus served appropriately as Dehkhodā's byline for most of his similarly faux-naïf columns.

By issue 15 he appeared on the masthead as the editor of the paper. He wrote most of *SE*'s editorial articles and all of the *Charand-o Parand* columns. *SE* stopped publication with issue no. 32 on June 20, 1908, a few days before the royalist coup of June 23, which led to the arrest and eventual exile or execution of a number of constitutionalists.

After the coup, Dehkhodā took sanctuary at the British legation in Tehran and eventually fled the country. He moved to Paris and then left for Yverdon, Switzerland, a small town that had welcomed one of Dehkhodā's favorite writers, Jean-Jacques Rousseau, when he was under attack. There Dehkhodā lamented the death of his colleague Mirza Jahāngir Khan, who was killed by order of the

---

36. See, e.g., *Dakhownāmeh*, pp. 11 (Obeyd) and 12 (Mollā Nasr al-Din); and *SE* no. 6, note 64, referring to a Dakhow anecdote recorded in Dehkhodā's *Amsāl va hekam*.

Masthead of *Sur-e Esrāfil*, series 1, no. 27 (Rabi' al-Avval 27, 1326 / April 29, 1908). This issue identifies Dehkhodā as the editor of the paper.

shah.[37] All three constitutionalists killed in those early days of the coup—Malek al-Motakallemin, Sayyid Jamāl al-Din Vā'ez, and Mirza Jahāngir Khan—had Azali Bābi sympathies. At Yverdon, with the assistance of Mo'azzed al-Saltaneh Pirniā, another influential social democrat, Dehkhodā composed three more issues of *SE*, which were printed in Paris between January and March 1909. But the logistics of publishing in Europe proved too daunting, and the paper permanently folded on March 8, 1909.

In the spring of 1909, Dehkhodā and Taqizādeh settled in Istanbul, where the Young Turk Revolution of 1908 had created a more hospitable environment for Iranian constitutionalists who had taken refuge in that city and now provided Dehkhodā and Taqizādeh with financial support.[38] Dehkhodā joined La Fraternité Musulmane, an association established by the Young Turks, and the Sa'ādat Anjoman, an organization of Iranian immigrants. With the backing of merchants in the Sa'ādat Anjoman he published fifteen issues of the Persian-language newspaper *Sorush*.

When the constitutional order was reestablished in Tehran in the summer of 1909, Dehkhodā returned to Iran and was elected to the Second Majlis as the representative for Kerman and Tehran. Although there is no indication that he abandoned social democratic ideas, Dehkhodā surprised everyone by joining the more conservative Moderate Party instead of the social democratic Democrat Party, with which many of his old friends were affiliated and which was led by Taqizādeh, the staunch supporter of *SE*.

37. The elegy that Dehkhodā composed at Yverdon for his friend appears as poem no. 2 in his *Divān*. It was translated into English by Browne (*Press and Poetry*, pp. 200–204) and is the subject of an article by Hasan Javadi, "'Yād ār ze sham'-e mordeh . . . .'"

38. See Farzin Vejdani, "Crafting Constitutional Narratives."

Soon, however, Dehkhodā became disillusioned by the bitter feuds between the Democrats and the Moderates, which led to several assassinations, and by the paralyzing influence of the Great Powers, which objected to the nascent democratic movement in Iran. He withdrew from politics and instead devoted himself to literary and scholarly pursuits.

During the First World War, when Russian, British, and Turkish troops occupied Iran and German agents instigated southern tribes to oppose both the central government and the Allied forces, Dehkhodā, like many constitutionalists who feared for their lives, fled Tehran. He went to a remote Bakhtiyari village, where he laid the foundation for his subsequent scholarship. His first major publication, *Amsāl va ḥekam*, a four-volume collection of Persian proverbs and witticisms, was published in 1930–34. Dehkhodā edited many works of classical Persian literature, including collected poems of Farrokhi Sistāni (d. 1037), Manuchehri Dāmghāni (d. 1040), Nāser Khosrow (d. 1088), Masʿud Saʿd Salman (d. 1121), Suzani Samarqandi (d. 1166), and Hafez of Shiraz (d. 1390). But his primary occupation for the rest of his life was the compilation of the *Loghatnāmeh*, the first Persian encyclopedic dictionary, a massive work that draws examples from classical and folk literature, history, and religious texts and remains crucial in the field of Iranian studies.

Dehkhodā was a professor at Tehran University and held several other academic positions. He served as president of the university's School of Foreign Affairs and its School of Law and Political Science. He was also a member of the Iranian Academy of Language and Literature.[39] In the last decade of his life, the Majlis recog-

39. See Mohammad Moʿin's "Dehkhodā," introduction to *Loghatnāmeh*, part 1.

nized the scale of Dehkhodā's contribution with the *Loghatnāmeh* and allocated a budget and a staff for the completion of the work. After his death it was continued by a team under his collaborator since 1945, Mohammad Moʻin (1918–71), who produced his own dictionary, *Farhang-e Moʻin*, between 1963 and 1973. Eventually the entire project was moved to Tehran University and became the nucleus of the Dehkhodā Institute of Tehran. The lexicon was finally published in 1980 in fifty folio volumes.

In the turbulent 1950s Dehkhodā once again became involved in progressive politics. He joined the Society of the Supporters of Peace, an organization with leftist politics. Dehkhodā was a strong backer of Prime Minister Mohammad Mosaddeq in his efforts to nationalize the Anglo-Iranian Oil Company (AIOC). Britain complained about this to the International Court of Justice at The Hague, but the court found in Iran's favor. In 1952 when Mosaddeq returned triumphant from The Hague, Dehkhodā sent him the significant amount of ten thousand tumans, the last of his personal savings, with a note that it should be used for the nationalist movement.[40] Despite ideological differences with the communist Tudeh Party, Dehkhodā backed its activists in their national campaign to eradicate illiteracy. He headed the National Society for the Struggle Against Illiteracy (Jamʻiyat-e Melli-ye Peykār bā Bisavādi) and asked his students and supporters to join this effort.

After the August 1953 coup that returned Mohammad Reza Shah Pahlavi (r. 1941–78) to power, security forces took Dehkhodā into custody and interrogated and mishandled him for his

---

40. Nosratollāh Nuh, *Barrasi-ye tanz dar adabiyāt*, pp. 3–6. The funds were returned to him with a thank-you note.

support of the nationalist movement; he was even accused of having presidential aspirations in the event the shah was removed from power. However, the state could ill afford to make a martyr of such a distinguished figure, and he was soon released. Despite the trauma he endured under interrogation, a feeble Dehkhodā continued to work on the *Loghatnāmeh* until shortly before his death in 1956.

## The Ulama and the New Constitution

In addition to his remarkable literary achievement, Dehkhodā has to be appreciated for his insistence that Shi'ism ought to reform itself for a modern world, and for his greater tolerance of what today we would call ethnic and gender diversity. These ideas were not academic concepts expressed in the safety of an educational institution. They were responses to an ideological battle between supporters of the new constitutional order and those who planned to use the constitution to institutionalize the supremacy of the mojtaheds in the new order.

By early 1907 the ulama had realized, much to their surprise, that the new order intended to revamp both the shari'a and the 'orf legal systems and overturn hitherto inviolable cultural and religious hierarchies. Soon many clerics turned against these reforms and joined hands with the incensed new monarch, Mohammad-Ali Shah (r. January 1907–July 1909). The shah immediately tried to overturn the constitutional order through a number of canards, first by claiming that his father had been mentally incapacitated when, shortly before his death, he signed the August 1906 Royal Proclamation, and then by asserting that the new order was anti-

Islamic. He was backed by the leading conservative cleric of the nation, Shaykh Fazlollāh Nuri, who had joined the constitutionalist camp for a brief few months in 1906. Many clerics and wealthy landowners were also terrified by the proposed reform of the tiyul land allotments. Together they argued that the new order was incompatible with Shi'ite religious law and tried to reverse it.

In the winter of 1907, social democratic and liberal constitutionalists, many of them members of the National Revolutionary Committee, pushed for the ratification of a bill of rights that would guarantee the achievements of the revolution. The new bill, known as the Supplementary Constitutional Law (SCL), would further limit the authority of the sovereign and the powers of the religious establishment and grant greater powers to the Majlis and more autonomy to provincial anjomans. It accepted the participation of non-Muslims in the new political process. Article 8 granted equality before the state law to all (male) Iranians, regardless of their religion or ethnicity.

Ratification of the SCL proved to be a daunting task. Mohammad-Ali Shah and clerics headed by Shaykh Fazlollāh Nuri fiercely opposed the first draft, which would have substantially reduced the powers of the king and the authority of shari'a. They argued that the constitution and most of its supplements were against shari'a. Eventually the anticonstitutionalist coalition gained the right to form a Comparison Committee. Its responsibility was to make sure that the SCL was compatible with shari'a.

Progressive anjomans mobilized the public and organized strikes and *bast*s in Tehran, Azerbaijan, and Gilan against the Comparison Committee. They forced the leading mojtaheds of Tabriz and cities of Gilan out of their towns. Shaykh Fazlollāh Nuri fled from Tehran and set up shop at the Shah Abd al-Azim

Shrine, where he was flanked by more than a thousand clerics of all levels, shopkeepers, servants, and freeloaders who joined the gathering for its free meals.

In his newspaper, *Lavāyeh-e Shaykh Fazlollāh Nuri*, he castigated the modernist newspapers, especially *SE*, for daring to question sacred Shi'i rituals and hierarchies. He warned that the constitutionalists had interfered with four sacred principles of Islam: the belief in one God; the acknowledgment of Mohammad as his prophet; the recognition of the twelve Shi'i imams; and the belief in life after death. If constitutionalists had their way, he warned, a day would come when religious taxes (*khoms* and *zakāt*) would be used for building modern factories and industries, social hierarchies between Muslims and non-Muslims would be ignored, and women would start wearing pants!

Nuri received substantial financial and political backing from the royal court, the Ottoman government, and the conservative Najaf cleric Sayyid Kāzem Yazdi. Had it not been for the support of the two other, more liberal grand ayatollahs from Najaf, Mohammad Kāzem Khorāsāni and Abdollāh Māzandarāni, the public might have rejected the constitution at this point. Ultimately the two sides reached a compromise. The new SCL guaranteed certain rights to citizens, such as freedom of association and equality before the state law. However, most of these rights were burdened with the added stipulation that they adhere to shari'a. In addition, Article 2 set up a Council of Clerics with veto power over deliberations of the Majlis. Its purpose was to guarantee that none of the laws discussed in the Majlis came into conflict with shari'a dictates. While this council did not function in the constitutional era, Article 2 did block the constitutional process, which would have ended Iran's binary legal system.

By early 1908 the two sides had moved further apart, as even constitutionalist clerics opposed reforms that interfered with shariʻa laws. Sayyid Abdollāh Behbahāni, an early supporter of the revolution and leading mojtahed, blocked all efforts to reform the judiciary, including mild measures to unify and codify existing shariʻa laws. He and his allies also placed additional restrictions on freedom of the press, some of which were aimed at *SE*. They passed a law forbidding the publication of articles and books that offended religious sensibilities, though Article 20 of the SCL already did the same.

## *SE* and the Project of Reforming Shiʻism

Dehkhodā and Mirza Jahāngir Khan were convinced that fundamental social and economic change could take place only if there were substantial reforms in cultural and religious practices, at the heart of which were Shiʻi orthodoxy—its teachings, institutions, rituals, and attitudes toward women and non-Muslims. The project of creating a more modern and (social) democratic Iranian society went beyond building better roads, trains, factories, and schools or even establishing a parliament and a constitution. Rather, it placed human beings at the center of the universe, a deep humanism Dehkhodā called *ādam-parasti*.[41]

41. "Baqiyeh az nomreh-ye qabl," *SE* no. 19, p. 2. Dehkhodā's role model in this discussion was the French Socialist Jean Jaurès (1859–1914), who campaigned for the separation of church and state and for the inclusion of some elements of Marxism into the body of nineteenth-century rationalism. Jaurès devoted the last years of his life to preventing the First World War but was assassinated by a French nationalist. He is buried in the Panthéon.

*SE*'s vision of an Iranian enlightenment included cultivating a healthy skepticism toward Muslim religious leaders and Qajar authorities and adopting scientific methods of investigation. This new humanism challenged blind faith and superstition, exposed the abuses of both the mosque and the royal palace, encouraged rational interfaith dialogues with Christians and Jews, and argued for greater social inclusion of Iran's religious minorities. It also discouraged absolute trust of those in power, including even Majlis deputies and the leaders of grassroots anjomans.

At the same time, the journalists' commitment to a secular politics did not prevent them from recognizing the sensitive nature of the task at hand. Modern Western values of humanism, enlightenment, social democracy, and women's rights could not simply be grafted onto a people whose main source of identity was religion as it was defined by the clerical establishment. The editorials and columns in *SE* attempted to establish a link between these two very different modes of thinking, an approach that was baffling and at times offensive to contemporary readers. The authors condemned many Shi'i practices as backward and superstitious yet maintained that early Islam was devoid of such superstitions. They exhibited an informed view of social democratic principles and practices in Europe yet argued that the humanistic tenets of early Islam were compatible with both constitutionalism and socialism and that Qur'anic laws that had been introduced "thirteen hundred years" ago could be applied to the modern world.[42]

42. When, for example, royalist supporters savagely beat a journalist, leaving him nearly paralyzed, Dehkhodā argued, "As for Islamic law, it has never condoned the beating of respectable persons, especially ulama and sayyids" ("[On Victimization of Jounalists]," *SE* no. 17).

One might argue that this type of discourse, the linking of modern values to early Islamic principles, was common to the rational liberalism of Muslim reformers such as Jamāl al-Din Afghāni and his student Muhammad 'Abduh. Afghāni had dabbled in Western philosophy and campaigned for an anticolonial Pan-Islamism while forming alliances with clerics in the Tobacco Protests of 1891–92.[43] But more than fifteen years and vast ideological differences separated him from the authors of *SE*. Afghāni's goal of building an alliance with the religious establishment aimed at recruiting the masses for the purpose of unleashing an anticolonial revolution. It was not meant to introduce a more democratic society in the Muslim world. In contrast, *SE* was published after a successful nationalist and democratic revolution in Iran, which had been the product of an alliance with the religious establishment. The newspaper appeared after the formation of the Majlis and after the passage of a mostly secular constitution in 1906, at a time when the monarchy was stripped of a great deal of its powers and blanket concessions to Western powers had halted.

By 1907, secular revolutionaries had realized that the task of reforming the nation and crafting a more progressive Iranian society was far more complicated than they had imagined. Many concluded that cultural and religious practices also had to change. Hence, contrary to what their opponents said, and whatever Dehkhodā and Mirza Jahāngir Khan's personal beliefs might have been in their hearts and in their private lives, their writings in *SE* were not antireligious per se but rather one of the first attempts to reform Iranian Shi'ism for a general audience. Both men maintained

43. For one of the first detailed studies of Afghāni see Nikki R. Keddie, *Islamic Response to Imperialism*.

that they were scraping away ossified, superstitious, and ritualistic layers of Shiʻism—layers they compared to *shirk* (the sin of associating other beings with God, which might be considered tantamount to polytheism)—in order to recover the religious purity of early Islam, a *tawhid* (monotheism) that was devoid of ritual sacrifice and the worship of imams, a monotheism centered on the Qur'an. They maintained that this more rationalist interpretation of Islam was open to change and progress and, if revived, could become the basis for a modern Shiʻism.

Multiple attacks on *SE* by the ulama, the royalists, and even Majlis deputies led to its periodic closing and its eventual demise in the spring of 1908. The tragic murder of Mirza Jahāngir Khan, the extreme hardship that Dehkhodā endured during exile, and the factional fights that ensued among constitutionalists with the return of the constitutional order in 1909 left the paper's religious project unfinished. But in looking back at Dehkhodā's writings in *SE*, both the editorials and the *Charand-o Parand* columns, we can glean the main strands of this reformist project: he and his colleague bravely hammered away at old orthodoxies and the enormous power of the Shiʻi hierarchy—even the class of mojtaheds—in an attempt to clear the ground of old dogmas and plant fresh interpretations. They maintained that a rationalist interpretation of Islam could coexist harmoniously with the modern values of science, constitutionalism, and even social democracy.

## Chipping Away at Religious Traditions

*SE*'s criticism of the religious establishment centered on the argument that popular and ritualistic Shiʻism, which focused on veneration of the imams, was anathema to both early Islamic principles and the requirements of a modern, rational religion. In their rituals, Shi'i believers prayed and offered sacrifices to the imams so that the imams might intercede with God on their behalf, grant their wishes in this world, and secure them salvation in the next. In an interpretation of Qur'anic verses on shirk, which built on the earlier work of Shaykh Hādi Najmābādi, Dehkhodā criticized these rituals as a form of shirk. His criticism of both clerics and popular expressions of Shi'ism in *Charand-o Parand* columns covered the following practices and institutions, among many others.

## Clerics as Enablers of Superstitious Beliefs

Islam had to rid itself of divination, magic and talismans, soothsayers, fortune-tellers, and Sufi leaders in order to become more compatible with a scientific world view. Yet this appeared to be an impossible task. As Dehkhodā lamented in a poem, it seemed easier to resurrect the dead than to rid Islam of magic and the influence of Sufi *morsheds* (leaders): "From magic and *murshids* can Islám win free? / Bid the dead come to life, for 'twill easier be!"[44] Employing a Marxist analysis of this cultural malaise, Dehkhodā argued that superstition thrived because it helped provide hundreds of thousands of people with jobs, from the high-ranking mojtaheds, who were in charge of charitable endowments and bestowed blessings

---

44. "Literature: 'O Kablāy!'" (Browne's translation), *SE* no. 17. For a humorous illustration of a Shi'i superstition at work in society, see the dialogue at the end of "The Year in Review—*continued*," *SE* no. 27.

on pilgrims, to the low-ranking fortune-tellers and snake charmers on the streets, who sold healing amulets and talismans.

For this reason the clerical establishment was terrified by the rationalists' appeal to modern philosophy and the sciences: "I knew that if my newspaper condemns traditional practices, then 299,641 sufferers from a sore throat, some of whom tie a thread from the druggist's store round their throats and wrists, will all die of their ailment; and because as a gradual result of the publication of my articles, 227,000 prayer writers, 546,000 fortune-tellers, 151,000 geomancers, 462,000 superintendents of charitable drinking fountains, ascetics, dervishes, snake charmers, crystal-ball gazers, numerologists, and astrologers will lose their livelihood." There were also important political reasons for maintaining superstition. Both the clerics and the court believed in keeping the masses ignorant so they could easily be ruled. However, even when clerics recognized that freedom of thought, modern sciences, and social democratic principles were not "anti-Islamic," they maintained that these were just not suitable for ordinary people: "One of the senior ulama, after I had read out to him the first article of *Sur-e Esrāfil* no. 12, and he had listened carefully and understood it all, declared, These things are not blasphemy. None of this is contrary to Islam. It is all correct—however, these matters are not for the common people to read" ("[Religion for the Elite, Religion for the Masses]," *SE* no. 14).

## Poverty of Religious Education

Another of Dehkhodā's major criticisms was that the vast majority of mullas and *ākhund*s (low-level clerics) were poorly trained and had little formal religious education. Their learning was limited to rote memorization of texts in a Qur'an school (*maktab*). Hence they shut down any attempt at argument, because they were incapable of explaining or reasoning through the most basic tenets of Islam. The malignant ulama (*olamā-e suʾ*) expected blind obedience (*taʿabbod*) from their followers, reducing the people to toiling animals that turned the mill but always remained in the same place.[45] But even the more educated clerics forbade nonclerics from discussing religious matters or offering opinions about controversial matters. As a result, only those in clerical garb were permitted to discuss the basic tenets of Islam, but the vast majority of people was not: "Although you and I, according to the prevalent opinion in this day and age, have no right to inquire into the principles of our own beliefs, let me tell you confidentially that in the early days of Islam, religion consisted in 'believing with one's heart, affirming with one's tongue, and acting with one's limbs and members.' Nowadays, however, since the likes of us are not dressed in clerical garb, we cannot lay claim to having religion" ("Response," *SE* no. 6).

## Political Abuse of Shi'i Rituals

Clerics had an arsenal of religious weapons in the battle against their opponents, especially those who interpreted Islam more liberally. One was the accusation of ritual pollution. In orthodox

---

45. *Olamā-e suʾ* (literally "evil clergy") usually referred to worldly and venal clerics, but when used by progressives it could also emphasize reactionary attitudes and arrogance. See Soroudi, "Sur-e Esrafil, 1907–08," p. 235.

Shi'ism, an individual becomes polluted through improper ablution, as well as through contact with objects and persons deemed impure. In the course of the Constitutional Revolution, conservative clerics such as Nuri routinely labeled reformers ritually impure (calling them Bābis, Bahā'is, or simply heretics) and urged their own followers to avoid bodily contact with the nonbelievers or even to eradicate them. Most clerics had no qualms about using such heavy-handed tactics despite their grave implications. Once labeled infidel, people were considered ritually impure, and any objects or persons they touched also became impure. The public was to shun them and might kill them with impunity.

One example of the ease with which clerics leveled accusations of apostasy appears in a *Charand-o Parand* column on bribery (*SE* no. 15). The wealthy governor of Kerman sent carpets to the offices of the newspaper. A discussion ensued as to whether this was a gift or a bribe. A majority agreed that it was a bribe and should be returned. But the local cleric, who approved of the bribe, argued that the rejection of charity was religiously reprehensible (*makruh*). When others took issue with this blanket condemnation of their decision, the cleric escalated the debate by stating that anyone who rejected charity was also an apostate and that it was permissible to shun or even kill such a person.

Yet the same ranking clerics who labeled reformers ritually impure were secretly colluding with Russian and British diplomats who had opposed the new constitutional order. Behind closed doors, they shook hands with "infidel" European ministers, informed them about the nation's affairs, and parted without washing their hands of this dastardly deed in either the ritual or the ethical sense:

We bumpkins imagined that sayyids, mullas, and mojtaheds, out of a strict regard for the sacred, when they hear a foreign name, ritually purify their mouths with the prescribed quantity of clean water. Now that we've come to the city we see a person who is a sayyid, a mojtahed, an ākhund, the brother of a mojtahed, and the head of the granary keepers' guild, in Zargandeh; we see him and another person . . . in private conversation with . . . the Russian chargé d'affaires. An hour and a half later . . . he goes to see His Excellency the [British] ambassador, spending an hour and a half in private with him. Finally the sayyid shakes hands with these gentlemen and climbs aboard his droshky; . . . and off he goes, without even washing his hands in the flowing streams of the Zargandeh. ("[A Villager Goes to the City]," *SE* nos. 7–8)

One of the tragic consequences of this opportunistic labeling of the opposition was that clerics lost the ability to argue rationally with Christian or Jewish religious leaders about the merits of Islam. The same Muslim clerics who stifled the nation's educational growth had created a situation in which in the entire nation "there was not one scholar who could debate a Christian priest or a Jewish rabbi" for an hour without having to resort to the "stick of heresy," which is the last resort in attacking an enemy.[46]

46. "Zohur-e jadid" (New revelation), *SE* no. 4, p. 6. See also Janet Afary, *Iranian Constitutional Revolution*, p. 122. Such tactics were not exclusive to Shi'i clerics, nor to this late period. The Ziyarid ruler of Gurgan Kai Kā'us, in his classic mirror for princes, the *Qābus-nāma* (1082 CE), advises the would-be cleric to deal with critical or hostile written questions by tearing up the papers and declaring, "This is the kind of question put by misbelievers and heretics; the questioner is a heretic" (Persian text, p. 91; translation, pp. 149–50).

## Use of Seminarians as Praetorian Guards

Another criticism of the clerical establishment was that it used young seminarians as a paramilitary force to silence its opponents. The superintendent of shrines gathered thuggish seminarians, who shouted together, "Long live the glorious Qur'an! Down with the new law! Long live God's Qur'an! Down with European laws!" ("[Servants of the Privy Chamber]," *SE* no. 18). The same superintendents warned against bodily contact with constitutionalists: "Do not associate with constitutionalists! Send a second, louder blessing upon the Prophet and his family to ward off this evil!" ("[Letter to the Russian Diplomat Shāpshāl Khān]," *SE* no. 19).

Dehkhodā was writing from personal experience. After the publication of issue 12, fifty theology students descended upon the offices of *SE* in search of the writers. Dehkhodā went into hiding for fear of his life and later wrote, "I was afraid, and I had a right to be. Because I had seen the madrasa students of Tabriz beating people, and witnessed how when one of them struck someone the whole pack of ākhunds would descend on that person, and often enough after the poor wretch had died from the clubbing they would ask one another, 'So what did he do, this cursed fellow?'" ("[Religion for the Elite, Religion for the Masses]," *SE* no. 14).

## Clerical Sexual Abuse and Subjugation of Women

Dehkhodā's discussion of the religious establishment included a sharp and revealing criticism of the clerics' sexual abuse. As teachers, judges, legal advisers, and marriage counselors, clerics were involved in the intimate details of their clients' lives, and many took advantage of this position to engage in sexual relations with male and female students and visitors in the privacy of the seminary. Dehkhodā was not necessarily critical of consensual same-sex relations per se. Indeed, in speaking of the boy concubines of the Qajar elite, he rhapsodized about their beauty and their unavailability to common folk: "A disk of a face like the moon, a pistachio-shaped mouth, straight nose, stature straight as a box-wood bough, almond eyes, eyebrows extending all the way to the temples, neck slender as a rose stem . . . why go on?" ("[Servants of the Privy Chamber]," *SE* no. 18). But he did lambast the mullas and theology students who engaged in pederasty at the madrasa, shut the flimsy screen door of their cubicle tight when tutoring "handsome young male students," or took advantage of the institution of temporary marriage, which allowed male-female sexual unions that might last only a few hours. Under the guise of providing religious and legal aid to unmarried or divorced women, some clerics engaged "in temporary marriage with female clients who had not reached menopause" ("[Religion for the Elite, Religion for the Masses]," *SE* no. 14).[47] Temporary marriage is a religiously sanctioned form of concubinage that can last from a few hours to a lifetime. Hence in Dehkhodā's fictional story "Gum," a senior mulla offers Mulla Abbās, a younger, aspiring one, the following amenities: "Since you're a stranger here, my cell is your home. Friday and Saturday are my days off, when some postmeno-

47. Mullas were approached to draw up contracts and arrange matches for temporary marriages (*sigheh*), which a divorcée or a widow might seek to support herself; an unscrupulous cleric could then marry her himself in lieu of payment.

pausal women hoping for marriage, sometimes widows, and young virgins too, come around; you can come—I am at your disposal" ("Gum—*continued*," *SE* no. 28).[48]

The Tbilisi newspaper *Mollā Nasreddin* had earlier accused clerics of using the privacy of their madrasa cubicles to engage in sexual relations with adolescent boys and female clients; *SE* was continuing this discourse.[49] Dehkhodā, who was one of the first male supporters of women's rights in Iran, also blamed the clerical class for the subordinate position of women in society. In the tale "Gum" we read about the semiliterate Mulla Abbās, who, after years of using his cubicle in the madrasa for a variety of sexual liaisons, decides to get himself a proper, formal wife. He marries a rich orphan who is eleven years old and goes on to take three more wives, including a prostitute whom he marries after purifying her through "the ablution of repentance" ("Gum—*continued*," *SE* no. 28).

Clerics also abused their authority as vakils (trustees or attorneys) and cheated their clients, especially female clients. It was not uncommon to hear that a woman had appointed a mulla as her vakil and given him power of attorney to resolve a legal case, only to find that he had taken her in marriage unbeknown to her. Dehkhodā linked the common clerical abuse suffered by women

48. This line of attack apparently riled the clerics, but that did not dissuade Dehkhodā. In a fictitious letter to *SE* we read that clerics were furious with the newspaper for dwelling on the sexual escapades of mullas and theology students, and the seminarians' relations with "hairless young boys, and enjoyment of nonmenopausal females," instead of focusing on supposedly more important issues ("Text of the [Shaykh's] Translation," *SE* no. 16).

49. See Janet Afary, *Sexual Politics in Modern Iran*, pp. 134–40.

and children to that of the nation as a whole. The vakils (MPs) of the Majlis were subjecting the nation to a similar type of fraud. They ignored the petitions of their constituents and did as they pleased with the authority that was conferred upon them ("Letter [Distrust of 'Vakils']," *SE* no. 22).

In general, Dehkhodā painted a highly sympathetic portrait of the ordinary urban Iranian woman, even if she was steeped in superstitious beliefs. Shrouded in a veil, she endured relentless poverty, was denied a first name after marriage, suffered multiple pregnancies and infant mortalities, and often lived with a husband who had little concern for her welfare or happiness. She sought refuge with mullas and faith healers who offered her talismans and potions that promised to change her husband's behavior, cure her children's ailments, and ameliorate her life. However, one category of women received little sympathy in the writings of Dehkhodā: outspoken Qajar princesses. As in many modern nationalist narratives, these women were accused of sexual improprieties, and their actions (and those of their male accomplices) stood for the corruption of the regime as a whole and as a justification for its overthrow.[50]

---

50. Thus, writing from abroad after the 1908 coup, Dehkhodā catalogued some of the immoral indulgences of Mohammad-Ali Shah and the Qajar elite as a whole. He claimed that if "the Queen Mother, the mother of Nāser al-Din Shah, didn't put on chambermaid's clothes every night and consort with the guards and soldiers, she became unwell; and likewise Omm al-Khāqān, Hajji Nasir al-Saltaneh's wife, if she didn't spend some time each night in private with Mohammad-Ali Khan, she became ill. Likewise Mohammad-Ali Mirza, if, during the first year of his reign, he didn't consort with his aunt Tāj al-Saltaneh every day, became sick" ("The Speech of Kings Is the King of Speeches,'" *SE*, series 2, no. 1).

## The Case for a Rationalist Islam

These criticisms of Shiʻi clerics and rituals were also discussed in a series of editorials written by Dehkhodā (*SE* nos. 12 through 16) that called for the establishment of a rationalist Islam based on the Qurʾan and the legacies of early Islam. These editorials, in which Dehkhodā primarily referenced the Qurʾan and prophetic hadiths, wove a new narrative about the history of humanity.[51] Imams other than Ali and other Shiʻi hadiths were rarely referred to. The first of these essays was a call for freedom of thought and the emancipation of citizens from the forced tutelage of guardians and elders, government, and clerics. There was no outward limit to human development. Nor had the greatest philosophers exhausted the potential of human beings, not "Socrates, nor the thought of Plato, nor the knowledge of Spencer or Kant." The assistance of benevolent kings or religious leaders was of little help in furthering human progress. Only when human beings were given freedom, allowed to achieve self-consciousness, and offered the opportunity to find their own path to self-development—and which was not blocked—did humanity progress. The only limit to this freedom was where it interfered with or harmed the rights of another person. Neither clerics nor leaders of Muslim countries discussed this concept, yet individual freedom was implicit in the Qurʾan and early Islamic doctrine. The only question was what limits should be placed on it so it would not lead to "corruption [and] forceful

51. The authorship of these *SE* editorials, which are not signed, has long puzzled scholars. But the *Loghatnāmeh* states that Dehkhodā wrote all the *Charand-o Parand* columns and all the editorials, except for the one in no. 20, which Mirza Jahāngir Khan Shirāzi wrote. See Dehkhodā's *Loghatnāmeh*, s.v. "Sur-e Esrāfil."

acquisition of the rights and freedoms of others." The essay ended with a frontal attack on the *kohneh-parastān* (upholders of traditional views), who refused to accept these new ideas: "The flood of the new ideas, either through your own initiative or else unfortunately through the force of others, will soon wash the dirt of your illusions and superstitions from the face of the earth."[52]

In the subsequent issues, after deflecting attacks on this editorial and once again affirming the writers' adherence to Islam, Dehkhodā employed Marxism to explain the evolution of human beings from barbarism to civilization. He argued that in prehistoric times, humans lived an animal-like existence. Economic necessity gradually pushed people to form "cooperatives" and engage in an "exchange of ideas," which materially improved their lives (*SE* no. 13, p. 2). Next he moved to a theological explanation of human development, using contemporary tropes which presented human civilization as a lost ship, caught in the midst of a rough sea, moving dangerously close to a tumultuous whirlpool. Prophets provided the basic moral principles for an ethical life. Finally, with Islam, "the broken ship" of humanity landed safely on the shores of progress, and with the death of Mohammad the age of prophecy came to an end.

Did the end of prophecy mean that human beings no longer needed guidance? Was it possible that "fourteen centuries ago, humanity reached perfection and all secrets were revealed to humankind"? Did Muslims no longer need "to decipher, translate, abridge, or expand the laws according to the requirements of the period in which they lived"? Dehkhodā continued: "The more

52. Editorial in *SE* no. 12, p. 3. See also Afary, *Iranian Constitutional Revolution*, p. 125.

human beings progress, the greater their knowledge becomes and the more they find new truths." So why did the Almighty end the era of prophetic revelations? Why did he deprive human beings of the wisdom of his messengers? Because Islam "finally put human beings on the highway of humanism [*ensāniyat*] and placed in their hands the rules through which they could decipher all the necessities of life and perfection." Henceforth "all that was left for us Muslims was to deliberate on the Qur'an and to extract laws from that abundant treasure and eternal sea, laws that suited the needs of each era."[53] Here we have a dramatic reinterpretation of *khātamiyat*, the notion that the Prophet Mohammad was the Seal of the Prophets. The ulama maintained that humanity had reached its highest degree of perfection with Islam and that the task of the mojtaheds was simply to safeguard this tradition. Dehkhodā was now challenging this interpretation. With Islam, human beings had achieved the stage of ensāniyat and gained the potential to decide important matters of life on their own.

In the next issue, despite frequent attacks on the paper, Dehkhodā brazenly continued this line of argument. Once again he confirmed that he and other writers of *SE* were indeed Muslims (and not, for example, Bābis or Bahā'is) but believed it was their ethical duty to shed light on these issues. He then repeated the argument that there was no limit to human progress, that no one could predict when human beings might reach a state of perfection. No "mojtahed," "governor," or "doctor" could predict such a time. This statement was not "injurious to our Muslim religion." It harmed only "those who had convinced others that *they* had

53. Editorial in *SE* no. 13, p. 3.

reached the state of perfection—that no one else was worthy of such a high rank and dignity" in the universe.[54]

Dehkhodā proceeded to argue that early Islam had a constitutional form of government and that after the Rāshidun Caliphate (comprising the first four caliphs of Islam) the practice was lost to Muslims. By invoking the legacies of all four early Muslim caliphs and not just Ali, whom Shi'ites revere as the sole legitimate heir to the Prophet, Dehkhodā attempted to bridge the divide between the Shi'i and Sunni worlds. He also established continuity between early Islam and modern (Christian) constitutional forms of government, suggesting that the Western world had only perfected early Islamic principles. He argued that "we need to borrow terms from Western languages," in which much effort had been exerted to "further" the notion of constitutionalism. New terms had been coined via French, such as *pulitik*, "politics," *riāksiunir*, "reactionary," and *konsirvātur*, "conservative"—terms that still had no Persian equivalents. *Pulitik*, for example, referred to issues pertaining to one's livelihood and not matters of "Judgment Day or somebody's religion." In its efforts to castigate superstitious beliefs, *SE* was simply following the example of the Qur'an, while discussing contemporary political issues in Western terms.[55]

Soon after the publication of the issue of *SE* with this argument, the Majlis shut down the paper. After some parliamentary debate, the ban was lifted.[56] *SE* tried henceforth to soften its tone

54. Editorial in *SE* no. 14, p. 3.

55. Ibid., p. 4.

56. See especially the public discussions in *Majlis* vol. 1, Sunday, Ramadan 19, 1325 *Hq* (October 27, 1907), p. 359, and Wednesday, Ramadan 22, 1325 *Hq* (October 30, 1907), pp. 359–60. Some clerical deputies, such as Sayyid Abd al-Hoseyn

by giving examples from Judaism and Christianity before turning to Islam. The most important message of the Qu'ran was tawhid (the oneness of God), the idea that multiple deities, overseeing the seas, oceans, and mountains, did not rule the universe. Yet soon after Moses had delivered this message of tawhid, the Israelites returned to their earlier polytheistic beliefs and made sacrificial offerings to idols. The same thing had happened in Christianity. Jesus maintained that he was a messenger of God, the only creator of the universe. As proof, Dehkhodā wrote, "In chapter 5 of the Gospel of John, Jesus says, 'I have come not at my volition but at the volition of the one who sent me.'"[57] Yet later Christians took the phrase "my father in Heaven" (Matthew 12:50) to mean that God was the biological father of Jesus. They ignored other biblical applications of the term *father*, examples which showed that it conveyed the kindness and love of God toward his creatures rather than his literal paternity of Jesus. Soon after, Christians adopted the concept of the Trinity. In doing so, they combined their old polytheistic beliefs with the monotheism of "Jesus (Peace

Shahshahāni, now took offense at constitutional provisions that guaranteed the freedom of the press, if newspapers were going to write about such sensitive matters. Others, such as Vakil al-Tojjār, the merchants' deputy, complained that Iranian newspapers such as *SE* and *Habl al-Matin* were going too fast. They acted as if "our constitutionalism is like that of Germany or France, whereas we have had a constitutional order for only one year, and it must fit our circumstances." Iranian constitutionalism should not be "harmful to religion," nor should newspapers "displease our neighbors [presumably the Russians or Ottomans] with harsh words" and turn them into enemies (Ramadan 22, 1325 *Hq*, p. 360).

57. This seems to be a loose rendition of John 5:19 (English Standard Version), "Truly, truly, I say to you, the Son can do nothing of his own accord, but only what he sees the Father doing. For whatever the Father does, that the Son does likewise."

Be upon Him)" and destroyed the essence of tawhid as Jesus had presented it.[58]

The same process had taken place in Islam. Qur'anic verses demonstrated that tawhid was the focal point of the Qur'anic revelations. Yet soon after interacting with other nations, Muslims reverted to shirk. "They retrogressed to the practices of barbarity and in their desire to compete with their neighbors engaged in polytheistic rituals."[59] Thus the blame for the supposed retrogressions in Islam was placed squarely upon the Muslims themselves, rather than upon neighboring Christians, Zoroastrians, or Jews. Nor was there a hint of anti-Sunni sentiment in these statements of a Shi'i writer.

In *SE* no. 16, in an editorial titled "Muslims and Shirk," Dehkhodā criticized another central tenet of Shi'ism, the religious intercession (*shafā'at*) of holy persons (such as imams).

A short digression on the significance of shafā'at is necessary before we turn to this discussion. In the institution of the imamate, the Fourteen Innocents (Mohammad; his daughter Fatima; and the Twelve Imams) are a reservoir of justice and merit, by virtue of their noble lineage. They can mediate on behalf of other faithful Muslims, whom they ask God to forgive, grant wishes, or save on Judgment Day. As the anthropologist Mary Elaine Hegland has pointed out, Hoseyn, the third imam, has served as "an intercessor between God and human beings."[60] His martyrdom earned him a special place in the heavenly pantheon. He has the ability to appeal to the Prophet and to Allah on behalf of penitents

58. Editorial in *SE* no. 15, pp. 3–4.
59. Ibid., p. 4.
60. Mary Elaine Hegland, "Two Images of Husain," p. 221.

and to request absolution for them. The rituals of Moharram—the mourning processions on the streets, self-flagellations, continuous narration of the Battle of Karbala in *rowzeh-khāni* social gatherings, and dramatic reenactments of the martyrdom of Hoseyn in ta'zieh passion plays—are all carried out in the hope that Imam Hoseyn might intercede on behalf of sinful individuals and secure redemption for them. The imams are not the only ones with the power to facilitate redemption; Shi'i clerics often lay claim to this power. Even quite low-level mullas and sayyids might claim to have performed miracles, known as *karāmat*, in order to establish their bona fide link to their *marja' al-taqlid* (source of emulation, a senior mojtahed), to the Prophet, or to God himself and claim the same power to intercede.[61]

In an earlier essay in *SE*, Dehkhodā had mocked these "fraudulent prophets." Low-level Shi'i clerics who looked disheveled and lacked basic hygiene claimed to be imams, or even prophets, when given the opportunity: "If you tell them, Mr. Sayyid! Become a prophet, and Shaykh! Claim that you are an imam—the reverend representative of the imam immediately begins to roll his eyes in awe, adopt a sad expression, soften his voice . . . His whole being prepares itself for receiving revelations."[62] This essay was both a criticism of popular Shi'ism and a condemnation of the new Bābi and Bahā'i religions. In addition, it served to confirm the credentials of *SE* writers as non-Bābis and non-Bahā'is. But the same essay can also be read as a veiled attack on another central tenet of Shi'ism, the belief in the reemergence of the twelfth imam as the Mahdi on Judgment Day. Thus Dehkhodā was un-

61. Moojan Momen, *Introduction to Shi'i Islam*, p. 235.
62. "Zohur-e jadid" (New revelation), *SE* no. 4, p. 6.

dermining three central pillars of Shi'ism—khātamiyat, shafā'at, and *mahdaviyat*.[63]

In "Muslims and Shirk" he went a step further, linking the very notion of intercession to shirk. He claimed that according to the Qur'an, one could appeal to God or Mohammad but not to anyone else for intercession. To prove his point, he quoted a number of suras, as he generally did in other arguments. These included Yūnus (Jonah) 10:3, "Surely, your Lord is Allah, who created the heavens and the earth in six days, then was established on the throne, regulating all things. No intercessor [can plead with him] except by His leave. That is Allah, your Lord; so worship Him." In addition, Islam approved of only one manner of repentance (*tawba*), whereby the believer promised to not engage in the same act again and to observe other requirements. Furthermore, the possibility of repentance was open only to the living, not the dead. The sura Ghāfir ("Forgiver [of sins]," also called al-Mu'min, "The believer") warns about Judgment Day, "when the hearts will be choking the throats. The wrongdoers [*zālimīn*] will have no friend nor intercessor who might be heeded" (40:18). From these and many other verses where the term *shafā'at* appears, Dehkhodā concluded that "appeals to those other than God, in any name or any manner, suggested belief in the power of intercession." And according to the Qur'an, belief in intercession is tantamount to shirk.[64]

Dehkhodā lamented that he and his colleagues dared not open up this discussion as they had planned and "compare the beliefs of contemporary Muslims with the teachings of early Islam, since neither was the public ready to hear such things nor had we

63. Soroudi makes a similar argument in "Sur-e Esrafil, 1907–08," p. 236.
64. "Muslimīn va shirk," *SE* no. 16, pp. 1–5.

remained courageous."[65] Instead, he turned to the Book of Jeremiah to talk about the message of that prophet.

In 626 BCE, Jeremiah had warned the misguided Israelites about the impending fall of the kingdom of Judah to the Assyrians. Dehkhodā compared the invading Assyrians to the imperialist Russians and British, and the victimized Israelites to the Iranian people of his time. The Israelites had remained monotheistic only in name. They had performed ablutions, built numerous shrines to religious leaders, and offered sacrifices to those who might intercede on their behalf, yet they ignored God's central command to them when he placed them in Jerusalem, "that they learn kind deeds, be just to others, free the innocent, attend to the orphans, and support the widows."[66]

Dehkhodā thus likened himself and *SE* to the prophet Jeremiah, who intensely loved his people, could see that their continued disobedience would lead to their destruction, and did everything in his power to reform them. Dehkhodā argued in this last essay on rationalism as follows: "Yet again we repeat, of all the forms of intercession, all that come in conflict with what the Qur'an has stated, are, according to the Qur'an itself, forms of shirk and cause destruction of this world and the other" (*SE* no. 16, p. 4).

After this editorial, Dehkhodā moved from a discussion of religious freedom to one of economic matters. He wrote a series of social democratic articles on peasants and workers, including the

65. Ibid., p. 3.
66. Ibid. This seems to be a loose rendering of Jeremiah 22:3 (English Standard Version), "Thus says the LORD: Do justice and righteousness, and deliver from the hand of the oppressor him who has been robbed. And do no wrong or violence to the alien, the fatherless, and the widow, nor shed innocent blood in this place."

need to change social attitudes toward manual labor in Iranian society, to dignify labor, and to implement land reform. In editorials and columns he called upon the Majlis to implement a program of land distribution, "making peasants owners of the piece of land they cultivated."[67] He also discussed the political platforms of various Russian socialists.

Dehkhodā recommended that Iranians struggle for the adoption of male and female suffrage, the eight-hour workday, the right to strike, freedom of education, free distribution of crown and waqf properties, and the sale of land owned by major landowners to the peasants. While the nation was fighting for a constitutional government and a democratic social order, he warned of the limits of democracy under capitalism. Capitalism was a barbaric system: "Neither Nero of Roman history nor Zahhāk of Iranian mythology nor any priest of the Inquisition had as much power as the present capitalists of civilized Europe, nor did they commit as much murder." Iran could learn from this experience and take advantage of the fact that it had a very small capitalist class. Perhaps the country could bypass the inhumane capitalist system of Europe and speedily move toward a more egalitarian, socialist society. The original precepts of Islam, its "poor-loving principles," were generally in harmony with "tenets of socialism" and could be revived for such a purpose. Now was the time to embark on such a project. Later, when Iran had developed native "Rothschilds" and "Carnegies" and "vast amounts of capital [had] accumulated in a few centers," such a transition would prove impossible.[68]

67. "Baqiyeh az nomreh-ye qabl" (continued from the previous issue), *SE* no. 19, p. 2.
68. *SE* no. 29, p. 2. For a detailed discussion of Dehkhodā's thoughts on socialism, see Afary, *Iranian Constitutional Revolution*, ch. 5.

## Dehkhodā and Other Muslim Reformers

How groundbreaking were Dehkhodā's ideas? His essays on economics and social democracy were truly unprecedented in Iranian society. Although Azerbaijani and Iranian social democrats and their anjomans had discussed such ideas, their publication in *SE* marked the first time that these concepts were presented to the larger literate public in such detail.

What about his project of reforming Islam? There are some similarities between his criticism of Shiʻi traditions and those of the radical Azeri playwright Mirza Fath-Ali Ākhundzādeh (Akhundov; d. 1878) and the freethinker and socialist Mirza Āqā Khan Kermāni (d. 1896), who also condemned the Sunni-Shiʻi divide, mocked Shiʻi rituals and the cult of imams, and shared *SE*'s strong support for gender-based reforms. However, neither Ākhundzādeh nor Kermāni was a religious reformer in the sense that Dehkhodā tried to be, nor did they present their views in a public newspaper published in the nation's capital city; rather, they circulated their ideas privately among a small group of the elite.

In Ākhundzādeh's *Maktubāt*, a fictional exchange of letters between two princes, one of the characters, Kamāl al-Dowleh, maintains that when he criticizes Islamic practices, he is not favoring other religions, nor does he think that Islam is any worse than others. In fact, he prefers Islam to other religions. However, he simply does not take religion seriously: "I believe that all religions are meaningless and nothing but myths."[69] Kermāni, in his *Seh Maktub* (Three letters), a fictional response to *Maktubāt*, condemns the entire Muslim enterprise in stronger language and repeatedly re-

69. Mirza Fath-Ali Ākhundzādeh, *Maktubāt*, p. 32.

fers to the "barbarous Arabs"—and occasionally the Jews—whom he blames for causing the collapse of the glorious Iranian civilization.[70] Dehkhodā shared Kermāni's criticism of Shi'i rituals. But he embraced neither Kermāni's blanket condemnation of the prophetic tradition nor his idealistic view of pre-Islamic Iran, where, according to Kermāni, "no beggars or poor could be found on the streets"[71] and where elite women, who lived a free and joyful life, were "equal and companions to their husbands," except that they did not rule.[72]

If we compare Dehkhodā to the Egyptian Muslim reformer Muhammad 'Abduh (d. 1905), who was roughly his contemporary, we do see more possible overlap. 'Abduh might have influenced Dehkhodā, but again, Dehkhodā's writings are unique in content, style, and intended audience. In his *Risālat al-Tawhid*, published in 1897, 'Abduh wrote about the Qur'an as a logical text which "spoke to the rational mind and alerted the intelligence" (p. 32).[73] He condemned the rote memorization of religious texts and blind adherence to religious leaders (*taqlid*), insisting that "man was not created to be led by a bridle" (p. 127). He also argued that the Qur'an had anticipated the Christian Reformation in ensuring that divine scripture was available for all to read, and even quoted a "Western philosopher" to the effect that intellectual awakening came to Europe as a result of increased contact with Islamic culture and scholarship in the sixteenth century (p. 128). 'Abduh also devoted much space to the doctrine of free will and

70. For a discussion of Jews in Kermāni see Jaleh Pirnazar, "Chehreh-ye Yahud."

71. Mirza Āqā Khan Kermāni, *Seh Maktub*, p. 122.

72. Ibid., p. 126.

73. Page references are to Muhammad 'Abduh, *Theology of Unity*.

its discussion and limits in the Qur'an (p. 32). Finally, he emphatically denounced the practice of intercession (shafā'at): "[Through Islam] man's initiative was released from its captivity to mediators, intercessors, divines, initiates, and all who claimed to be masters of 'hidden' cults and pretended to authority over the relations men have with God through their works. These 'mediators' set themselves up as disposers of salvation with the power of damnation and bliss. In sum, man's spirit found freedom from the slavery of deceivers and charlatans" (p. 125).

However, we should remember that 'Abduh was a Sunni Muslim who found easy scapegoats in non-Muslims and Shi'i Muslims for the downfall of the Muslim empire. Shi'ites had caused the first civil war (*fitna*) in the Muslim community after the death of the third caliph, Uthmān, and "exalted Ali and some of his descendants to divine or near-divine status" (p. 33). 'Abduh also managed to find a Jewish culprit for this religious transgression so that he could spare Ali. He pointed to a certain Abdallāh ibn Sabā, who had embraced Islam and was "an excessive admirer of Ali (whose face God honors)," as the true cause of the fitna (p. 32).

In contrast, Dehkhodā's vision of reform was nonsectarian vis-à-vis Sunnis and respectful of non-Muslims. He was far too sophisticated to blame the derailment of early Islam, or the fall of the Muslim empires, on Sunnis or non-Muslims. His praise of early Islam included the first three caliphs, also claimed by the Sunnis, a bold position in a country where festivals celebrating the murder of the second caliph, Umar, were annual events Nor did he blame only non-Muslims for Iran's past or present problems. In revealing the machinations of the Great Powers, he never reduced Western politics to Christianity's hostility toward Islam, though he was fully cognizant of anti-Muslim prejudices from having lived in the West. Instead, he always looked for native shortcomings when responding to Western adversaries. His various references to recognized minorities of Iran—Armenians, Zoroastrians, Jews—were also always full of compassion, as he insisted on legal equality (*mosāvāt*) for non-Muslims.

The one exception lay in his characterization of the Azali Bābi and Bahāʾi communities of Iran. Conservative clerics routinely accused *SE* writers of harboring Bābi tendencies. Mirza Jahāngir Khan had espoused Bābi sympathies before establishing the paper, while Dehkhodā knew and worked with Azali Bābi and Bahāʾi intellectuals before and during the constitutional movement. Like many Muslim reformers of his time, Dehkhodā shared their criticisms of Shiʿi orthodoxy without adhering to the new religions. For these reasons, *SE*'s writers chose to be prudent in this one arena and simply denied the accusation that anyone affiliated with the paper was a Bābi.[74]

Times have changed since the twilight of the Qajar dynasty. Seventy years after the Constitutional Revolution, the political upheaval later to be known as the Islamic Revolution inspired a new crop of critical and humorously satirical journals in exile, aimed not at the defeated regime but at its successors; notable was *Asghar Āghā* in London, edited by Hādi Khorsandi, which (with an online edition) is published still. Today, in Iran as elsewhere, print journalism as a medium for satire has given way to the Internet. In addition to blogs, choice television skits and homemade videos (and, of course, poetry) with a critical and mocking message find a discerning audience there.

74. For a discussion of *SE*'s treatment of non-Muslims and other minorities, see Mozaffari, "Crafting Constitutionalism," pp. 187–93.

Yet more than a century after the publication of *SE*, Iranian supporters of democracy continue to turn to it for inspiration. In 2012 a special issue of the online publication *Tārikh-e Irān* (Iranian history), produced in Tehran, was devoted to *SE*.[75] A number of academics were interviewed or asked to write essays on the significance of the paper and to mine it for insights for today. The commentators came from diverse ideological backgrounds inside and outside Iran. Some held religious beliefs and said the publication had been born from "the blood of the martyrs on the road to liberty."[76] More secular-leaning contributors extolled its radicalism in propagating social democratic ideals.[77] Yet all shared a sense of awe at the manner in which the paper had built a bridge between progressive intellectuals and the popular classes in such an astonishingly short time. Dehkhodā and his colleagues planted the seeds for an authentic Iranian modernity. So long as this goal seems out of reach, *SE* and its *Charand-o Parand* columns will be part of the Iranian psyche.

75. "*Sur-e Esrāfil* ru-ye pishkhwān-e tārikh" (*Sur-e Esrāfil* on display for history; 23 Khordād 1390 / June 13, 2011), accessed November 25, 2013, available at http://tarikhirani.ir/.

76. Javād Mojābi, "Dar bāreh-ye *Sur-e Esrāfil* ke mashhurtarin ruznāmeh-ye mashruteh bud" (On *SE*, which was the most famous newspaper of the constitutional period), ibid.

77. See contributions by, e.g., Touraj Atabaki, Ali Gheissari, Mansoureh Ettehadieh, Negin Nabavi, and Pardis Minuchehr.

*Charand-o Parand*

# Sur-e Esrāfil, Series 1, No. 1, pp. 2–3

May 30, 1907

## [A Cure for Addiction]

*Dehkhodā never visited India. Here he is situating his satirical per-sona, Dakhow, in the tradition of writers (such as Sa'di before him and Sādeq Hedāyat after) who visited, or claim to have visited, the exotic land from which so much wisdom and inspiration had reached Iran and the rest of the world. This inaugural column also sets the tone and displays some of the techniques of satire his readers would come to anticipate and enjoy: a deadpan, tongue-in-cheek chain of pseudo-scientific non sequiturs and false analogies in which the absurdities and*

*corruption of government, clerical authorities, and the rich and power-*
*ful are "unwittingly" laid bare by the naïve observer.*

*Edward Granville Browne reproduced this and the following*
Charand-o Parand *column (SE no. 2) in Persian, together with an*
*annotated English translation, as specimens of "excellent and original*
*prose writing" in his* LHP, *pp. 469–82.*

After several years traveling in India, where I saw the invisible saints[1] and acquired skill in alchemy and the occult sciences, I have succeeded, God be praised, in a great experiment: to wit, discovering a cure for the opium habit! Now, if someone in any foreign country had made such a discovery, he would undoubtedly have patented it and grown wealthy on the royalties. His name would have been trumpeted in the press, but what can one do—in Iran, no one appreciates genius!

Habit is second nature; once a person is accustomed to doing something, it isn't all that easy to quit. There is only one cure, and that is by some special procedure gradually to cut down the dose

---

1. Dehkhodā here uses the terms *abdāl* and *owtād*. *Abdāl* refers to seven mysterious wise beings aware of the secrets of the universe. Each has dominion over one of the Seven Climes of the earth and represents one of the prophets who lived before Mohammad, such as Joseph, Moses, or Jesus. The abdāl are not immortal, and upon their deaths the Almighty replaces each one with another saint. *Owtād* refers to the Seven Sleepers of Christian martyrology: seven youths who were accused of holding Christian beliefs during the reign of the Roman emperor Decius in 250 CE. Refusing to recant, they took shelter in a cave, where they prayed and fell asleep. As punishment Decius ordered the mouth of the cave sealed. When it was reopened nearly two hundred years later, during the reign of the Christian emperor Theodosius II (408–50), the youths were miraculously found alive. A reference to this legend appears in sura 18 of the Qur'an, known as *al-Kahf* (The Cave). It also has analogues in Western literature (e.g., the story of Rip Van Winkle); it is Aarne-Thompson tale type 766.

over time until one loses the habit. I now proclaim to all my zealous opium-ingesting Muslim brethren that it is possible to kick
their addiction, as follows. First, they must be firmly resolved to
quit. Second, someone who consumes, say, two *mesqāls* of opium
[about 9 grams] per day should reduce his intake by one barleycorn
[about 0.07 grams] and add two barleycorns of morphine instead.
Someone who smokes ten mesqāls of opium a day should cut back
by one *nokhud* [about 0.2 grams], adding instead two nokhud of
hashish per day.[2] He should persevere in this way until the two
mesqāls of opium he used to consume is replaced by four mesqāls
of morphine, or the ten mesqāls he used to smoke is replaced by
twenty mesqāls of hashish. After this he will find it very easy to
switch from morphine pills to injections, or from smoking hash to
eating "yogurt of union."[3]

My zealous opium-using brethren! Since God has made it so
easy, why not spare yourselves the annoyance of people's silly remarks and the waste of all this time and money? Quitting the opium
habit by this method has no side effects and is very simple.

Invariably, eminent and important persons who want to wean
the ordinary people from some bad habit use this method. How
true is the poet's dictum that intelligence and prosperity go hand
in hand! For instance, when the great see that the people are poor

2. The term translated as "barleycorn" is *gandom*, "[grain of] wheat" (also
called *jow*, "barley," or *gandom-e jow*, "barleycorn"); *nokhud*, "pea," is likewise
a traditional unit of weight for cereals or pulses, also used in pharmacy. This
enhances the bland analogy of the large-scale adulteration of cereals described next, and Dehkhodā's tongue-in-cheek evocation of the micro-macro
connection.

3. *Dugh-e vahdat*, or *banjāb*, is a mixture of curdled milk, hashish, and the
herb pennyroyal, which dervishes drink in a special ceremony on Imam Ali's
birthday. See *MD*, p. 6, note 7.

and can't afford to eat wheat bread, and the peasantry spend their whole lives growing wheat while themselves going hungry, here's what they do: On the first day of the year, the eminent owners bake bread with pure wheat flour. On the second day, into each hundredweight [*kharvār*, about 300 kilograms] of wheat flour they mix one *man* [about 3 kilograms] of bitter-apricot pits, barley, fennel-flower, sawdust, alfalfa, sand, and, say—to keep the example short—around eight mesqāls of assorted clods of earth, broken bricks, and the like. Obviously, in a hundredweight of wheat flour, which is one hundred man, one man of these things will not be noticed. On the second day they substitute two man, on the third day three, and after a hundred days, or three months and ten days, a hundred man of wheat flour has become a hundred man of bitter-apricot pits, barley, fennel-flower, sawdust, straw, alfalfa, and sand, without anyone noticing, and the habit of eating wheat bread has been forgotten! Sure enough, intelligence and prosperity go hand in hand.

My zealous opium-using brethren! You are aware, of course, that a human being is a microcosm, perfectly analogous with the macrocosm, which is the world at large. Which means, for example, that anything that can happen to a person can happen also to an animal, a tree, a stone, a clod of earth, a door, a wall, a mountain, or the sea, and anything that can happen to these things can likewise happen to a person, since human beings are microcosms and they form part of the macrocosm. I mean, for example, that just as it is possible to wean people from a habit, so it is possible to wean a stone or a clod of earth from a habit, because there is a perfect analogy between the microcosm and the macrocosm. Where is the person who is less than a stone or a clod of earth?

For instance, the late *mojtahed* Hajji Shaykh Hādi built a hospital and endowed it with funds in perpetuity for eleven patients.[4] So long as the shaykh was alive, the hospital was accustomed to having eleven patients, but as soon as he passed away, the madrasa students told his eldest son that they would acknowledge him as the master only if he spent the endowment funds on them. Now see what this worthy successor did by dint of his wisdom. During the first month he reduced the number of patients by one, the second month by two, the third month by three, the fourth

4. Hajji Shaykh Hādi Najmābādi (d. 1320 *Hq*/1902), a leading mojtahed of Tehran, was known for his open-mindedness and integrity. Nearly all the progressive intellectuals of the Nāser al-Din Shah era were part of his circle, and as a youth Dehkhodā also attended their gatherings. Najmābādi's house was open to all social classes and even to religious minorities. He was a member of Malkom Khan's Freemason organization the House of Oblivion (Farāmush-khāneh), lived an austere life, and contributed much to the community he lived in, both spiritually and materially. Some of his followers and students said Najmābādi had Bābi sentiments. Orthodox clerics called him a heretic but could not touch him while he lived, as he had strong supporters at high echelons of society. He died before the Constitutional Revolution but left a lasting influence on a number of his supporters, who became leaders of that revolution. See Edward Granville Brown, *Persian Revolution*, pp. 405–7.

The hospital mentioned here, officially named the Vaziri Hospital, was made possible by Mīrzā 'Isā Tafrashi Vazir, one of Nāser al-Din Shah's ministers, who had bequeathed one-third of his wealth for the construction and operation of a small hospital and a mosque, in which he was buried. (The combination of a mosque, a hospital, and the founder's tomb is clearly modeled after the traditional *dār al-shefā*; see S. Sajjādi, "Bimārestān," in *EIr* [1989], also online.) Construction started in 1898 under the supervision of Najmābādi, who had been appointed the *motavalli* (administrator) of the Vaziri endowment. The hospital was completed in 1900. After Najmābādi's death, its work was hampered because the foundation (waqf) that he had created questioned the hospital's finances. See Willem Floor, "Hospitals in Safavid and Qajar Iran," p. 56.

month by four, and so on up until the present day, when the number of patients has fallen to five. And by dint of this arrangement, in another five months the few remaining patients will also have disappeared. So you see, by good management one can wean anyone or anything from a habit, just as a hospital that had gotten accustomed to eleven patients has now lost the habit entirely with no ill effects. Why? Because it too is a part of the macrocosm, and like humans, who are a microcosm of the world, it can be weaned from a habit.

Dakhow

# *Sur-e Esrāfil,* Series 1, No. 2, pp. 9–10

June 6, 1907

## Letter from the City [The Battle of Thermopylae]

*The target of this supposed letter from a friend in Tehran, and Dak-how's reply to it in the following column, is the indiscriminate sale of high-sounding titles to personalities, functionaries, or nonentities un-der the Qajar monarchy. Nominally conferred by the sovereign, many such honorifics were in fact obtained by bribes from the honoree or his associates. Dakhow's mock-indignant reply, extolling the virtues of an arguably even less patriotic functionary, Arfaʿ al-Dowleh ("Highest in the state"), shows that already possessing a title did not disqualify one from adding more. (Arfaʿ al-Dowleh comes in for a further spot of ridicule in* SE *nos. 14, 26, and 27.)*

Kablāʾi Dakhow:[5]

In the old days you used to help people; if your friends had a problem, you would solve it. Recently we haven't seen hide nor hair of you, and I've been wondering whether perhaps you'd taken to opium and were lounging in a corner of the room next to a brazier. Now don't tell me, you sly devil, that (as you wrote in *Sur-e Esrāfil*) you had gone and sneaked off to India without a word, to study alchemy or the occult sciences or something? I suppose you've found a treasure map too. Of course, if my suspicions are unfounded, you must forgive me and accept my humble apologies! Anyway, thank God you are safely back, which is cause for everlasting thankfulness; you have arrived in the nick of time, for things are pretty chaotic.

May God have mercy on everybody's dear departed, and may the earth not bring him news [of them]![6] We had in Qāqāzān[7] a

---

5. *Kablāʾi* is a colloquial form of *Karbalāʾi*, "one who has made the pilgrimage to the Shiʿi religious center of Karbalā" (in present-day Iraq). It is used as a term of respect. *Dakhow* is a dialect form of *Dehkhodā*, "village headman," and means "rube, simpleton" in the idiom of Qazvin; Dakhow is also the protagonist of a cycle of humorous folktales. The columnist Dehkhodā, whose family was from Qazvin, used it as a pen name (see "Ali-Akbar Dehkhodā: Diplomat, Radical Journalist, and Scholar" in the introduction).

6. A common formula among Zoroastrians, as they pass round a cup of wine and drink to the memory of the departed. See Edward Granville Browne, *Year Amongst the Persians*, p. 375 (1893 edition), pp. 410–11 (1926 edition and later reprints).

7. A district to the west and southwest of Qazvin.

certain Mulla Inek-Ali, a *rowzeh-khwān* with a sense of humor.[8] He and I used to be very close. Whenever he recited a *rowzeh* he used to preface it with a long-winded introduction, saying (and I quote), "This way the matter will be perfectly intelligible even to asses." There's no arguing with a motto like that. So it occurs to me that it might not be a bad idea to provide you with an introduction as well, just to orient you to the matter at hand.

In olden days there was in the world an empire called Persia, and next door to Persia was a country called Greece. In those days the Persian Empire was puffed up with pride and was mighty pleased with itself. Its jug, if you'll pardon the expression, held a lot of water.[9] Its aim was no less than the king-of-kingships of the world. In those days in Persia there was no Darling of the Realm, Sweetheart of the State, Honey of the Province, Beau of the (Royal) Boudoir, Charmer of the Imperial Presence, or Mignon of the Empire.[10] They hadn't yet built slides in their palaces.[11]

---

8. *Inek* is Turkish for "cow"; the compound "Ali's cow" is a pseudo-Shi'i name coined on the analogy of *Kalb-Ali*, "Ali's dog." A *rowzeh-khwān* is a low-grade cleric who is paid to recite the passionate story of the martyrdom of Imam Hoseyn and the Prophet's family on Friday evenings and at other religious commemorations. The term *rowzeh* refers to the book *Rowzat al-Shohadā*, "Garden of the martyrs," written by Hoseyn Vā'ez Kāshefi (d. 1005/1504), one of the original scripts for such performances.

9. Referring to the earthenware jug used for ablutions; metaphorically, an allusion to a man's sexual endowment, hence to his power, influence, and arrogance. See Amir-qoli Amini, *Farhang-e 'avām*, s.v. "lulahingesh besyār āb migirad."

10. These mock-honorifics allude to well-known boy and man concubines in the Qajar court.

11. In a number of royal palaces, such as the Saltanatābād Palace and the Negārestān Garden, large slides were built for entertainment. Browne writes

The mullas in those days didn't include in their number a Bludgeon of the Sacred Law or Chamberlain of the Sacred Law or Park of the Sacred Law. In short, in those days there was no Carriage of Islam or Table and Chair of the Faith or Russian Horse of Religion. And fine days they were too, truly the Time of Good King Vezvezak.[12]

But to our tale. One day Persia mustered its legions and stealthily advanced up to the walls of Greece. There was only one way into Greece, through which the Persian army had to pass. Ah, but behind this path, unknown to the Persians, was a secret narrow lane, a veritable Kucheh-ye Āshti-konān[13] of the mosque of Āqā Sayyid Azizollāh. When the Persian army reached the wall, they found that those crafty scoundrels of Greeks had blocked the way with troops. Well, here was a pretty mess! The Persian army found to its consternation that it could neither advance nor retreat. It was stuck, bewildered and humiliated. God bless the poet who so aptly wrote, "Neither have I happiness in exile nor honor in my native land," etc.

---

about a "beautiful marble bath, furnished with a long smooth *glissoire*, called by the Persians *sursurak* ('the slide'), which descends from above to the very edge of the bath. Down the slope, the numerous ladies of Fatḥ-'Alí Sháh's harem used to slide into the arms of their lord, who was waiting below to receive them" (*Year Amongst the Persians*, p. 105).

12. An imaginary ruler of ancient times. His era may be evoked in allusion to an old-fashioned style or practice or, as here, to the "good old days," a supposed golden age when the clerics and rulers were not pretentious and morally and financially corrupt (Sayyid Mohammad-Ali Jamālzādeh, *Farhang-e loghāt-e 'āmmiyāneh*).

13. Located in the Tehran bazaar; the name means "Reconciliation lane," perhaps from the necessity for all who wished to squeeze through to put aside their differences and make peace.

But as luck would have it, all at once the Persians saw one of those Jaʿfar-qoli Āqās, the sons of Cossack leaders,[14] in other words a hospitable, altruistic friend of strangers, detach himself stealthily from the Greek army and sidle up to them. "*Salām aleykom*, welcome, nice to see you, may you have a safe journey!" said he, all the while pointing surreptitiously to that narrow back lane. "We Greeks don't have any troops there; if you take that path, you'll be able to conquer our country." The Persians accepted, marched that way, and invaded Greece. But that's beside the point. Incidentally, before I forget—the name of this foreigners' friend (though it doesn't trip lightly off the Persian tongue, but that can't be helped) was Ephialtes, God curse the Devil.[15] Somehow, whenever I hear that name it puts me in mind of certain Iranian ambassadors. Anyhow, let's get to the point.

When His Excellency, that embodiment of zeal, that sum of science and statecraft, Abd al-Razzāq Khan, an engineer and lecturer at the school of the Cossack barracks, after a three-month tour on foot drafted a military map of the Mazandaran highway

14. The name is a generic reference to the sons of Iranian officers of the Cossack Brigade. Nāser al-Din Shah founded this outfit in 1879 on the model of the Cossack cavalry regiments of the Imperial Russian army. Originally all the officers were Russians, in the service of the Russian army, while the other ranks were mostly Iranians; however, numerous mentions in *SE* indicate that by this time the brigade had Iranian officers of all ranks (see F[iruz] Kazemzadeh, "Persian Cossack Brigade"). The Cossack Brigade was used against the constitutionalists; in June 1908, by order of Mohammad-Ali Shah, it shut down the First Majlis (1906–8) and arrested many constitutionalists.

15. Ephialtes of Trachis showed the Persian army a secret path around the pass at Thermopylae, which helped them win the battle there against Greece in 480 BCE. (The battle was distinguished by the heroic last stand of the Spartan rear guard under Leonidas, "the Three Hundred.")

for the Russians, we his friends thought it a pity that such a talented man should be without a title. Twenty of us sat for three days and nights racking our brains for a suitable title, without coming up with anything. Worst of all, he is a man of taste. "Any title obtained for me," he says, "must be virgin; that is, nobody should have borne it before me." We consulted the state accountants, who told us there were no virgin titles left. We looked through the dictionaries and discovered that neither in Persian, Arabic, Turkish, nor any European language from A to Z was there any word that had not been used at least ten times as a title. Well, now what could we do? Would it be pleasing to God that this man should remain untitled?

But since all things must have a happy ending, one day, feeling extremely dejected, I picked up a history book that was lying near at hand to take my mind off things. As soon as I opened the book, there in the first line of the right-hand page[16] I read: "From that day forth the Greeks called Ephialtes a traitor and proclaimed him an outlaw whom anyone might slay." Curse you, Greeks! What had Ephialtes done to you to deserve the name of traitor? Is altruism blasphemous in your creed? Don't you believe in kindness to strangers?

In short, as soon as I saw this name I told myself that this was the best possible title to adopt for Mirza Abd al-Razzāq. It was not only virgin, but these two people were exactly alike: the one was kind to foreigners, and so was the other; the one was hospi-

---

16. The place where one should expect to find the solution to a problem or a good omen for the future when "taking a *fāl*," i.e., opening a book, such as the Qur'an or the divan (collected poems) of Hafiz, at random.

table to guests, and so was the other; the one said, "If I hadn't done this, somebody else would have," and so did the other. The only difference between them was that the buttons of Ephialtes's coat were not made from our native forest wood—a negligible detail. In brief, we friends got together for a celebratory dinner and immediately sent a telegram to Kashan with an express order for five bottles of Qamsar rose water[17] and two boxes of sugared walnuts to give [to the shah] in order to obtain the title.

In the midst of all this, His Excellency Hajji Malek al-Tojjār conceded the Astara highway to the Russians,[18] and some wretch leaked the tale of this title to him, whereupon he put his foot down and declared that, as he was a heaven-sent genius, this title was his right and due. For several months now there has been such an uproar as you wouldn't credit, between Mirza Abd al-Razzāq Khan on the one hand, wielding the power of geometry, and on the other Hajji Malek al-Tojjār, with the force of rhetoric and literature quoting the poems of Imru' ul-Qays and Nāser-e Khosraw . . .[19] Kablā'i Dakhow, you've no idea what a mess we are embroiled in!

17. Qamsar, some twenty-two miles south of Kashan, was famous for its rose water.

18. The honorific Malek al-Tojjār, "King of the Merchants" (designating an informal representative of the merchants at court), refers to Hajji Mohammad Kāzem. Browne (*LHP*, p. 481, note) remarks that his "accomplishments were reputed greater than his honesty." The Astara highway, along the southwestern coast of the Caspian, was the historical route of Russian invasion of Iran.

19. Imru' ul-Qays ibn Hujr ibn al-Harith al-Kindi was a celebrated pre-Islamic Arab poet of the sixth century CE. Nāser-e Khosraw (d. 1088 CE) was one of the greatest Persian poets, as well as an Isma'ili scholar and philosopher. Malek al-Tojjār was, in the estimation of a contemporary, "certainly the most foulmouthed man in Persia" ("*Balivernes*," *RMM* 3, no. 6, p. 321).

If you can deliver us from this calamity it would be as if you had freed a slave for God's sake, and may God, if it please him, keep your sons safe! May he make one day of your life equal to a hundred years! Today is a day to do the right thing; for the rest, you may judge yourself. That's all I have to report.

Your faithful servant,
Gadfly

# Sur-e Esrāfil, Series 1, No. 3, p. 8

June 13, 1907

## News from the City [A Case of Indigestion]

*Dehkhodā introduces another of his specialized types, Meddler, shown here in a first-person composite of the self-interested fixer who, for a consideration, will offer his services to provide a foreigner, the government, or other interested individuals with privileged information or access. His incidental gossip, social contacts, and pious self-justification provide further pretexts for broad social and political satire.*

Last night, after I took the Majlis report to the Russian embassy, I delivered the order of the day from the embassy to the *polkovnik.*[20] I saw the English to discuss a few issues and met with Akbar-Shah.[21] On my return I transmitted to the chief superintendent of the waqf endowed properties the list of new petitions from the sayyids of Qom.[22] Then I went back to see the son of Hajji Āqā Mohsen and put in an appearance at two or three secret anjomans that I had managed to wangle my way into.[23]

When at last, dead tired, I was walking back through the park, there in front of the Armenian school I caught sight of the esteemed Dr. X and Dr. Y, riding past in separate carriages at full gallop. I was suddenly terrified that the rumors that Hajji Z's leg had been amputated might be true. I rushed up and, relying on our former friendship, doffed my hat, wished them good evening, and inquired what was the matter. Nothing, they replied, only that the Honorable Hajji, having within the past few days wolfed down[24] several

20. *Polkovnik* is the Russian for "colonel," referring here to the commander of the Cossack Brigade (see *SE* no. 2, note 14). The Majlis should not have sent a report to the Russian embassy and the (Persian) Cossack Brigade was not supposed to receive its orders from the Russian embassy, both treasonous acts.

21. Sayyid Akbar-Shah, a close ally of the anticonstitutionalist cleric Shaykh Fazlollāh Nuri. All of these actions would be considered treasonable, as they undermined the Majlis and the new constitutional order.

22. Sayyid (male) and Sayyida (female) are honorific titles in the Shi'i branch of Islam held by those who claim to be descendants of the Prophet Mohammad, through his daughter Fatima and her husband Ali. In Iran, as well as in Pakistan and India, sayyids are numerous and often have unverifiable lineage. Here the sayyids are presenting bogus petitions to be compensated out of religious endowment funds.

23. Supporters of Mohammad-Ali Shah had infiltrated some of the secret constitutionalist societies, known as anjomans, where they gathered information for the royalist side.

24. The Persian verb *khordan* means literally "to eat" but metaphorically "to unjustly take another's money or property; to borrow without paying back." This ambiguity is here used to satirical effect.

thousand tumans from Hajji Āqā Mohsen, another thousand or so from Heshmat al-Molk,[25] a further few thousand from Āsaf al-Dowleh,[26] and again from Qavām [al-Molk][27] in quick succession, had contracted indigestion and been diagnosed with an intestinal obstruction—you know how these people can't stop eating, and the weather *is* hot; this kind of thing happens. It's not serious.

God forbid! said I. The Lord should visit the trials and sufferings of such clerics upon us Shi'ites; let him reduce the length of our lives and add to theirs.

Meddler[28]

## A New Invention

An Austrian doctor by the name of F. Schneider, having heard all about the bread one gets in Tehran,[29] has invented a steel shield to protect the teeth from losing their enamel coating and falling

25. Probably a reference to Amir Ma'sum Khan Heshmat al-Molk, one of the provincial leaders of Sistan and Qā'enāt. Nuri wanted him appointed the governor of Sistan and Qā'enāt, but the Majlis refused to honor this request. This was seen as the primary reason why Nuri left Tehran for Shah Abd al-Azim in protest (Ahmad Kasravi, *Tārikh-e Hejdah-sāleh-ye Āzarbāyjān*, p. 379).

26. The autocratic governor of Khorasan, whose harsh tax policies forced peasants to sell their daughters to Turkman tribes in the summer of 1905, creating a major controversy in the constitutional era: see *SE* no. 4.

27. Perhaps a reference to Habibollāh Qavām al-Molk IV, the *kalāntar* (mayor) of Shiraz and chief of the Khamseh tribal confederacy.

28. The Persian is *Sag-e Hasan Daleh*, "Hasan Daleh's dog," said of someone who pokes their nose into others' business or turns up and hangs around where they are not wanted.

29. See *SE* no. 1.

out. With the help of this shield, one's teeth acquire the strength of a four-horsepower millstone and can pulverize stones, gravel, bricks . . . Address: Von Kuhilachstal, Lazarettgasse 21.

## Reply to the Letter [of June 6]

My dear Gadfly:

People like you will never die peacefully in your beds! What do you mean by meddling in affairs of state, picking up titles here and bestowing them there—haven't you ever heard of the saying "Kings know what's best for their kingdoms"? And on top of this, why are you so ungrateful as to ignore all that Mirzā Rezā Khan, Prince Arfaʿ al-Dowleh,[30] has done for us? Haven't you read the text of the agreement on Iran's loan from Russia? Aren't you aware of his kindness and hospitality to foreign guests? Don't you read the foreign press, where every day the poor prince deplores the brevity of his title? If I were you, I'd give that title to the prince and have done with it, and henceforth I would address him thus: Most Sapient Ambassador Ephialtes, Prince of Peace, Dr. Amir Noyon[31] Mirzā Rezā Khan Arfaʿ al-Dowleh.

Sincerely yours,
Dakhow

30. Prince Arfaʿ al-Dowleh "Dānesh" (wisdom), an Iranian diplomat, served as the consul general in Tiflis and later became the ambassador to Turkey and Russia. He was not related to the Qajar family but claimed (according to some, falsely) descent from royalty in Yerevan. For his ambiguous attitude toward the revolution, see, e.g., *RMM* 2, p. 543; vol. 6, pp. 683–84.

31. A Mongol title, *noyon*, "a prince of the blood."

# Sur-e Esrāfil, Series 1, No. 4, pp. 7–8

June 20, 1907

## Literature [Verse: Girls of Quchān]

*This column refers to two incidents in Quchān district in Khorasan, near the Russian frontier, in 1905. In the summer, after a plague of locusts, the peasants of one village could not pay their exorbitant taxes and had to sell their daughters in lieu to local officials—who resold them at a profit to Turkman traffickers from north of the border, allegedly with the connivance of the provincial governor, Āsaf al-Dowleh. Then, in November, Turkman raiders, subjects of Russia who had long carried out regular cross-border raids for Persian captives to sell as slaves in Bukhara, hit another village, killed a dozen peasants, and carried*

*off some sixty captives, including a number of young girls. The scandal
became a cause célèbre for the constitutionalist press and, the following
year, a challenge for the new Majlis. A court of inquiry was set up (mentioned
in SE no. 6), and Āsaf al-Dowleh was removed from his post.*[32]

*Dehkhodā's ironic response is cast as a cabaret performance supposedly
given by the captive girls in Tiflis (now Tbilisi, Georgia, which
was certainly a plausible venue for a Parisian-style cabaret but nowhere
near the Turkman steppes or Bukhara) for the amusement of
their captors and their confederates. Their* tasnif *(akin to the revolutionary
ballads composed by poets such as ʿĀref) is an opportunity for
Dehkhodā to highlight the impotence and complacency of Persia's rulers
in the face of domestic and foreign oppression.*

*This translation closely follows that of Browne* (Press and Poetry,
*pp. 174–79).*

Persian Concert, which the girls of Quchān, at the request of
the Russians and Turkmen, give at a café chantant[33] in Tiflis.

(Girls in chorus, to the tune of the popular song "O God, Leylā
doesn't care for me!")

Our nobles all are drunk with pride,
  (*O God, nobody cares for us!*)
From justice and virtue they stand aside,
  (*O God, etc.*)

---

32. Āsaf al-Dowleh then went to Tehran and briefly became the minister
of the interior in the cabinet of Nāser al-Molk. (See Mahdi Bāmdād, *Sharh-e
hāl-e rejāl-e Irān*, vol. 3, pp. 14–16. For the full story and discussion, see Afsaneh
Najmabadi, *The Story of the Daughters of Quchan*.)

33. A café chantant (literally "singing café") was an outdoor café in France
that hosted performances of popular songs or cabaret music.

The people are ignorant, blind, tongue-tied.
　(*O God, etc.*)
*Seventeen, eighteen, nineteen, a score:*
*Nobody cares about us any more!*


You see how Fate with us does play,
　(*O God, nobody cares for us!*)
From kith and kin we are torn away;
　(*O God, etc.*)
Who served us thus will surely pay!
　(*O God, etc.*)
*Seventeen, eighteen, etc.*


Though exiled far from our home so dear,
　(*O God, nobody cares for us!*)
And plunged by exile in sorrow and fear,
　(*O God, etc.*)
We love it still, and yearn for it here!
　(*O God, etc.*)
*Seventeen, eighteen, etc.*


*(A girl of twelve, solo)*
Pause, my breath, for it seems as though
　(*O God, nobody cares for us!*)
I catch a scent as the breezes blow:
　(*O God, etc.*)
A delicate scent from a land I know!
　(*O God, etc.*)
*Seventeen, eighteen, etc.*

*(The girls, in chorus)*
How sweet the breeze from the homeland smells!
  *(O God, nobody cares for us!)*
New life it gives, and grief dispels!
  *(O God, etc.)*
But alas, of exile it also tells!
  *(O God, etc.)*
*Seventeen, eighteen, etc.*

Are our menfolk all asleep, do you know?
  *(O God, nobody cares for us!)*
Where did their sense of honor go,
  *(O God, etc.)*
That they gave their loved ones to the foe?
  *(O God, etc.)*
*Seventeen, eighteen, etc.*

*(The girl of twelve, solo)*
Who to the Majlis my message will bear,
  *(O God, nobody cares for us!)*
Of heart's surrender and hope's despair?
  *(O God, nobody cares for us!)*
Is our name no longer remembered there?
  *(O God, nobody cares for us!)*
*Seventeen, eighteen, nineteen, a score:*
*Nobody cares about us any more!*

The spectators in unison:

*Hurrah, hurrah, hurrah!*
*Slava gratsioznym dyevitsam*          *Yaşasın İran'ın güzel*
                  *Persii!*                      *Qızları!*
*Slava Āsaf al-Dowleh!*                *Yaşasın Āsaf al-Dowleh!*
*Slava ministyerstvu Persii!*         *Yaşasın millet vezirleri!*

—In Russian and Turkish, i.e.,
"Long live the pretty girls of Persia! Long live Āsaf al-Dowleh! Long live the Persian ambassadors!"

# *Sur-e Esrāfil*, Series 1, No. 5, pp. 7–8

June 27, 1907

## [Hazards of Journalism]

*Several hundred newspapers began publication in the course of the Constitutional Revolution, but except for a dozen or so, most folded after a few months. This was partly because of lack of resources but mostly because journalism had become a hazardous occupation by the middle of 1907, so that the lives of publishers and writers were in grave danger (on the press in this period, see Negin Nabavi, "Readership, the Press, and the Public Sphere in the First Constitutional Era," and Pardis Minuchehr, "Writing in Tehran: The First Freedom of Press Law," both in H. Chehabi and V. Martin, eds.,* Iran's Constitutional Revolution*).*

*Dakhow mocks the overzealous journalists who abandoned their newspapers in midcourse. He also reports on the atrocities committed by tribal brigands loyal to the king; the financial corruption, forgery, and theft of the supporters of the shah; and attempts by parliamentarians to limit democratic reforms to Tehran and major urban centers.*

I hate to be a nuisance, but what can I do? Speech is for humankind what the cud is for the cow; if a person doesn't speak, his spirit atrophies. I have a friend called Fickle [Damdami].[34] This Fickle has been pestering me for more than a year: Buddy, he goes, you're older than these journalists, you've seen more of the world, your experience is broader—you've even been to India, for heaven's sake! Why don't you start a newspaper?

My dear Fickle, I would protest, first of all, if I did, then you—who are now my friend—would become my enemy. Second, quite apart from that, suppose I did sit down to produce a paper—what would I write about?

And he'd sink his head deep in thought for a while, then look up again and say: What do I know? The same kind of thing all the others write about, I guess—expose the shortcomings of the high and mighty, identify the friends and enemies of the nation . . .

My dear man, for God's sake, I would retort, this is Iran: that sort of thing just isn't done! Well, in that case, he would finish, you're just as much a despot as they are! Yeah, you too!

And whenever I heard this, I was at a loss for words, for I knew that his "you too!" was fully justified.

---

34. Cf. the Persian *damdami-mezāj*, an irresolute person who changes his mind all the time.

Anyhow, to cut a long story short, he kept on pestering me till finally I succumbed. Now that he has gotten his way, he has pulled in his horns and forgotten all those bold challenges. Whenever he sees a red-coated bailiff his heart skips a beat, and as soon as he catches sight of a policeman he turns pale. He keeps saying he will be tarred with the same brush as me and go down in the same boat.

My dear fellow, I remind him, I used to be just a simple farmer; I had four small vineyards. The gardeners watered them and took the grapes to town and dried them to make raisins while I simply relaxed in a corner of the vineyard and, in the words of the poet of blessed memory,

> I fix no trellis and ply no spade,
> I munch grapes, lounging in the shade.

You are the one who forced me into this. As the Tehranis say, you tied my hands—and henna-dyed them in the bargain! So why are you kicking up a fuss?

No, no, he says, but too-rapid growth brings an early death.

I see that he's still the same old Fickle.

Very well, my dear Fickle. Show me what I've said so far that has put such a scare into you.

It's outrageous! says he. People are not complete idiots, you know. As soon as you write "F," I know you mean Farahzād;[35] how the rest of the article will read is perfectly obvious from the open-

35. Farahzād was a popular summer resort north of Tehran. The expression means "I see where you are going."

ing lines. Maybe tomorrow you'll get it into your head to write that the factions of our ruling elite are handpicked at the whim of the Russians and the British. Or maybe you'll decide to write that some of our mullas, now they've stopped selling their pious endowments, have started selling off the country. Or that in the Cossack regiment, those [Persian] officers who are not prepared to betray their country are p-poisoned—(at this point, his tongue failed him and he began stuttering)—and this, and that, and God knows what else; and then what will I do, how will I dare admit in public to being a friend of yours? No, no, it's impossible. I have a wife and children, I'm young, I have hopes for the future!

My dear fellow, I tell him, as the old saying goes, "A thief is a king till he's caught." Until I've actually written something, who has the power to accuse me? God has created the imagination free, without recourse to any fatwa from the clerics. Let me think whatever I like, then when I write it you can say what you like.

If I wanted to write everything I know, I would have written many things by now.[36] For instance, I would have written that a certain Cossack officer who has not betrayed his motherland has been on the run for two months, poor fellow, and that a Cossack officer who *has* sold out, with twenty other Cossacks, has been

36. By this point, it is obvious that Dehkhodā is using a column from a recent issue of *Mollā Nasreddin* (from April 21, 1907, five weeks before this issue of *SE*) as a direct model. This was a sincere form of flattery rather than plagiarism, indulged in at times by both papers. In his "Reply to a Letter from Demdemeki" (a Turkish diminutive form of Damdami), *Mollā Nasreddin*'s editor Jalil Mammed-qulizadeh had treated his naïve correspondent to a barrage of hypothetical exposés of scandalous stories too sensitive to print. See Dzh[ehangir] Dorri, *Persidskaia satiricheskaia proza*, pp. 79–80.

ordered to find and kill him. I would have written, for example, that if one examined B's account at the British Bank[37] one would find twenty crore[38] [ten million tumans] of Iran's national debt. Or I would have written that Eqbāl al-Saltaneh in Maku,[39] Rahim Khan's son in Azerbaijan,[40] Hajji Āqā Mohsen in western Iran,[41] Qavām in Shiraz,[42] and Arfaʿ al-Saltaneh in Tālesh (Tavālesh)[43] are all showing through their deeds that "the Lord giveth, and the Lord taketh away."

I would have written, for instance, that a map of the route to Tabriz, drawn by the Belgian engineer Monsieur de Brucq after

37. The Imperial Bank of Persia was established by the British government in 1889 and had branches in major cities of Iran and India.

38. In Indo-Persian, *korur*; a unit of enumeration equal to five hundred thousand items.

39. The anticonstitutionalist governor of Maku Eqbāl al-Saltaneh was removed from his post by the Tabriz Anjoman because of mass peasant discontent. Maku soon became a center of peasant resistance supporting the constitutionalist movement. In 1908, during the civil war of Tabriz, Eqbāl al-Saltaneh raised an army that defeated the Maku peasants.

40. Rahim Khan Chalabiānlu, the leader of the Shāhsevan tribe, and his son plundered Azerbaijan in the service of Mohammad-Ali Shah.

41. Hajji Āqā Mohsen (d. 1910) was one of the wealthy elite of the city of Arāk (formerly Sultanabad, some 163 miles southwest of Tehran) and a strong foe of the Constitutional Revolution (Farhang Rajaee, *Islamism and Modernism*, p. 53).

42. The Qavām clan in Fars also opposed the constitutional government at this time.

43. Arfaʿ al-Saltaneh, a son of Amid al-Saltaneh, the governor of Tavālesh in the Caspian Sea region, was the principal landholder in that area. Arfaʿ al-Saltaneh jailed many peasants, including women, who sympathized with the constitutionalists, and he threatened to sew up the mouth of anyone who dared to speak of anjomans or the constitution. In the first months of the Constitutional Revolution an anjoman was formed in Anzali, where the residents of Tavālesh took their complaints.

five months' hard legwork and an outlay of several million tumans from the state purse, one day took wing from a minister's desk and flew heavenward, never to be seen again, and that the poor Belgian engineer, whenever he recalls the trouble he took over that map, still bursts into tears.[44]

When the conversation reaches this point, Fickle gets flustered. Stop it, he begs, don't say such things! These walls have ears! I respond: Yessir, I accede—whatever you command, I shall obey. In any case, I'm older than you; I have been through the wringer before. I know myself what topics to write about and what to avoid.

And have I written anything untoward so far? Why, on Saturday the twenty-sixth of last month, when the interior minister's representative came to the Majlis and said those harsh and hurtful things, did no one respond?[45] Did I write that the forgery of documents is considered a major crime in other countries, so why is it condoned and applauded in Iran? Did I write, "How is it that we can overlook seventy poor immigrant students at the American School but can't overlook one school director?"[46]

44. A. de Brucq was under contract to the Persian government from February 1901 until 1913 as the director general of roads and bridges (see Annette Destrée, *Les fonctionnaires belges*, pp. 67, 333). This anecdote no doubt derives from personal experience: on his return from Europe in 1905, Dehkhodā first found employment as an interpreter for de Brucq, who was building a road in Khorasan.

45. A reference to Mohtashem al-Saltaneh Hasan Esfandiāri, the deputy minister of the interior. See *MD*, p. 21, note 7.

46. In 1907, members of the Assyrian community became fearful of emerging conflicts around the city of Urumiyeh, and they began to send a number of their children to the Presbyterian schools in Tehran. The director of the American School for Boys at this time was Dr. Samuel Jordan; for more on Jordan see M. Zirinsky, "Jordan, Samuel Martin," in *EIr* (2009), also online (updated 2012). Thanks to Thomas R. Ricks for this information.

These are all state secrets. They are matters that can't be broached anywhere. I didn't get my beard white in the flourmill, nor did I pick up my wits in the countryside. Don't you worry: I will never write about any of this. What do I care that they want to unseat deputies of city [anjomans] who have great insight into the affairs of their own city, once provincial anjomans are formed?[47] Why should it bother me if Nasr al-Dowleh [Ebrāhim] Qavām's son brags before the assembly of nobles of Tehran, "I am the drinker of the Muslims' blood, the bearer of the honor of Islam; I am he who subjugated one-tenth of the land of Fars Province with fire and sword, who slew seventy-five Qashqa'i men and women with shot and shell"? What do I care if, at the conclusion of his speech, the nobles of Tehran yell "Hurrah!" and "Long live Qavām!"?

Why should I care if every night two figures shrouded in their *'abā*s and a certain official together slip through a certain big door? Never mind me—there is an accounting to be made in the hereafter; let them go and answer for it in the next world.

When Fickle hears this, he cheers up, embraces me, and kisses me on the cheek, saying, I always trusted your intelligence. Bravo! Bravo! Don't ever change! Then, perfectly happy, he shakes my hand, says good-bye, and leaves.

Dakhow

47. In 1906–7, many small cities and towns and even some large villages formed their own anjomans. The Majlis ordered them closed and asked that all matters before them be referred to provincial anjomans, in the capital city of each province. This was highly contested by local anjomans, which the Majlis sent forces to shut down in some cases. See Afary, *Iranian Constitutional Revolution*, ch. 6.

# Telegram from Fars

*The pseudotelegram as a satirical device was used more than once in* Mollā Nasreddin, SE's *forerunner in Tbilisi. This "telegram" reads like one of the secrets that Dakhow-as-journalist in the previous article would never (well, hardly ever) have leaked. The conservative Shaykh Fazlollāh Nuri joined Mohammad-Ali Shah in opposing the new order. He insisted on additions to the Supplementary Constitutional Law that would give five top-tiered mojtaheds veto power over the deliberations of the Majlis. This proposal was ultimately accepted and appears as Article 2 of the Supplementary Constitutional Law (for the text of the law see* Browne, Persian Revolution, *pp. 372–84).*

To

HIS GRACE PROOF OF ISLAM—REFUGE OF HUMANKIND—
REVEREND HAJJI SHAYKH FAZLOLLĀH—
LONG MAY HIS BLESSINGS ENDURE

THE FIVE PROPOSED ARTICLES REGARDING TOP-TIERED
[MOJTAHEDS] RECEIVED STOP—BE ASSURED THEY WILL BE
REPRINTED AND DISTRIBUTED TO EVERY VILLAGE
TOWN AND CITY IN REGION STOP
YOUR HUMBLE SERVANT YAHYĀ EBN ABU TORĀB[48]

48. Mirza Abu Torāb Khan Kāshi was the personal secretary and a close confidant of Mohammad-Ali Shah. He accompanied the king when the latter was deported, and returned to Iran only after the king's death.

## Announcement

To anyone who wishes to meet the writer: from early morning until lunchtime he is busy attending a trial at the Dār al-Fonun school. After lunch—that is, from two hours later up until sunset—he is at the office of *Sur-e Esrāfil*, Alā al-Dowleh Avenue, opposite the Central Hotel.

# *Sur-e Esrāfil*, Series 1, No. 6, pp. 6–8

July 4, 1907

## Letter from the City [Looking for Religion]

*This miniature first-person* bildungsroman *is perhaps Dehkhodā's most daring departure from verisimilitude among the many elastic near-fantasies in the* Charand-o Parand *narratives; at least so it might appear in translation. The polysemy of the verb* raft, *"has gone; disappeared; deserted (us); is dead," in the author's cannily manipulated scenarios, which is the primary reason for this, has been explored in the introduction (in the section "The Work and Its Title"; see also Christophe Balaÿ and Michel Cuypers,* Nouvelle persane, *p. 74). Suffice it here to note that the naïve young Kerendi, or Candide, makes his mystified*

*way after a perfunctory religious "education" through a selfish and cor-*
*rupt society where "religion" (*din, *an unidentifiable object which he has*
*been told is essential for his salvation) eludes him, as it seems to elude*
*so many others. At least he is a sufficiently modern creation to send his*
*cri de coeur to a newspaper, where his correspondent—perhaps feeling*
*obliged to heed the censor—is sympathetic but enigmatic.*

People, for God's sake help me! Newspaperman, for fear of the dawn of doomsday write to me, a Kurdish country boy, a response to my question!

My name is Āzād Khan Kerendi. My father fled with me from the oppression of Hosayn Khan Qal'eh-zanjiri in Kerend [a district in Kermanshah Province, in the west of Iran] to Tehran, and he died there. I was a child; I went to stay as a houseboy with an ākhund who taught elementary school, and whenever I was free I sat in with his students. The ākhund saw that I was eager to learn and taught me to read. I became a mulla.[49]

It was written in the book that you had to have religion; anyone who didn't would go to hell. I asked the ākhund what religion was. He told me it was Islam. I asked him what "Islam" meant. He said a few words, which I memorized; he said that this was the religion of Islam.

Then I grew up. The ākhund told me, You're no use to me anymore. I need a houseboy at home that my wife needn't veil herself in front of. You're a grown man; go away! So I left the ākhund's home and went begging. Another ākhund told me to go the house

49. The Persian *mollā* (our "mulla"), as well as designating a Muslim cleric in general, especially a low-ranking Shi'i cleric, was also at this time a vernacular term for any literate or reputedly learned person. *Ākhund*, in contrast, often connoted a theologian, preacher, or religious tutor.

of the *emām-jom'eh*, the leader of the Friday prayer: he would feed me and give me some money.

It seems that Mirza Hasan Āshtiyāni[50] had taken the endowment of the Marvi School[51] from the emām-jom'eh and was now feeding those who came to his house and also paid them some cash.[52] When I got to the emām-jom'eh's house I saw a crowd of people in the courtyard. They were all lamenting, "Religion has deserted us!" I was at a loss to understand how religion could have left. I remembered the words that the teacher-ākhund had said to me and wondered if maybe he didn't know that religion is actually the endowment fund.

Night fell, and they threw me out. The ākhunds ate the rice and stew and were each given two *qerāns*.[53] I didn't go back the next day.

In the bazaar I heard them saying the same thing: "Religion has deserted us!" There was quite a hubbub, and I walked around for a while. I gathered that Mirza Hasan was about to leave. I thought Mirza Hasan must be religion. How, I wondered, could

50. A leading mojtahed of Tehran, who played an important part in the opposition to the tobacco concession of 1891. He died in 1901. Nāser al-Din Shah briefly threatened to expel him from the city but ultimately backed down and repealed the concession. See Bāmdād, *Sharh-e hāl-e rejāl-e Irān*, vol. 1, p. 316.

51. A madrasa in the Bāzārcheh-ye Marvi opposite Shams al-Emāra, built by a khan of Marv earlier in the Qajar period.

52. The funds of a pious endowment (waqf) were supposed to be used only for charitable purposes, such as the upkeep of a designated mosque or madrasa or the feeding of the poor. The ulama who managed these trusts often interpreted the rules liberally, living off the funds themselves and subsidizing madrasa students, who would become their political supporters and strong-arm men.

53. A small-denomination copper coin, later replaced by the rial.

I "have" Mirza Hasan so as not to go to hell? I couldn't make any sense of it.

Not long after, Mirza Hasan died. His son took over the Marvi School. One day about that time I was at the Shah Abd al-Azim shrine when a crowd of divinity students arrived, crying, "Religion is no more!" Later I found out that Sālār al-Dowleh had summoned the coffee shop lad Ahmad Qahvechi to Arabistan, and Mirza Hasan's son had sent the students to Shah Abd al-Azim to turn him back.[54] So now I thought that Ahmad Qahvechi was religion. As it happened, when I saw Ahmad I fell for him. I told myself the students must be right, but I could never have him. This boy would have cost me a fortune. I was a beggar. On top of that, how could a boy who was the object of a feud between Sālār al-Dowleh and Mirza Hasan's son ever be mine? I saw that I was bound to go hell, since I had no way of getting religion.

After that I became an errand boy for a dealer in secondhand goods. He had a very pretty daughter and had made a temporary marriage [*sigheh*] with a pretty girl. Khadijeh the singer charmed his temporary wife, who left the dealer for Ayn al-Dowleh.[55] The

54. Sālār al-Dowleh was a Qajar prince who aspired to the throne, a younger brother and rival of Mohammad-Ali Shah; at the time of this article, he was in revolt in the province of Arabistan (now known as Khuzestan). Shah Abd al-Azim was the first stage of any journey southward from Tehran. Sālār al-Dowleh evidently had, or intended, a homosexual relationship with the coffee boy.

55. Prince Ayn al-Dowleh was the chief minister in 1903–5 and a vociferous opponent of the constitutional order. At the time this column was published he was without an official post, though later in 1907 he was sent at the head of government troops to put down the popular rebellion in Tabriz (see *SE*, series 2, no. 2).

dealer had also arranged the marriage of his daughter to a sayyid whose brother was a mojtahed, but later the girl was abducted from her husband's house. The dealer lamented that religion had forsaken him, though I couldn't figure out which girl he meant. Whichever one it was, I reckoned religion was a good thing! Since I despaired of ever getting it for myself, I resigned myself to hell and gave up hankering after religion.

These days, now that feudal land grants [*tiyul*] are overseen by the state and there is talk of monthly salaries and pensions, and the powers of some of the governors have been reduced, and some people have lost their income, I'm hearing "Religion has deserted us" yet again.[56]

One evening there was a rowzeh held in the house of a Shirazi man. I went there to drink tea. There was a guy there who was the great-grandson of the treasurer of Shiraz. He claimed that he had left a deposit of three thousand tumans on trust with a certain shaykh, who now swears he never had it. "Religion has deserted us!" Many agreed that Religion had up and left, except one man who said, "Why didn't you entrust your money to Jamshid, who is honest?[57] It isn't religion that has deserted you—it's your common

56. Land reform was a hot topic in the Majlis in the spring of 1907. Traditionally, members of the nobility, the military, and the ulama were assigned annual revenues from a village in return for services they performed for the court. This was known as *tiyul*, a land grant. Reforms of the constitutional era granted the state the right to collect the revenue and pay the tiyul holders a fixed annual amount. As a result, the revenue of some tiyul holders was reduced.

57. This might be a reference to the Zoroastrian merchant Arbāb Jamshid, who had opened a branch of his office in Shiraz and was known for his honesty in business. The advice given here would be insulting to some Muslim

sense, along with that of other people, that's deserted you!" And there was a lot of talk that I didn't understand.

Anyway, I'm at a complete loss to fathom which of all these is meant by "religion." Is it what the teacher-ākhund told me? Or the funds of pious endowments? Or the beautiful Ahmad Qahvechi, the coffee shop lad? Or the broker's sigheh and his daughter? Or the three thousand tumans? Or the land grants, salaries, and pensions? Or something else? For God's sake, and for fear of the dawn of doomsday, tell me, because I'm terrified of going to hell!

The Beggar Gholām Āzād Khan Ali-Allāhi

## Response

My dear boy Āzād Khan:

Although you and I, according to the prevalent opinion in this day and age, have no right to inquire into the principles of our own beliefs, let me tell you confidentially that in the early days of Islam, religion consisted in "believing with one's heart, affirming with one's tongue, and acting with one's limbs and members."[58] Nowadays, however, since the likes of us are not dressed in clerical garb, we cannot lay claim to having religion. But Hajji Mirza Hasan

---

merchants, who regarded themselves as morally superior to non-Muslims and refused to deal with them.

58. This dictum sounds more like the Zoroastrian exhortation to have "good thoughts, good words, good deeds" than like any familiar Muslim motto.

Āqā[59] and Shaykh Fazlollāh, when they left Tabriz and Tehran respectively, declared, "We are leaving, but so is religion."

The Newspaperman

## Criticism and Objection [to *Habl al-Matin*]

*The newspaper* Habl al-Matin *(The firm cable), edited by Sayyid Hasan Kāshāni, was the most influential Tehran daily in 1907–8. Kāshāni's older brother Mo'ayyed al-Eslām was the editor of the illustrious Calcutta-based* Habl al-Matin, *which had started in 1893 (see* Browne, Press and Poetry, *p. 74; N. Parvin,* "Habl al-Matin," *in* EIr [2002], *also online [updated 2012]). Residents of Kerman complained to the Majlis about the atrocities committed by the son of their governor (also the nation's minister of justice) in the area bordering Baluchistan and asked Majlis deputies to come to their aid. Various versions of this episode appeared in newspapers of the time, including* Mozākarāt-e Majlis, *11 Jomādi al-Avval 1325/June 22, 1907.*

My dear *Habl al-Matin*:

Some people say (wrongly, I'm sure) that even though you had read the discussions in *Majlis* about the high-handed and un-just conduct of the son of the minister of justice Farmānfarmā

59. Mirza Hasan Mojtahed, the leading cleric of Tabriz, who opposed the new order and was expelled from that city by the Tabriz Anjoman in April 1907, as was Shaykh Nuri from Tehran.

[in Kerman], as published in issue no. 122 of *Majlis* [the official newspaper of Parliament], you were still scared of the governor of Kerman and so took up the pen and, in your own words, "wove together foul and fair with our usual flair" and churned out an article critical of *Sur-e Esrāfil*.

But then, one cannot charge you with cowardice, because look where you hail from! If I remember rightly—aren't you from Azerbaijan?

Of course! Has any Azerbaijani showed fear so far, that you should be the second? Oh no, that's a silly idea. If you had lacked boldness and been afraid, you would not have backed up like a fighting ram and charged like a lion to butt heads with the *Sur*. But look here—after all, you're just a human being; even if you *were* afraid, don't be ashamed, just tell me about it in confidence. I have a box of first-class ointment I'll send you.[60] You should take a pinch of salt as well, but, pardon my insolence, be careful not to take the salt from a stranger, or I'm afraid you may be obliged to return the favor.

Some people even imagine—God forbid, and heaven save us!—that you were forced by the high price of bread and meat and the increased cost of publishing to allow some of those lightweight, high-value packets into the editorial office. I don't believe it for an instant. How could you, for the sake of money, take the side of an eighteen-year-old youth [Farmānfarmā's son] and deny the reports of the Kerman deputies bearing a box of written complaints from the residents?

There are a few ākhunds and sayyids who take bribes and go to the shrine of Shah Abd al-Azim. But you and I, thank God, even

---

60. Possibly camphor, used to revive one who has fainted (Dehkhodā, *Charand Parand*, ed. Sayyed Ali Shāheri-Langarudi, p. 37).

if we are ākhunds and sayyids, taking our cue from the generosity of Hajji Mo'in al-Tojjār[61] of Bushehr, have donated all our efforts and resources to the national cause. Nay, I will be the first to slap the face of anyone who says otherwise about you!

Again, some who are unacquainted with the power of your pen fancy that you might have lifted this article from the introduction to the oeuvre of Prince Malkom Khan,[62] so fluently and elegantly was it penned, and by virtue of its eloquence it quite stripped the country's readers of their powers of resistance and delivered the nation bound and gagged into the hands of hired goons. No, never in a hundred years; this allegation is likewise rubbish! I've been following you closely, and I know that the effect of your pearls of wisdom on their silken string is much greater than those people know. None of these allegations is true. Whoever imputes such things to you is gravely mistaken.

But now we are friends again, wasn't it you who on the very first day asked me shyly, "Did you fake the letter?"

And I, in roguish friendship, told you, "I swear on your manly moustaches that it is a real letter from a real big shot, who is ready to defend it to his last breath."

So how does it happen that somewhere along the way you lambasted me with that farfetched and mendacious criticism and outright defamed me? Don't you know that Iranians are touchy about their honor, and with that 95 percent duty free allowance that the

61. One of the wealthiest and most influential merchants of Tehran, who sided with the constitutionalists.

62. Malkom Khan (d. 1908) was one of the most important reformers of the late nineteenth century, an Armenian-Iranian convert to Islam and the editor of the influential Persian newspaper *Qānun* (published in London, 1890–98; reprinted in Iran ca. 1908—see *SE* no. 11).

late Monsieur Naus decreed, which we promised on our honor would not cross the border, the cry of "Honor! Honor!" is still raised against us every day in the Ministry of Justice?[63]

Anyhow, let's get to the point. I know for sure that you didn't take any "nauseous" money, nor did you resort to the mockery of ignoring your debt, and you are no coward. So why did you write that stuff? We need Dakhow to settle this—he's the only one who could get the cow's head out of the pot.[64]

So what is Dakhow's solution in this case? I'll tell you. But look, I'm afraid you might be offended! I beg you, don't take offense; if

---

63. On December 25, 1892, the Iranian government decided that henceforth 5 percent would be collected from British merchants on both imports and exports through Persian Gulf ports and that no further inland duties would be levied. However, complaints continued about the collection of inland duties. To address these, the government of Iran abolished the system of farming out the customs revenues in the Persian Gulf as of 1898, when they were assigned as a guarantee to service a foreign loan. Shortly thereafter, the government created a national Customs Administration with one national customs tariff to replace the system of varying rates plus local taxes. In March 1900, Belgian customs officials took over the management of the new administration, which collected 5 percent ad valorem. The Belgian Joseph Naus was the minister of customs in this period. Protests against this uniform tariff and Naus's role in implementing it and other reforms played an important part in bringing about the Constitutional Revolution. See Destrée, *Les fonctionnaires belges*, pp. 126–60.

64. A Persian saying, alluding to a situation where solutions are worse than the problem. The story goes that a cow put its head into a clay pot to drink the water within. When it tried to take its head out, its horns got stuck inside the pot, which the cow walked off with over its head. The villagers asked Dakhow how to free the cow's head from the pot. After a moment's thought, he decided that the only way was to cut off the cow's head. But after they did so, the villagers still couldn't free the head. Dakhow then advised them to break the pot. See Dehkhodā, *Amsāl va hekam*, vol. 2, pp. 967–68; and *Dakhownāmeh*, pp. 31–32.

you do, we'll have a real falling-out. And then that single-sheet newspaper that is published with our poor Iranian funds, crippled by scholarly and stylistic anemia, will perforce become a personal battleground for the Kashani and the Azerbaijani. Keep the topic in mind, and we'll digress for just a few words in the margin.

Once upon a time, there was a Ministry of Justice. There was an Āsaf al-Dowleh and a Matter of the Quchān Captives [see *SE* no. 4]. There was also a Journalist. And then over a period of time there was a Court of Inquiry held in the Ministry of Justice. The Journalist attended these sessions every day to write up the developments. The inquiry would last until close on noon. The weather was hot, and in the Journalist's house—which in any case was some distance away—there was nothing to eat but cheese and cress. The aroma of chicken kebab and eggplant stew filled the ministry. The sound of the noonday gun was heard . . .

I forget what happened after that.

Dakhow

## Good News [A Minister's Munificence]

A few days ago our Ministry of the Interior,[65] purely out of the goodness of its heart, granted seven other ministers with port-folio permission to sit on chairs while in its presence. This regal munificence is surely worthy of the highest praise. We hope that

65. A reference to Amin al-Soltān, known as the Atābak-e A'zam (see Sohrāb Yazdāni, "Siāsat," p. 232). He was soon promoted to the premiership: see *SE* no. 12, likewise a cryptic allusion.

His Excellency the Minister will continue to manifest such beneficence and condescension toward us his loyal subjects and that as long as our poets sing praises, and our soothsayers and dervishes cast horoscopes and interpret good and bad omens, and the noble Hajji Najm al-Dowleh's[66] calendar determines auspicious days for important deeds, he might sit securely on the throne of glory and greatness.

## Strike of Workers at Shah Abd al-Azim

Yesterday, workers in the Bazaar of the Religion Vendors downed tools in protest of their insufficient wages. They were each granted a raise of five *shāhi*s[67] by their employer.

66. "Star of the state": Hajji Mirza Abd al-Ghafur, one of the first graduates of the Dār al-Fonun, received this title after being appointed the chief astrologer to Nāser al-Din Shah (see Bāmdād, *Sharh-e hāl-e rejāl-e Irān*, vol. 2, p. 273).

67. One quarter of a *qerān* (see note 53 above), a paltry sum.

# Sur-e Esrāfil, Series 1, Nos. 7–8, pp. 14–16

August 1, 1907

## [A Villager Goes to the City]

*After selling his fresh produce in Tehran, the smart but naïve Owyār-qoli reports to his stunned fellow-villagers on city affairs. He waxes enthusiastic about corrupt politicians, clerics who secretly collude with foreign diplomats, and journalists who are in the paid service of the shah.*

May the countryside go to the dogs. Really, a villager is very un-civilized, very uncouth. Not to mince words, the villager is utterly beyond the pale, a complete boor, a veritable animal. We villagers, unless we go to the city, never become human. Our eyes and ears will never open. The poet was dead right, bless him, when he warned, Shun the countryside, it makes a man a fool.[68] Elsewhere he says, A bird whose tail points toward the town and whose head points toward the countryside—that bird's tail has more sense than its head.

I mean to say, let's take someone who, from morn till night, trudges after cows or sheep or goats, or (seriously) after an ass. And at night he beds down with these same creatures till morning. I ask you, what will become of such a person?

As the poet of blessed memory said, May my companion become a better person, so that I may become better than he. Villagers come home from the fields at nightfall and dip their flat bread into a fatty egg stew. A milking pail of well water is set down beside them, and, hey presto, they tuck in with greater gusto than any prosperous shaykh ever enjoyed a chicken breast and fresh-squeezed lemonade. After supper, they all gather round; a night-time grazing!

Little woman, bring in the raisins and dried mulberries and apricots! There is a wooden platter of toasted peas, and a sackful

68. The verse (whose second hemistich Dehkhodā does not quote) is by Jalāl al-Din Rumi: "Deh marow, deh mard-rā ahmaq konad / Aql-rā bi-nur o bi-rownaq konad [It dims and tarnishes the mind]." Coincidentally, Sadr al-Din 'Ayni (or Aini; 1878–1954), a Bukharan reformer-turned-revolutionary and a contemporary of Dehkhodā, quotes this same verse in the first volume of his Tajik autobiography *Yoddosht'ho* ("Reminiscences"; English translation, *The Sands of Oxus* [1998], p. 189). He puts it into the mouth of a disdainful city youth who is visiting 'Ayni's village, whom the young 'Ayni subsequently beats in a verse-capping contest.

of parched wheat has been tossed on top of the *kursi*.[69] And now let's hear how Owyār-qoli,[70] just back from the city after selling his fresh produce, regales the company. Just like the special correspondent for *Le Matin* returning from the Far East or—not that there's any comparison!—the *mojāhedin* of Shah Abd al-Azim returning from a raid on the Jewish quarter.[71] Our Owyār-qoli waxes enthusiastic about the shah, the vizier, the mojtahed, his listeners all agog for more.

For instance:

He says the crown jewels belong to the nation. Nader Shah brought them from India at the cost of two million Iranian lives.[72]

The livestock sellers were driving a large flock of sheep to the city, and the governor ordered them turned back at Saveh, for fear that on a full stomach the people might start thinking about the constitution.

---

69. The *kursi* (or *korsi*) is the Iranian village version of central heating: a wooden frame is placed over a brazier in the middle of the room and covered with quilts. The family can sit around this, their legs warm under the quilts, and even sleep under the quilts on winter nights.

70. This dialect Persian term (the literary form would be *ābyār-qoli*), meaning "slave of the assistant irrigation manager," implies an unschooled country yokel.

71. Dehkhodā is here using the term *mojāhedin* sarcastically, in reference to anticonstitutionalist forces stationed at the Shah Abd al-Azim shrine and their raids on the Jewish community. Supporters of Nuri demanded that Jews take their side in the nation's political battles. These attacks led to the migration of some Jewish families to Palestine. See David Yeroushalmi, "Israel ii. Jewish Persian Community," in *EIr* (2007), also online (updated 2012).

72. At one time there was a rumor that the shah had pawned the crown jewels to the Russian Bank so he could pay the anticonstitutionalists (Yazdāni, "Siāsat," p. 222).

One of the royal attendants went and kissed the knee of a venerable old mojtahed[73] and asked him to go with them to Shah Abd al-Azim. The cleric protested that since the start of the revolution he had not stepped outside his house, on purpose to avoid giving aid to an oppressor during these last days of his life.

They have built a "House of Oblivion,"[74] and they're taking people there to swear an oath together to make all the other viziers into the personal flunkies of the minister of the interior.

Anyway, to cut a long story short, he told so many of these tall tales that it seemed during the two hours that this cursed devil was selling his load in the hay seller's square—everyone had come to see him with one story or another, among them the tobacconist, the sorcerer, the Sā'ed, the Manshur,[75] the gov-

73. Apparently a reference to Mojallal al-Soltān, the king's special attendant. The "old mojtahed" probably refers to Sayyid Abu Tāleb Zanjāni (ibid., p. 223).

74. Farāmush-khāneh, "house of forgetfulness," a phonetic imitation of the French *franc-maçon*, "Freemason," was the name of a semisecret organization modeled after the Freemasons and established in Tehran in 1895. Its founder was Malkom Khan, an Armenian intellectual, nominally a Muslim convert, who had become acquainted with Freemasons while living in France (see *SE* no. 6, note 62). The organization attracted a number of intellectual reformers, including Amin al-Dowleh, the prime minister to Mozaffar al-Din Shah, and Sayyid Sādeq Tabātabā'i, whose son Sayyid Mohammad Tabātabā'i became a leading constitutionalist figure and a prominent Freemason (see Amir Nejāt, *Jam'iyat'hā-ye Serri*, p. 340; and Hamid Algar, *Religion and State in Iran*, p. 284). However, the term was also (as here) a catchall phrase for any secret political organization in which the elite were involved (Yazdāni, "Siāsat," p. 242, note 26).

75. "Sā'ed" and "Manshur" refer to the politicians Sā'ed al-Dowleh and Manshur al-Nezām, secret members of the Farāmush-khāneh. Dehkhodā does not divulge their full identity, but he gets his point across. Thanks to E. Malekzadeh for clarification on this point.

ernment official, the broker, several clerical sayyids, the *fokoli* bunch[76]—as if every reporter in town had come to see him and told him all his secrets. Now, to get back to the point: as I said, until you come to the city, your eyes and ears are closed, and that's a fact.

A few years earlier this same Owyār-qoli had come to the city to buy stuff for his son's wedding. That evening, round the communal bread oven, he told everyone how word was going about the city that in Tabriz there was a certain money changer, Hajji Mohammad Taqi Āqā, who had forty hundred million crore of cash, five hundred times twenty flocks of sheep, each consisting of a thousand sheep, probably ten to fifty complete villages, dogs, cats, mares, camels, mules, this, that, and the other . . . We were amazed how a respectable God-fearing hajji could have so much money, since obviously this kind of wealth can't be gotten by honest means. Surely he must have taken over the property of Hajji Abbās by force.[77] Surely he must have kidnapped someone or clubbed orphans and widows and children and robbed them. Then our Owyār-qoli added that Hajji Mohammad Taqi Āqā was also pretty thick with the government of Tabriz.

We all protested, For God's sake, these are no secrets! Everyone knows that anyone who has money is in cahoots with the shah and the government—this is not news you should be bringing from the city and broadcasting to us!

No, hear me out, he said. The best part is still to come.

76. *Fokoli*: from the French *faux col*, "false collar." A disparaging name given by traditionalists in the reign of Nāser al-Din Shah to men who affected a formal European style of dress, including the starched detachable shirt collar.

77. The term for "the property" in the original is *Lakki Dizi*, which according to Dabirsiāqi was apparently the name of a place. See *MD*, p. 41, note 8.

OK, go on, we agreed.

Well, this Hajji Āqā happens to be a tough guy . . .

At this juncture we became skeptical. You see, we village folk call the city people "Tajiks," by which we mean cowards. Not only us; even the city folk call that kind of person—Hajjis and their ilk—"three-slit gownies," which, like the epithet "waterskin" in the townies' parlance, implies a fat coward.[78]

So now he stands revealed as a city slicker, and a hajji to boot! How could such a person be a tough guy?

At this point, let me add a couple of marginal notes. We villagers have a right to call the city people Tajiks and cowards because, for instance, when visiting officials give us a hard time, however many they are there's always ten or twenty of the village youths ready to pick up an almondwood cudgel and lay into those agents, even if they number fifty or a hundred. Hey, Mister Tax Man, what did you eat for breakfast—mushy peas? Take this for lunch, if you please! Just like a few years ago in the village of Jowqābād near Varāmin [south of Tehran] when sixty Cossacks came to force us to sell them our wheat for nine tumans per hundredweight, so that the hajjis of Tehran could mix sawdust with it and sell it in the city for forty tumans. Twenty of us ganged up and pounded those Cossacks so hard with the butts of their own rifles that the poor devils galloped nonstop for thirty miles before halting for

78. The reference is to a particular style of *qabā* (a gown or robe worn mostly by clerics) with an open front and a slit up each side almost to the waist. "Waterskin" is *khik*; the adjective *khiki* means fat and bulging, suggesting that the person so called is out of shape and inactive. The term *Tājik*, nowadays reserved for Persian speakers of Central Asia, was formerly applied (especially by Turks of Iran) to sedentary urban Persians in general.

a breather, and a pipe of opium, at the Mozaffari coffeehouse in Shah Abd al-Azim.

Let's get back to our topic. We left off where Hajji Mohammad Taqi the money changer was, according to Owyār-qoli, a tough egg. He told us how one day another money changer, a creditor of Hajji Āqā, came to his shop on the upper story to get his money back. Hajji Āqā hit him so hard in the chest that the man fell off the balcony and landed flat on the ground. The hajji punched a second creditor on the nose so hard that he became one with the ground and went to meet his maker ahead of the first creditor.

At this point we all exclaimed to Owyār-qoli, Get out! Come off it! However stupid we might be, we're not so stupid as to believe everything you tell us. When the poor man saw that we really didn't believe him, he swore, If I tell a lie, may my tongue not confess the faith on my deathbed! May I not see my son's wedding! May the sins of Shemr, Yazid, the governor, the footman, and the headman be on my head![79]

Well, now that we've been to the city, we suddenly see that poor Owyār-qoli was telling the truth.

We see, as it were, that until one has been to the city one doesn't understand these things properly. Because once we *have* been to the city, we see that this same Hajji Mohammad Taqi Āqā was actually a lot tougher than Owyār-qoli had said. It seems that quite recently, according to general report, he gave money and guns to five men and sent them, on the pretext of a dispute over water

---

79. Yazid I (d. 683) was the son of Muʿāwiya, the founder of the Umayyad dynasty. Yazid's army, led by Shemr, fought and killed Hoseyn b. Ali and his supporters in the famous Battle of Karbalā in 680 CE.

rights in Bahārestān Square,[80] to kill Mohaqqeq al-Dowleh[81] and two other Majlis deputies in the residence of Hajji Moʻin al-Tojjār. And in the excess of his power and toughness he ignored the fact that Mohaqqeq al-Dowleh, in addition to being a people's representative and universally popular, had taught five hundred students in this city, the least of whom is Dakhow, who takes on our biggest roughnecks, no holds barred.

So that's the kind of person who is a tough guy: the kind who carries a lot of weight about town, *not* a Hajji Āqā. But a country bumpkin who has never been to the city doesn't understand these things. No, a country bumpkin who has never been to the city just doesn't understand these things. For example, one of the things that we villagers didn't understand is when, during these past few years, our children came back from the city to the village, they would tell us: In the city there is a sort of syrupy vinegar called cognac. The landlords drink it at night and get drunk and quarrelsome, then yell to their servants, Hey, boy! Go fetch that goddamn peasant who brought us chicken and *lavāsh* bread this morning. The servants come and take us from the caravansary to wait on their boss, but then the boss, who has gotten drunk on cognac, flies into a towering rage such as no God-fearing man should have to suffer. I'm barely in the door when he confronts me with "I hear that this year you, you bastard, have stored fifty man of wheat in a dry well?" And when I protest abjectly that I too am a Muslim, with a wife and children, who works hard from one year's end to the next and depends on the landlord's charity for a crust of bread,

80. The location of Iran's parliament, the Majlis.

81. Mohaqqeq al-Dowleh, a son of Mirza Hāshem Khan Amin-e Darbār Kāshi, graduated from the School of Political Science of Tehran. He was a deputy in the First Majlis, representing the merchants' class.

the landlord's eyes bulge from their sockets and he lays into me with his stick like nobody's business: "See how the bastard sings like a nightingale for me now! Beat him, boys!"—and a score of coachmen descend on me to thrash me till I can't take any more.

Now, where was I? Oh yes, I was saying that until we country folk have been to the city we don't understand these things. Like this cognac, for instance, which we thought was grape vinegar; now that we've been to the city, we realize that Cognac is a person. It isn't grape vinegar.

Yes, Cognac is a person; Cognac is in fact a woman. My God, if Cognac doesn't forgive us now, what are we supposed to do? Isn't it a sin that for so many years we've been slandering someone, calling a poor, weak woman a "grape vinegar?"

Yes, this is a great sin. I here and now declare in the presence of you Muslims all that Ms. Cognac is a person. She is a woman [a madam] in the household of His Highness's butler. Ms. Cognac ripped off the silk merchants, the grocers, and the druggists, for four or five thousand tumans, and now that she has displaced the bride, the poor suitors have been thrown out. Anyone who demands his money is slapped, jailed, or banished. And if—God forbid!—someone says that some of the . . . [82] of Isfahan flirted with Ms. Cognac, the matter became public knowledge, and these men then banished her from Isfahan and sent her to Tehran in order to swindle the tradesmen there, the story is deemed so outrageous that the person is labeled an unbeliever twice over.

Yes, the point is that we country folk understand nothing until we have been to the city. For instance, we bumpkins imagined that

82. The omission marks here probably (in view of what follows) allude to the ulama.

sayyids, mullas, and mojtaheds, out of a strict regard for the sacred, when they hear a foreign name, ritually purify their mouths with the prescribed quantity of clean water.[83] Now that we've come to the city we see a person who is a sayyid, a mojtahed, an ākhund, the brother of a mojtahed, and the head of the granary keepers' guild, in Zargandeh;[84] we see him and another person on Tuesday the fifth of this month at 9 a.m. European time in private conversation with Minorsky,[85] the Russian chargé d'affaires. An hour and a half later, together with the same Mr. Minorsky and that same other person, he goes to see His Excellency the [British] ambassador, spending an hour and a half in private with him. Finally the sayyid shakes hands with these gentlemen and climbs aboard his droshky; they seat that large sayyid in the front of the droshky, and off he goes, without even washing his hands in the flowing streams of the Zargandeh.[86]

No, unless he goes to the city, the villager doesn't understand these things.

83. Persian *kor kashidan*: the *kor* is a quantity of water (about 3.5 cubic feet) prescribed by shari'a which, provided it retains its volume, color, taste, and smell, can legally purify any unclean object that it rinses or that is dipped into it.

84. A village north of Tehran known for its river and cool weather in the summer. Mohammad Shah Qajar (1808–48) granted it to the Russian legation for diplomatic use. He gave the neighboring Golhak to the British legation. The British government built a massive compound in the area, composed of summer houses for the ambassador and other diplomats.

85. Vladimir Minorsky (1877–1966), a Russian scholar and Iranologist, after the Russian Revolution left his diplomatic post in Tehran for Paris and subsequently England, where he continued his brilliant academic career: see C. E. Bosworth, "Minorsky, Vladimir Fed'orovich," in *EIr* online (2004).

86. According to Shi'i doctrine, a Muslim should perform the ritual ablution after touching an impure object, in this case the hand of an infidel.

For instance, when we villagers heard the words *brigadier, officer, colonel,*[87] our bodies would tremble and our mind's eye would visualize something like the boogeyman; we would tell ourselves that surely these creatures were man-eaters, surely they had no sense of fair play and none of the mercy of [Imam] Ali in their hearts. Whereas in fact this was not the case. Because we saw these same officers, when they picked up issue no. 3 of the newspaper *Hekmat-e Emruz* [Philosophy today] and read there such an eloquent and persuasive notice of the [Russian] colonel's proclamation of protection—all of a sudden, from these hearts that we would have said held not a whiff of fairness there welled up as it were a fountain of compassion and generosity! They immediately opened the cash ledger of financial assistance and collected five, six, eight thousand shāhis out of their own pockets, and as much as twenty-five tumans and sixty-seven hundred and a half shāhis in all was sent to the editor of the periodical.

Yes, we country folk don't understand a thing until we've been to the city. For example, during recent days when there was all this talk about justice and oppression, we always thought that a tyrant and oppressor had to wear a [tall] hat, hard leather shoes with his heels tucked inside, and an old-fashioned robe with folds around the waist. And, of course, tight trousers. By the way, to change the subject, what was I saying? The point I wish to make here is that homespun cloth of Yazd has a much longer life than imported Western cloth.[88] Need I say more?

Dakhow

87. *Sartip, sāhebmansab, sarhang* in the original.
88. Dakhow might be referring to the endurance of native, homespun forms of corruption.

# *Sur-e Esrāfil,* Series 1, No. 11,[89] pp. 5–8

August 22, 1907

## Razi-ye Ghaznavi [and Other Indian Mystics]

. . . Desirous of going to India, I looked up Shaykh Abu Rezā-ye "Ratan"—whose origins, according to some, go back to the apos-

89. There is an unexplained gap of two issues of the paper (and two weeks) between the double issue nos. 7–8 and issue no. 11. In a letter to one of the co-owners of the Tarbiat Library, which financially supported the paper, Managing Editor Mirza Qāsem Khan Tabrizi wrote that he owed 140 tumans to the print shop, "which won't publish the issue until paid." For an excerpt of the letter see Iraj Afshār, "Sur-e Esrafil" (this appears in an issue of *Āyandeh* devoted entirely to Dehkhodā's life and publications).

tles of Jesus, and according to others to the Companions of the Prophet of Islam, and who lived for one thousand and fourteen years—and found the following circumstantial extract in the books of this sect (*Riāz al-'ārefin*, p. 79):[90]

> Abu Hafs-e Khuzi: One of the great men and leaders of this sect, and the true successor of the revered Shaykh Abdollāh Yaqzān al-Khuzi. He was a contemporary of Shaykh Abu Sa'id Abi Khayr, with whom he had a strong bond. He was a master of many sciences and held minds in thrall, for which reason he was given the sobriquet "Shaykh of the Jinn" (idem, p. 43).

## Letter from a Lady [Cure for a Sty]

*In these "letters" Dehkhodā is not merely showing off his knowledge of Persian folklore and popular superstition. Behind the mockery is a sympathetic understanding of the dimensions of the social straitjacket imposed on Iranian women, even in the capital. However loving and caring of their children and intuitively in tune with adolescent psychology,*

90. The source that Dehkhodā cites is not the well-known *Riāz al-'ārefin* (Gardens of the gnostics) by Rezā-qoli Khan Hedāyat (1800–1871), a memoir and anthology (*tazkereh*) of recent and contemporary Persian poets of Iran, but rather a memoir of Indo-Persian mystical poets with a similar title, *Tazkereh-ye riāz al-'ārefin*, by a younger Indian contemporary, Āftāb Rāy Lakhnavi. In the modern printed edition of this work (Islamabad, 1977–82), the brief notice of Shaykh Razi al-Din Lālā-ye Ghaznavi is in vol 1, p. 269: he was a cousin of the poet Sanā'i and died in Isfahan in 643/1245. References to Shaykh Abu Rezā and Abu Hafs-e Khuzi have not been located in this edition. Abu Sa'id (967–1049) was a famous mystic of Khorasan: see *EIr* (1983), also online (updated 2011).

*these veiled "captives of the sack" were denied free access to education and support in the public sphere (by financial and patriarchal restrictions sanctioned by long social tradition and reinforced by religious rulings). They were thus left at the mercy of neighborhood quacks, prayers and pious rituals, talismans, and magical spells.*

Kablā'i Dakhow:

God preserve all the Muslims' children from the evil eye; may he not begrudge me this one spot of balm. Kablā'i, after burying twelve children, I have just this one left, and the onyx-eyed[91] enviers never take their eyes off him. Yesterday my boy was skipping hale and healthy along the street, hopping on the back of carriages, and singing a verse or a ghazal for the Europeans. A relative of his father's, damn his envious eyes, was staying with us last night; next morning one of my boy's eyes closed, and the lower lid swelled up—he had a sty. His uncle called it by a crude expression![92]

---

91. Persian *bābā quri shodeh'hā*, literally "those afflicted with staphyloma." This refers to an eye disease that causes the uvea, the pigmented layer of the eye, to bulge out, making it resemble an onyx stone (*bābā quri*). People with abnormal eyes were believed to have malignant powers to disfigure those they looked at.

92. Persian *sendeh salām*, referring to a folk spell to cure a sty. The person so afflicted should go to the toilet early in the morning and recite a rhyme asking his excreta (*sendeh*) to please remove the sty (see below, in "Reply to Letter," where Dakhow quotes this rhyme but modestly omits the indelicate word *sendeh*; and further in Jamālzādeh's *Farhang-e loghāt-e 'āmmiyāneh*). The treatment of eye diseases (very prevalent in Iran) was a recognized medical specialty, and in some treatments (especially of cataract) local physicians (*kahhāl*) performed better than European ophthalmologists (Willem Floor, *Public Health in Qajar Iran*, pp. 28, 105, 136–40).

They're forever scolding me for letting the boy out into the streets bareheaded and barefoot in this heat. But what can I do—I've been blessed with only one child, how can I help it? May no meal be limited to a single loaf, dopey or crazy. A spoiled only child is naturally foolish and wild.

Anyway, for all of four days now, morn and eve, his playmates have been throwing stones at carriages and poking knives (if you'll pardon the expression) under the asses' tails, placing stones in the horse-tram lines, and throwing dirt at pedestrians.[93]

Now my Hasan is sick at home with me. I've tried every remedy and drug I can think of, but he just gets worse and worse. They tell me to take him to these doctors and suchlike; I say, a plague on them and their medicines, what do I know about these new-fangled quack cures and what sort of stuff I might be giving to my child? I entrust my boy's welfare to you, today, here, tomorrow, till doomsday. God keep even your blind and scab-headed children from the evil eye. God requite you a thousand times over. May you never see them perish in your old age. I beg you, I need whatever medicines you know of to make my boy well again within a couple

93. In 1879, on returning from a European tour, Nāser al-Din Shah instituted a metropolitan police force (*nazmiyyeh*) for Tehran under an Austrian chief of police. This official in 1896 issued a list of regulations, one of which forbade children to throw objects at carriages or otherwise disturb the passengers; the parents of violators would be subject to arrest and a possible term of hard labor in the coal mines. Most such regulations were routinely ignored (Willem Floor, "Les premières règles," pp. 176–77). By the early years of the twentieth century, Tehran had a horse-tram service. An American visitor in 1907 observed, "At intervals . . . a tramway crowded to the roof with native passengers goes jostling its way through the long files of camels and pack-horses" (ibid., p. 181, quoting Cresson, *Persia*, p. 67).

of days. Even though I have little to spare, I swear I will bring you a sugarloaf without fail. May God never take you old men from us!

Your humble servant,
Captive-of-the-Sack

## Reply to the Letter

Highly respected and esteemed Mrs. Captive-of-the-Sack:

First, it seems odd that a lady like you, a mature housewife, seeing that your children were not surviving, did not give them such names as Mashhadi or Māsha'allāh or Mirzā Māndegār![94] Second, on the very first day that the boy's eye swelled, why didn't you shoo it away?

Now, what's done is done. I am absolutely confident that his swollen eyelid is not, God willing, due to the evil eye but a result of the sun and the heat. This evening, first of all apply some smoke of Christians' amber[95] and see how it responds. If it works, that's fine; if not, then the next day boil a little rouge on a cotton or gauze pad together with a drop of breast milk from a woman who has given birth to a girl[96] and a little (pardon the expression) female donkey

94. Meaning, respectively, "Pilgrim to [the shrine of the eighth imam at] Mashhad," "What God wills," and something like "Prince stayhere"; such names were given to babies after previous children had died young, in hopes of their survival.

95. A mocking reference to donkey dung.

96. See Floor, *Public Health in Qajar Iran*, p. 28: "Infantile conjunctivitis was treated 'with fresh mother's milk squirted directly into the eye (good, sensible treatment this, for it is sterile, convenient, mild antiseptic).'"

dung in a fish's ear, pour that into his eye, and see what happens. If it works, fine; if not, then for three days at sunset take a cheap china bowl, fill it with water, place it in front of the boy, and look at the sty: if it is red, take seven bits of lean meat—and if it isn't, seven grains of rice or a clod of earth—and shake them for as long as it takes to recite an *'alam nashreh*,[97] and see how it responds. If it works, that's fine; if not, then for three days at breakfast time take the boy (you'll pardon the expression) to the toilet and teach him to repeat this jingle seven times:

Good morning, . . . —I humbly ask of you,
Take the sty from my eye—or else this day you'll rue!

—and hopefully you won't need any more medicines. If, God forbid, it still doesn't work, then I can offer no further aid. Go to the Hasanābād quarter and ask Āqā Sayyid Farajollāh the sorcerer to fix him a spell against the sniffles.

Servant of the Poor, Dakhow Ali-shāh[98]

## [Domestic Politics]

*In the pseudo-autobiographical sketch that begins this wide-ranging piece, Dakhow's mother seems to be following the advice of "an old witch" in a poem by the Azerbaijani satirist Ali-Akbar Sāber: "As no faithful*

97. A nonsensical phrase, from a popular misunderstanding of the Arabic *a-lam nashraḥ* [*laka ṣadraka*], "Have we not expanded [thy breast]," which begins a short sura (no. 94) of the Qur'an.

98. This satirical name takes a form typical of Ne'matollāhi dervishes.

*husband can possibly be found, a woman should spend the earnings of her husband on her women friends and be happy with them behind his back" (Hasan Javadi,* Satire in Persian Literature, *p. 212). Fictive bonds of sisterhood were common among women and could involve sexual relations (see Janet Afary,* Sexual Politics in Modern Iran, *pp. 101–3). The stream of reminiscence segues arbitrarily into a sketch of Yaḥyā Mirzā Eskandari, a deputy in the First Majlis with radical social democratic sympathies (for his political and literary career see Manouchehr M. Eskandari-Qajar, "Novellas as Morality Tales and Entertainment"). In a series of naïvely frank obiter dicta attributed to Yaḥyā Mirzā, the satirist reprises the technique he displayed in "[Hazards of Journalism]" (SE no. 5) to indirectly expose a selection of the governing class's dirty linen; some of the allusions here are too obscure to trace.*

God have mercy on all the dear departed. My late father, like all hajjis everywhere, was tightfisted, one who couldn't spend his money on himself. But my late mother was not like my father; she always said that a man's money never reaches his wife—as soon as he is wealthy enough to own a second pair of pants he starts to think about getting a new wife. No sooner did my father reach the end of the alley than she would dash up on to the roof and shout to the neighbor women: Auntie Robābeh, yoo-hoo! Sister Roqiyeh, yoo-hoo! Ma Fātemeh, yoo-hoo-hoo! Then suddenly you'd see the room fill up with my mother's soul mates; she would light the samovar, fill the hookah, and sit with them sharing their news and woes. This activity served two purposes: one, communal enjoyment, and the other, to fritter away my father's spare cash and keep him on a monogamous leash.

Now let's leave them at it; who and what they gossiped about can perhaps be told another time, but here it isn't the point. The point is that sometimes my mother, while chattering away and puffing nonstop on the hubble-bubble, would catch sight of me and say, Hey, cursed child, open your ears wide; see here—as soon as your father gets back, I know damn well you'll tell him every little thing that happened today. But if you breathe a word about the neighbors coming round, I'll tear your flesh from your body with my own teeth!

I would answer her with a laugh. And she would say, You'll be laughing on the mortician's slab.

Then she'd turn to her companion and remark, You'd think he was my stepson.[99] I can't stand the sight of him! Yes indeed, my mother knew her boy well. From childhood on, I was no respecter of anyone's secrets. I could never keep my mouth shut. Right from the word go I was a blabbermouth; even after my mother's injunctions, hardly had my father set foot in the hallway before I shouted, Daddy!

Go on! he said.

I told him: Today the neighborhood women came over again and Mommy lighted the samovar for them.

My father frowned. My mother looked daggers at me under her brows, but in my father's presence she didn't dare slap me for this indiscretion. Yet I tensed in expectation of the blow, since I knew that she would find an excuse to hit me anyway.

And indeed so it turned out. Not ten minutes passed before she attacked: Blasted child! I washed these clothes only

99. *Pesar-e havu-am*: strictly, "the son of my husband's other wife [in a polygamous marriage]."

yesterday, and you've gone and dragged them through the muck again—by God, may they be your shroud! I'll give you what you deserve, you little devil! Then she grabbed my cheeks and pulled as hard as she could, and punched me all over. Finally, when my father came to rescue me, she grew even angrier and bit me on the arms.

Yes, she bit my arms. I still have those bite marks on each of my forearms. Earlier, whenever I saw those marks I was reminded of my mother and would say a "God have mercy on her." But now, for no reason I can think of, whenever I happen to see them I remember Yaḥyā Mirza.

Poor Yaḥyā Mirza. Unfortunate Yaḥyā Mirza. That night when I stood in the courtyard of the Bahārestān, besides me there were 500 hajjis with red, henna-dyed beards, 450 Karbalā'is with close-clipped goatees, 350 Mashhadis with long beards and round heads, and at least 200 students of the school of Shaykh Abu'l Qāsem the Solver of [Doctrinal] Problems—and all of them listening to you. And you only told the truth about a Russian warship off the coast at Anzali, seventy-four votes in the Iranian assembly, Qur'ans hidden for two and a half months under the robes of three merchants, and midnight visits to the audience rooms of ulama and nobles. I was there, and so were 2,691 Hajjis, Karbalā'is, Mashhadis, and Qomis: that is, all the moral trustees of the city, and all of them would testify to your innocence. These are all persons two of whose testimony is enough to make what is lawful unlawful and vice versa, so how is it that in your case their testimony is invalid? Now it is alleged that you, God forbid, were disrespectful toward some representatives of the nation, saying that those who up until yesterday couldn't even hire a donkey, now that the End of Time is approaching, can buy horses for the price of a prayer.[100]

They say you said that a parcel of the lands of the Emerald Throne area belonging to Prince Farmānfarmā will be made into a private park.[101]

They say you said, I believe, that the delegate from Qandahar[102] to the Iranian national assembly asked some sayyid, in that dark area behind the Sepahsalar mosque, whether he approved of that article he had sent under his signature to the *Majlis Gazette*, and the sayyid had answered yes. They say you said that in that Majlis there was a quarrel over a financial distribution and one person walked out in a huff.

They say you said that if it's really forty thousand tumans, the Deutsche Bank won't be able to get back on its feet for four hundred years.

They say you asked, What sort of secret dealings do the hay merchant, the grocer, the druggist, and the greengrocer have with the government ministers that they bring their monetary drafts to the [wealthy] Zoroastrian merchants?[103]

---

100. Referring to a Shi'i belief that, as the time for the return of the Mahdi approaches, money will be superseded in business transactions by the pronouncement of a blessing (*salavāt*) upon the Prophet and his family.

101. *Pārk* in former times denoted a vast private estate, sometimes used for hunting. Dabirsiāqi indicates this was a place in Old Tehran later named Abu Sa'id (*MD*, p. 56, note 34).

102. There appear to have been informal representatives in the Majlis from regions that had been part of the Safavid Empire and Nader Shah's empire, such as the Russian Caucasus and Afghanistan.

103. Dehkhodā suggests some ministers were trying to garner support in the Majlis by paying off the deputies who represented various guilds (Yazdāni, "Siāsat," p. 222).

They say you said, Curses upon those that deny the Majlis, and likewise upon those who have taken refuge in the shrine of Shah Abd al-Azim, for they are evildoers upon earth,[104] but upon the companions of the robbers and the partners in the caravan alike, in whatever guise they be, curses!

They say you said that with daily expenses of two hundred tumans, how can they afford to deposit 120,000 tumans in the bank?

They say you said that after they fill the oil lamps, the sayyids relax on the wooden platform over the pond at the residence of Eqbāl al-Dowleh.[105]

They say you said that the representative from Tiyulābād[106] has been exempted from paying rent in return for implementing the memo from the shah concerning the transfer of the superintendence of shrines from Sufis.

They say you said that the election of the remaining parliamentary representatives will happen after 120 years, and then only after

104. In the summer of 1907 Shaykh Fazlollāh Nuri and a thousand of his followers left Tehran and took sanctuary at Shah Abd al-Azim. They turned the mosque into an alternative political center and published a newspaper, *Lavāyeh-e Shaykh Fazlollāh Nuri*, in which they condemned the new order. See Ahmad Kasravi, *Tārikh-e Mashruteh-ye Irān*, pp. 379–85.

105. Eqbāl al-Dowleh was a former governor of Kashan, Kermanshah, and Isfahan and a close ally of Mohammad-Ali Shah (see Bāmdād, *Sharh-e hāl-e rejāl-e Irān*, vol. 3, pp. 214–15). Almost every house had a shallow pool in its courtyard, which was used for ritual ablution. On festive occasions the pool was covered with wooden planks, and the added area was used to seat guests or stage performances.

106. "Landgrantsville," a satirical allusion to the officials responsible for awarding the revenues of landed estates (*tiyul*). The Majlis had modified this system in an attempt at land reform: the government would henceforth collect the revenue and pay a defined benefit to the tiyul holders.

the demise of Ehteshām al-Saltaneh, Moshir al-Molk, Amin al-Dowleh, and all the other intellectuals of Iran.

This is what they claim you said. Apart from these, they make a thousand other allegations. But really, I swear you never said any of these things; I was standing right there listening to every word you said! Apart from me, Mirza Sayyid Valiollāh Khān, a deputy of the assembly, was also standing there. You never said anything to disparage the honorable representatives. All you said was that Malkom didn't write his *Qānun* newspapers just to decorate his own library, that he should now send us a message not to reprint them.[107]

All you said was: That poor devil's soul [Malkom] is clueless about the composition of the [present-day] Tehran *Farāmush-khāneh*, and after forty years of knowing the gentleman inside out one can no longer be fooled by appearances.

All you said was that the interior minister should be alerted that the . . . of that Gushsāz-bāshi is not so remarkable that in these straitened circumstances her husband should be allotted a stipend of four thousand tumans directly from the treasury.[108]

All you said was that there are plenty of Russian Smirnovs in Belgium and Holland, in France and England and Switzerland, so why, when we have a six crore deficit, is *he* [Konstantin Nikolaevich

107. Malkom Khan's influential *Qānun*, originally published in London in 1890–98, was reprinted in Tehran by Hāshem Āqā in late 1907 or 1908 (Browne, *Press and Poetry*, p. 125; see also *SE* no. 6, note 62). These articles were meant for the public, so why would Malkom Khan ask that they not be reprinted?

108. We are unable to identify the person, or occupation, behind the name Gushsāz-bāshi. The term suggests a musician, and the remark doubtless implies that the payment mentioned was not for strictly professional services.

Smirnov] picked to teach Russian [to Crown Prince Ahmad] and paid a five-hundred-tuman stipend?

All you said was that a certain high personage [the Atābak, the prime minister] laid it on the line: The heads of departments and the ministers are all my personal servants, and their seal stamps are all in my hands.

All you said was that this fellow [Minister of War Mostowfi al-Mamālek] said: I swear, I'm so dense that even after so many years frequenting the cafés of Europe I still don't know how to play billiards! What do I know about war? And for a full twenty-four hours he begged not to be considered.[109] His Eminence said, Let the jellygraph horoscopes come through,[110] and don't embarrass me in front of the Russian envoy.

Yes, those are the things you said. And a lot more besides; I won't deny it, or I'll have to answer for it in the afterlife.

With my own ears I heard you say that the late minister of court did not die of a heart attack; it was an incubus.

I heard you say that Mirza Mohammad-Ali Khan did not fall off the roof of his own volition; his head was split open by a blow

109. See Yazdāni, "Siāsat," p. 220; also for the identity of the Atābak, alluded to above.

110. The jellygraph, hectograph, or gelatin duplicator is a printing machine that transfers an original, prepared with special inks, to a pan or pad of gelatin. Mikhail Aliso invented the mechanism in Russia in 1869. It had the advantage over existing processes, such as lithography, that it was not necessary to prepare the original as a mirror image, since it was impressed on the back of the master sheet with a stylus. Paper sheets were then applied to the pad (later mounted on a revolving drum) for a print run of between twenty and eighty. Here it appears to be serving as a government office mimeograph; it was also used at this period to print clandestine opposition leaflets called *shabnāmeh*, "night letters" (see Afary, *Iranian Constitutional Revolution*, p. 52).

from a club in the hand of a special agent, and he went to join the martyrs of Karbalā—that is, his pure ancestors.

I heard you say, The verse "God pardons what is past"[111] is specific to the earliest period of Islam, and those there addressed were products of the age of ignorance [pre-Islam]; one cannot reapply this sentiment every day, or else the world order will be destroyed. And furthermore I heard you say that if, God forbid, the clerics of Najaf wish to keep the sense of this verse in force, we as Muslims will not accept it.

These things I heard you say, and so did all the holy men in Tehran, and we are all prepared to testify to it. But you definitely did not insult the deputies of the assembly; you did not utter a word of complaint about them.

But let's see where we were. Yes, may God have mercy on all the dear departed, and may he even purify and redeem my shamefaced self. God forgive my mother when I blabbed to my father about her neighbor friends coming over and she beat me on the pretext of my dirtying her clean washing. Yes, she beat me on the pretext of my dirtying my clothes, just as the newspaper *Habl al-Matin* in the first column of its first issue got away with insulting the minister of the interior but was closed down on the pretext that in the last column of issue no. 1,694 it had published an announcement about a lottery. So go on, tell me to write down my testimony so that I will be rewarded by God. I've already written it, but let's see what day it is—I'm dead, you're alive; today is one, tomorrow is two, the day after tomorrow is three; if on the third day I am not

111. Qur'an 5:95. The context is the Islamic prohibition on hunting within the sacred precinct of Mecca or while on pilgrimage: God would overlook infractions of the law before it was promulgated but would punish a new offense.

called an infidel, I'll shave off this beard of mine. And this time I will be obliged to change my printing press, paper, pen, and ink too, to become a proper Muslim.[112]

Well, I won't trouble you any further. God keep you; but keep an ear cocked for the bell that will announce that the parliament has turned infidel. Never say Dakhow is a country bumpkin. What he says is all cock and bull.

Yours truly,<br>
Servant of the Poor, Dakhow-Ali

112. If he is considered an infidel and then reverts to Islam, all the items he has previously touched (including his writing and printing tools) become ritually impure and must be discarded.

# Sur-e Esrāfil, Series 1, No. 12, pp. 7–8

September 5, 1907

## News from the City [Lost Tempers]

*Meddler reports that an exasperated royal prince shot his own horse for moving too slowly and Meddler wants the tragic account published in* SE. *Dakhow counters with a long list of atrocities committed by the Qajar elite and their supporters against innocent citizens and even members of the Qajar family to show why there is no space in the paper to report on the more mundane cruelties of those in power. Included in this list is the infamous murder of 252 persons in Azerbaijan by the son of the brigand Rahim Khan, who was in the service of Mohammad-Ali Shah. Dakhow assures Meddler that these evildoers will eventually pay for their crimes, and he ends the column with the tale of Abbās Āqā of Tabriz, who several days prior had murdered the unpopular prime minister Amin al-Soltān (the Atābak), an event that the constitutionalists welcomed.*

Yesterday, Meddler[113] rushed panting and sweating into the office. As soon as he entered, without a word of greeting, he said, Quick, send so-and-so a memo about this, it's vital that it be inserted!

Friend, I told him, sit down and take a breather.

He replied, I'm very busy—hurry up and write it down before I forget; it's a very important matter.

I said to him, My friend, the material in the office in-tray alone is so copious that if our weekly paper were the length of the Kermanshahis' petitions, and a daily in the bargain, it would still be too much for it.

This material, he persisted, has nothing to do with your other stuff: it's a page-one story!

I had no option but to ask him. Go on, I said.

Get a pen, he said. I picked up a pen.

He said, Write: "A few days ago"—I wrote it.

Write: "On the way up to Zargandeh, the son of the crown prince"—I duly wrote it down.

"—found that the horses pulling his carriage were too slow."—I wrote it down.

"—His Royal Highness lost his temper—"

I said, Will you tell the rest, or shall I?

---

113. See *SE* no. 3, note 28.

Caught by surprise, he looked at me wide eyed and said, I hardly think you could know the story.

I said, "His Royal Highness lost his temper. He took out his revolver and shot one of the horses."

That's funny, he said.

You're the funny one, I replied.

He said, Upon my soul, who told you?

I said, My dear sir, do you imagine that it is only you, by virtue of your friendly relations with the high and mighty of this city, who are informed of events, and that we are perhaps unaware of goings-on anywhere in the world?

Not at all, he protested, I wouldn't dare.

I went on: As I said, we already have a pile of material in the office in-tray, and this story does not merit inclusion ahead of it. Apart from the fact that you yourself are aware that any European in the same situation would act in the same way, that is, kill a horse if it endangered its rider. Moreover, you said that His Highness lost his temper, and you know, I hope, that when a man loses his temper he sees red, especially if he is a high-ranking notable of the realm—then he is absolved of responsibility, for when men of high rank lose their temper they have the right to do anything.

Just as the powers that be lost their temper and executed the murderer of the overseer of the harem without trial, or as Habibollāh Afshār lost his temper a few days ago and on the orders of one of his superiors put a bullet through Seyfollāh Khan, the brother of Asadollāh Khan, the brigadier general of the Cossacks.

Just as [the governor of Kurdistan] Nezām al-Saltaneh lost his temper and carved up Ja'far Āqā-ye Shakāk [the chieftain of the

Kurdish Shakāk tribe] despite having sealed an oath [of safe conduct for him] on the Qur'an.

Just as those two persons lost their temper a month ago and butchered an Armenian behind the ice store at Hasanābād.[114]

Just as the men of Amid al-Saltaneh of Tālesh lost their temper and decapitated the supporters of the Majlis at Gorgāneh Rud.

Just as the Ottomans lost their temper over the demands of our ambassadors and four months ago martyred the pilgrims to Karbalā and even today are shelling the defenseless inhabitants of Urmiyeh.[115]

Just as the son of Rahim Khan Chalabiānlu[116] lost his temper and put to the sword 252 women, children, and old men in Azerbaijan Province.

Just as the executioners lost their temper and watered the hazel trees of the park in Tabriz with the blood of Mirza Āqā Khan Kermāni, Shaykh Ahmad-e Ruhi, and Hajji Mirza Hasan Khan Khabir al-Molk.[117]

---

114. At that time a separate township west of Tehran, Hasanābād was later incorporated into the city and now lies between the Bāgh-e Shāh and Tupkhāneh Square. See *MD*, p. 63, note 4.

115. For a discussion of this incident in the first week of August 1907, see Browne, *Persian Revolution*, p. 149. See also *SE* no. 13.

116. See *SE* no. 5, note 40. A chieftain of the Chalabiānlu tribe in the Russian border region of Qaradāgh and a notorious bandit, Rahim Khan (who also bore the titles Nasr al-Soltān and Sardār Nosrat) was a staunch supporter of Mohammad-Ali Shah and a sworn enemy of the constitutionalist party. For his checkered career, see Bāmdād, *Sharh-e hāl-e rejāl-e Irān*, vol. 1, p. 506; Brown, *Persian Revolution*, pp. 141–42, 148; and Richard Tapper, *Frontier Nomads of Iran*, pp. 247–29, 253–59, 264–65.

117. All were Azali Bābi intellectuals executed in Tabriz in 1896 during the reign of Mozaffar al-Din Shah. Their execution was overseen by the then–

Just as a certain doctor lost his temper and poisoned the minister of court in his bed at Rasht.

Just as the police lost their temper and split open the skull of Mirza Mohammad Khan Nuri with a blow from a club.

Just as Eqbāl al-Saltaneh in Maku lost his temper and spilled the blood of hundreds of innocent Muslims.[118]

Just as Mo'āven al-Dowleh's daughter lost it when they took her father away to Khorasan, and supposedly put an end to her grief by strangling herself.[119]

Just as the guest of Khosrow at Me'r in Azerbaijan lost his temper and behind that plane tree flayed his host alive, the bravest man in Iran.

Just as Mirza Ali-Mohammad Khan Sorayyā in Egypt and Mirza Yusof Khan Mostashār al-Dowleh in Tehran and Hajji Mirza Ali Khan Amin al-Dowleh in Lasht-e Neshā[120] lost their temper and took out their rancor and frustration on themselves.

---

crown prince Mohammad-Ali Mirza (see the entry "Ākā Khān Kirmānī" in *The Encyclopedia of Islam*, new edition).

118. Mortazā-qoli Khan Eqbāl al-Saltaneh, the chieftain of the Bayāt tribes of Maku as well as the governor of Maku, was entrusted with border security (against Russia and the Ottoman Empire). He sided with Mohammad-Ali Shah and opposed the formation of an anjoman in his area. His nephew Ezzat-Allāh Khan Sālār Mokram rebelled against him, set up an anjoman in Maku, and forced his uncle into exile in the Caucasus. Eqbāl al-Saltaneh's forces aided the royalist army during the siege of Tabriz in 1908. He was removed from power by Rezā Khan (later Rezā Shah) and died in prison (Mahdi Mojtahedi, *Rejāl-e Āzarbāyjān*, pp. 20–22).

119. Mirza Ebrāhim Ghaffāri Mo'āven al-Dowleh was a confidant of Nāser al-Din Shah and later the minister of commerce. He was appointed the consul general at Tbilisi in 1901 and the Iranian ambassador at Bucharest in 1902. See Abu'l-Hasan Alavi, *Rejāl-e 'asr-e Mashrutiyat*, p. 108; see also *SE* no. 26.

120. One of the oldest districts of the province of Gilan, nineteen miles northeast of Rasht.

Etc., etc., etc.

Yes, people—especially if they are someone of consequence or the child of the same—when they lose their temper, do these things. Moreover, in Isfahan one month ago the brother of this same Royal Highness killed his mother—did we report it at all? We have such a host of stories to write up that these incidents just don't make it. Apart from that, you know that some things, like some diseases, are hereditary. Who killed Hoseyn-qoli Khan the Bakhtiyari chieftain while he was fasting, under cover of an invitation to break his fast?

Yes, you're right, he said.

Wasn't it the father of this same Royal Highness?[121] I asked.

He said, It isn't necessary to go on at such length and in such detail. Out with it—just say you didn't catch my drift.

What can I say? said I.

Said he, Well, I'm deservedly red faced.

Oh, I wouldn't go that far, said I.

He said, Now let's change the subject. Do you think God condones these injustices? Will God forgive these murders of the innocent?

My friend, I replied, we dervishes have a verse that is apposite.

Go on, he said.

I recited [from Rumi's *Masnavi*]:

This world's a mountain, and our deeds are calls;
They come back echoes from the rocky walls.

121. Shāheri-Langarudi suggests that it was indeed Zell al-Soltān, on the orders of his father, Nāser al-Din Shah, who killed the Bakhtiyari leader: see Dehkhodā, *Charand Parand*, ed. Shāheri-Langarudi, p. 68.

What is that supposed to mean? he asked.

What it means, I replied, is this: you who call yourself Meddler and claim to know all that goes on in the world—why were you not in the Bahārestān on the evening of Saturday the twenty-first?[122]

But I was! he protested.

Swear it on my life, I told him.

On your life, said he.

And on yours, said I.

Bah, he said. You never stop with those jokes of yours, do you?

No matter, my friend, said I. Life's too short . . .

122. On the evening of August 31, 1907 (21 Rajab 1325), a junior banker and member of the revolutionary mojāhedin, Abbās Āqā of Tabriz, assassinated Prime Minister Amin al-Soltān (known as the Atābak-e A'zam, or Great Guardian) as he was leaving the Majlis (see Browne, *Persian Revolution*, p. 150). The Atābak had almost persuaded the Majlis to contract another much-despised Russian loan (see Mansoureh Ettehadieh, *Peydāyesh va tahavvol-e ahzāb*, p. 131). For the Atābak's career, see J. Calmard, "Atābak-e A'zam," in *EIr* (1987), also online (updated 2011); and Bāmdād, *Sharh-e hāl-e rejāl-e Irān*, vol. 1, pp. 387–425, s.v. "Ali-Asghar Khan Amin al-Soltān."

# *Sur-e Esrāfil*, Series 1, No. 13, pp. 7–8

September 12, 1907

## Letter from Urumiyeh [Ottoman Shelling]

*Frontier disputes with the Ottomans over the extensive pasturelands bordering Anatolia and northern Iraq (inhabited mainly by Kurds) had contributed to numerous wars in the course of the previous four centuries. Between 1843 and 1865, international boundary commissions were convened, and surveys produced a detailed map of the whole frontier area, but no lasting agreement was signed until 1914 (P. M. Sykes,* History of Persia, *pp. 469–70). The hostilities referred to here resumed in early 1906 and continued through 1908. Browne writes, "The Turks were clearly the aggressors, claiming and occupying points*

*on the Persian side of the mountains between Salmas and Margawar,*
*west of Urmiya, in which they had no shadow of right"* (Persian Revolution, *p. 125). In this fictional letter and its reply Dehkhodā suggests*
*that either the Shah or the Atābak had quietly colluded with the Ot-*
*tomans to get rid of constitutionalists' forces in Urumiyeh (see Yazdāni,*
*"Siāsat," p. 221).*

Eh, Kablā'i! By God, it's all over, our house is in ruins, my
wife, children, family, progeny, brothers and sons and everyone I
had have either been killed or died of fright. You've no idea what
a catastrophe it is—cash, kith, and kin all gone, we're reduced to
quitting the faith, we're just about ready to go over to the Russians. Half of us have already enlisted under the Russian banner,
and the rest are still held back by honor. By God, if we join the
Russians and lose our religion, then for sure our worldly lives
are safe, but then we will have "forfeited both this world and
the next!"[123]

Oh, Kablā'i! For the love of God, for the sake of the dawn of
eternity, tell our Ministry of War: Our rulers have canon, they have
rifles—if they want to have subjects too they have to send us help
very soon, or else we're done for; and if tomorrow we've become
Russian subjects, then don't say that the Urumiyans were dishon-
orable, renegades utterly without faith, unbelieving turncoats! We
beg you on bended knees, today and for the sake of eternity!

(Signed by "All the Urumiyans")

123. From Qur'an 22:11, "[Fair-weather believers who drop away when ill
fortune befalls them] lose both this world and the next." Dehkhodā alludes to
this sentiment several times in these columns.

## Reply from the Newspaper

By God, one is dumbfounded at the behavior of people in this day and age. One has no idea whether they are reasonable beings or lunatics, or indeed what they are at all. It leaves one gasping, lost for words. People have eaten donkey brains and lost their senses. Well, Gentlemen "All the Urumiyans"—what can I do? What should the minister of war [Mostowfi al-Mamālek] do? This is a disaster that has befallen you out of the blue; all these things are your fate. You yourselves have accepted all this through eternity. You should have kept your eyes wide open and your wits about you and refused to take it. What is fated cannot be averted. Just take two minutes to work it out for yourselves. You told me to go and tell the minister of war. So, if I disregard the accumulated experience of seventy years and go and tell him, do you know what the minister of war will say to me? He will say, Idiot! Madman! What can a poor mortal like me do about it? How can I possibly forestall the divine will? Will he not say, It is the fate of the Urumiyans that their women be taken captive, their men killed, their children massacred before their eyes, their villages burned, and their mosques turned into stables for the Ottomans' horses. I ask you honestly, is that or is it not what he will say?

Yes, he will. Finally, purely out of the sympathy and magnanimity that exists in the world of gentlefolk he will say one more thing: for instance, that in such circumstances a fourfold curse[124] is

---

124. Persian *la'n-e chahār zarb*, a shorthand formula used by Shi'is implying execration of the first three caliphs of Islam and Mu'āwiya, who allegedly usurped the position reserved by right for a relative of the Prophet (i.e., Imam Ali). The Ottoman Turks, as champions of these caliphs and enemies of Shi'i Persians, were also fitting targets of the curse.

also a trusted remedy for disaster. Or he will say that all this death and disaster that has befallen you is perhaps due to one of those you have buried chewing his shroud.[125]

Well, before I forfeit all remaining credit with you and you yourselves demonstrate your senselessness and folly to the minister of war, take the advice of this unworthy sinner and get busy reciting the fourfold curse, and maybe this death and disaster will leave you be. If it does, then ask a blessing for this unworthy specimen; if it doesn't, then it's obvious that someone in your cemetery has gotten his shroud between his teeth. Tell your community to have a man with a sharp spade go there and dig up the graves one by one until he finds the corpse that is chewing on its shroud, then with his spade immediately cut off its head. Mind you, the head must be severed from the neck with a single blow, or else the corpse will become even more stubborn. May God never bring such a day upon you, or you'll get a hernia.

Now let's see, where was I? Ah, I remember.

Poor miserable man (may the light stream upon your tomb), this Sabbath eve you too wanted a prayer. How true is the saying "A word at the right time can kill." Just imagine, it was only the other day at that very Vanak, residence of Mostowfi [al-Mamālek], that my late father and grandfather were sitting together. My father was discussing this question of the dead chewing their shrouds and said, There is no doubt about this. I myself in the year of the plague experienced a case in this very cemetery where they chopped off the head of a corpse that was chewing its shroud,

125. A popular belief was that widespread sickness and death in a community, such as from famine or an epidemic, resulted from one of the local corpses chewing on its shroud in frustration. Dakhow spells out the traditional remedy in what follows.

and immediately the plague stopped and the people were spared. Apropos, may God have mercy on everybody's dear departed, and for me, wretched sinner, may he grant a quiet grave.

So I had reached the point where I recommended you follow this course of action and see what happens. If this disaster is stopped, well and good, and if not there is no other recourse but patience. Be patient; God loves the patient. Let the Ottomans do their worst; there is a final reckoning in the next world. Bring them on in their blind malice, and on that day of the dawn of eternity let them stand bereft of all support for fifty thousand years and answer to you for their crimes. What could be better?

Dakhow

# *Sur-e Esrāfil*, Series 1, No. 14, pp. 7-8

September 19, 1907

## [Religion for the Elite, Religion for the Masses]

*Many clerics of Tehran were outraged by the editorial in issue no. 12, which was devoted to the controversial subject of human liberty. A group of seminarians attacked the offices of SE and called for the death of its writers. The paper temporarily shut down, though eventually, through the intervention of the progressive deputies in the Majlis and various anjomans in the city, it resumed publication in November 1907. This column deals with the very real threat the writers faced in this period. It ends with Dakhow's conclusion that the high clerics did not necessarily deem the paper's ruminations on human liberty and freedom of thought antireligious. They only wanted these discussions limited to elite circles and not shared with ordinary people.*

After a procession of some fifty theology students reciting their textbook the *Motavval*,[126] and when half of the Hajjis and Karbalā'is in the city and just about all the students in Shaykh Abu'l-Qāsem's seminar had pronounced a sentence of death on us, they launched several attacks on the *Sur-e Esrāfil* office—just like the Ottomans attack the frontier at Urumiyeh, and the Iranian consuls attack the Mecca pilgrims, and Prince Nosrat al-Dowleh attacks the millet-bread-eating peasantry of Kerman, and Sayyid Abbās Khan Yengi Emāmi attacks the peasants farming crown lands, and indeed just like some fine gentry attack dishes of rice and chicken breast. I panicked, gave myself up for lost, and finally, on the urging of friends and in fear for my life, took refuge at home, and (if you'll pardon the parallel)—just as when certain gentlemen receive Heshmat al-Molk in their homes, in order to slip him twenty-five thousand tumans to settle matters with the Russians in Qā'enāt, they instruct their servants to tell anyone who comes that the master is not to be disturbed[127]—I too gave orders to the effect that Dakhow was not to be disturbed. Then I retired to my bedroom, and—like some schoolmaster or (forgive

126. *Al-Mutawwal*, "The expanded [version]," is a commentary by the fourteenth-century scholar al-Taftāzānī on the treatise on rhetoric called *Talkhīs al-Miftāh*; also mentioned in "Meanings of a Phrase [Amān az dugh-e Leyli]," *SE* no. 24.

127. Refers to a controversy over the deputy governorship of Sistan and Qā'enāt between Heshmat al-Molk, backed by the Russians, and his uncle Amir Showkat al-Molk, backed by the British. See Pirouz Mojtahed-Zadeh, *Small Players*, pp. 110–12.

the analogy) some theology scholars of the Nezāmiyeh College in Baghdad,[128] who, when tutoring their handsome young male students or when engaging in temporary marriage with female clients who haven't reached menopause, shut the screen door of their cubicle—I also closed the door behind me.

Yes, I closed the door behind me, because it was necessary. Because they had threatened me with guns, because when I was a child my mother had always warned me against guns, because when I picked up an empty old matchlock (a relic from my late grandfather) she said, No! Promise me never to pick up a gun! I protested that the gun wasn't loaded, but she persisted: No! The devil will load it.

Yes, I was afraid. There's no shame in being afraid. I was afraid, just as the rulers are afraid of the Parliament.[129] Just as Hajji Malek al-Tojjār is afraid for his reputation.[130] As Nāyeb Hādi Khan and Ejlāl al-Saltaneh are afraid of the municipal anjoman, and the thieves of Tehran are afraid of Ejlāl al-Saltaneh's police, and as Prince Arfa' al-Dowleh is afraid of Iran's falling into disrepute, and as our ministers are afraid of foreign debt. Just as the English, in contrast to the Russians, are afraid of Heshmat al-Molk's government

128. One of a number of Sunni institutions of higher learning established by the celebrated Seljuk vizier Nizām al-Mulk Tusi in the eleventh century, which became a model for future madrasas. The innuendo that follows was evidently resented by the seminarians and brought more death threats: see "Text of the [Shaykh's] Translation," *SE* no. 16.

129. A mocking reference to the manner in which the Atābak and his representatives came to the Majlis and scolded its members (Yazdāni, "Siāsat" p. 222).

130. The Malek al-Tojjār (principal merchant) usually acted as an intermediary between his city's merchant community and the state. See Vanessa Martin, *Qajar Pact*, 33.

in Qā'enāt,[131] and as (stretching a point) some of our ulama fear the sequestration of their waqf funds and trusts for minors.

Oh yes, I was afraid, and I had a right to be. Because I had seen the madrasa students of Tabriz beating people, and witnessed how when one of them struck someone the whole pack of ākhunds would descend on that person, and often enough after the poor wretch had died from the clubbing they would ask one another, "So what did he do, this cursed fellow?"[132]

I was afraid because I knew that if my newspaper condemns traditional practices, then 299,641 sufferers from a sore throat, some of whom tie a thread from the druggist's store round their throats and wrists, will all die of their ailment; and because as a gradual result of the publication of my articles, 227,000 prayer writers, 546,000 fortune-tellers, 151,000 geomancers, 462,000 superintendents of charitable drinking fountains, ascetics, dervishes, snake charmers, crystal-ball gazers, numerologists, and astrologers will lose their livelihood.

Yes, all these things scared me. But of two things that should *really* have scared me I had no fear at all: this was because they simply never entered my head. Which was because I am a man of the common people, and the common people are blind—but when I went home I collected my thoughts and closed the doors,

131. For more on Heshmat al-Molk see *SE* no. 3.

132. Dehkhodā alludes to this accusation in lines 22–23 of his poem "In sha'allah gorbeh ast" (God willing, it's a cat), a satirical *masnavi* written in 1933: "Kaf cho az khun-e bigonah shuyand / sepas 'in sag cheh kardeh bod?' guyand" (When they wash their hands of innocent blood, only then do they ask, "What had this dog done?"). See *Divān-e Dehkhodā*, pp. 18–33; and for an annotated English translation by Paul Losensky, see "Inshallah gurbah ast: 'God Willing, It's a Cat'" (both s.v. "Dehkhodā").

as some of the gentry might close the door of their library to count their wrapped rolls of silver coins. And it was then that these two things occurred to me.

Yes, silly me, I had forgotten that thirteen is an unlucky number, and thoughtlessly had forgotten that issue no. 12 of *Sur-e Esrāfil* had been printed and we were now busy putting together no. 13. Inevitably we would be targeted for this bad luck. Well, man is not a universal almanac; a person can't remember every little thing.

The second thing that had slipped my mind was very important, and it was vital that I not forget it. This was that once I had read in a history book that the ancient Egyptians had two religions—one was the religion of the priests of the temples and the rulers, and the other was that of the common people. Pharaoh and the priests worshipped God, and the common people worshipped Pharaoh.

Now let's get to what I was about to say. One of the senior ulama,[133] after I had read out to him the first article of *Sur-e Esrāfil* no. 12, and he had listened carefully and understood it all, declared, These things are not blasphemy. None of this is contrary to Islam. It is all correct—however, these matters are not for the common people to read.

Need I say more? God bless the priests on this Sabbath eve, for they too worshipped God and were aware that Pharaoh is not God. I rest my case.

Dakhow

133. Possibly a reference to Sayyid Mohammad Tabātabā'i (1841–1921).

# *Sur-e Esrāfil*, Series 1, No. 15, pp. 7–8

November 5, 1907

## [Debate: Gifts for the Press]

*Many of the new anjomans published a newspaper. This piece seems to have in mind a fictitious anjoman affiliated with the newspaper SE, here serving in effect as the managerial board. As the anonymous chairman of the board mentions, the members need no introduction; we already know them as characters in previous* Charand-o Parand *columns. In the dramatic sketch provided by the verbatim reading of the minutes (a new format for Dehkhodā's satire) they meet under their same Dickensian names to discuss the independence of the press. Totally out of character, though, are Āzād Khan, formerly a confused Kurdish* *youth from Kerend (*SE *no. 6); Owyār-qoli, a peasant awed by the big city (*SE *nos. 7–8 and 16); and Mulla Inek-Ali, mentioned in passing by Dakhow as "a* rowzeh-khwān *with a sense of humor" (*SE *no. 2).*

The interim anjoman at the editorial office of *Sur-e Esrāfil* met on Sunday the fifteenth of the month. No doubt our esteemed subscribers would like to be introduced to the members.

Well, I am my humble self; this gentleman is well known to all of you; and this is . . . and this is . . . This gentleman, of course, needs no introduction, and the, ah, yes, the rest of the company are also quite familiar to you all.

Mr. Meddler read the minutes of the last meeting, as follows.

MR. GADFLY: Yes, in my opinion, such reprobates as he are fair game; why not take advantage of him and be done with it?

MR. FICKLE:[134] I hate to say this, but there's a very true saying, "A hair from the bear."[135]

OWYĀR-QOLI:[136] If you knew that the warp and weft of these rugs are made from the veins and arteries of us peasants, you wouldn't be happy to accept this offering.

ĀZĀD KHAN KORD-E KERENDI: Mr. Owyār-qoli is right—you live in the capital and have no idea of the wrongs inflicted on the peasants in the countryside.

FICKLE: This is what the great shaykh [Sa'di] of blessed memory has to say:

134. Persian *Damdami*; introduced in *SE* no. 5 (see note 3).

135. Persian *az khers mu'i*: said when one obtains something, however little and begrudged, from a miserly person. See Dehkhodā, *Amsāl va hekam*, vol. 1, p. 125.

136. Introduced in *SE* nos. 7–8 (see note 70).

"To talk of wasps is pointless—to one who has never been stung!"[137]

GADFLY: We must find out what would happen if we don't accept these rugs. Would the government return them to their rightful owners? Or would it keep and use them for a situation far more critical than this?

MULLA INEK-ALI: In my opinion, to give back these items as Mr. Gadfly suggests would be wrong, and tantamount to abetting a crime.

FICKLE: Hear, hear! Absolutely right! Well said!

ĀZĀD KHAN: Let's see just why His Excellency [the governor] is giving these items to Mr. Dakhow. If it's because Mr. Dakhow is in need, then he isn't; for the time being, he is keeping body and soul together by his meager earnings from journalism. If it's meant as an educational donation, then it would be better for the governor to choose two or three orphans without guardians, from within his own jurisdiction, and apply the annual revenues from this sum to their education.

MULLA INEK-ALI: What would be the harm if we say that he indeed means it for educational assistance? As for your saying it would be better to educate poor orphans with it, these matters depend on one's view of customary law: in my opinion, tendering assistance to a newspaper would be deemed preferable, in the eyes of the law, to helping orphan

137. A couplet from the *Golestān* (Rose garden) of Shaykh Mosleh al-Din Sa'di of Shiraz (ca. 1208–92), a compendium of mixed prose and verse on manners and mores that has contributed to Persian a wealth of aphorisms and humorous parables.

children, since a newspaper can persuade thousands of people to help educate needy orphans, whereas a scholarship for one or two orphans is limited and less useful in its effect.

FICKLE: I have a limited education and don't fully understand the gentleman's turn of phrase, but I think he's right, bravo!

OWYĀR-QOLI: But in my opinion, in common law, preference should be given to the education of poor orphans over assistance to a newspaper, since newspapers currently have revenue to cover expenditure and don't need assistance, whereas there are lots of poor children in this country who need all the help they can get. So it would have been better for our benefactors to give scholarships to a number of children from this fund, thereby encouraging other rich and important people to follow suit.

ĀZĀD KHAN: That's right; apart from the fact that, as Mulla Inek-Ali implied, there's no end to potential problems, his point is that it would be better to subsidize a newspaper on the grounds that it encourages others to support children's education, and on the other hand, whenever people wish to contribute to children's education there are newspapers in Iran, and, as he said, the newspaper will always take precedence.

FICKLE: The matter is settled.

MULLA INEK-ALI: You, true believer! This is specious reasoning and an invitation to grievous error.

OWYĀR-QOLI: Not so, sir! It is sound, since you yourself say that to assist a newspaper is good, because it can get people to contribute to the education of orphans. Therefore orphan children should never be educated, since subsidizing a newspaper is always preferable to subsidizing the schooling of orphans. Otherwise it would be a case of preferring the redundant over the recommended, and the preponderant over the preferred.

FICKLE: Mr. Owyār-qoli, please explain a little more clearly, so that I can offer my views!

MULLA INEK-ALI: I don't know about this stuff. The rejection of charity is both intellectually and religiously reprehensible. Muslims must avoid the company of a person who rejects charity. And, God save us, should his opposition lead him to apostasy, it would be incumbent to kill him.

FICKLE: God protect us from the evils of our base natures!

ĀZĀD KHAN-E KORD: My good sir, you're going too far! First of all, let's suppose this "rejection of charity" is a reprehensible act from the view of shari'a. How would a reprehensible act necessitate a Muslim's avoidance of the fellow, his apostasy, and finally his murder?[138]

MULLA INEK-ALI: Believer, do you know the proper protocol of the ritual prayer?[139]

The chairman rang the bell and said, Changing the subject is out of order! (Mulla Inek-Ali, visibly angry, rose and left the meeting

138. In Islam, human actions fall into five categories: obligatory (*wājib*), permitted (*mubāh*), recommended (*mustahabb*), disapproved but not unlawful (*makruh*), and unlawful (*harām*). A reprehensible act might be disapproved, but the penalty for committing it is not expulsion from the faith or murder.

139. At this point the mulla disrupts the hitherto polite tone of the debate by demanding sarcastically of Āzād Khan (using the familiar pronoun of address) whether he is a true Muslim.

without asking the chairman's permission and despite the pleas of the others replied only, I ignore the personal slights, but as for this insult to the profession, I take refuge in God!)

MEDDLER: When I was in Rasht and Isfahan and Shiraz and Azerbaijan and Mazandaran, and hobnobbed with the governors everywhere, I saw that the authorities always sent a little something every year to the newspapers, each in accordance with their importance. This annual retainer was provided, I gather, during the period of despotism, so why shouldn't it be continued nowadays?

OWYĀR-QOLI: Esteemed sir, for what reason does this unjust and godless governor—who pulls out earrings from village girls' ears and rugs from under the feet of some poor peasant family, who leaves not one chicken in an old woman's yard and draws the line at no source of illegal income, even from prostitutes—blithely provide an annual subsidy to journalists? Is his purpose not to make the newspaper reporters into accomplices of his evil deeds? Does he not intend, in an age when among all the civil institutions of the nations of the world, Iran has but four lightweight newspapers left, to co-opt even these to his regime? Is this not the very definition of bribery? And after the journalist has swallowed this corrosive poison, will his pronouncements garner any respect in the eyes of the nation? And will anyone listen any more to what the newspapers have to say? Alas that the veils of ignorance still block our vision, and that greed, caprice, and self-interest leave us no scope for introspection!

My dear members of the association! Does not Mulla Inek-Ali, who insists so forcefully on this course of action, intend nothing other than to open up the doors of bribery—nay, to share covertly with Dakhow in these unsolicited items? I tell you without risk of contradiction, that until corrupt clerics, and some . . . , and some of our journalists learn to curb their cupidity, Iran will never prosper nor Islam flourish. If I have overreached myself and acted in contravention of the bylaws of the anjoman, since I did so in the spirit of right and legality you will doubtless pardon me; if not, I am ready to resign.

(At this juncture, the majority declared themselves for Owyār-qoli, and a resolution was adopted to send a formal letter from the anjoman to the governor, as follows.)

To His Most Noble and Eminent Highness Prince Nosrat al-Dowleh, governor of Kerman, long may the days of his just rule endure:

Your Highness's ploy has fizzled out—that is, with all due respect, even Mulla Inek-Ali, who was in your camp, has been discomfited, and hence Your Highness's project has been left high and dry.

Your Highness, it is time for serious study in the schools of the English and the Germans, not for exercising responsibility for the province of Kerman in the wasteland of Iran. A consignment of complimentary rugs one hundred tumans in value with receipted invoices from Kerman was sent to the *Sur-e Esrāfil* office. Henceforth kindly recognize whom you are dealing with and look before you leap; *Sur-e Esrāfil* neither accepts bribes nor ignores the groans of the newly martyred souls and the peasants of Kerman Province who subsist on millet bread and sheep's blood.

Signed:
Chairman of the Anjoman of the Ruffians

# *Sur-e Esrāfil*, Series 1, No. 16, pp. 7–8

November 14, 1907

## [A Letter in Arabic?]

*Once again, using the epistolary form, Dakhow mocks the convoluted writing style of the clerics, a mixture of Persian and Arabic, which was often incomprehensible to the ordinary reader. He captures the clerics' impatience with any perceived criticism of their actions, and in the shaykh's garbled Persian version of the threatening missive fulminates against this column's recent aside on clerics' sexual indiscretions in their seminaries (*SE *no. 14).*

For the unlucky it never rains but it pours. A few days ago a letter arrived in the mail. I opened it and saw that it was written in

Arabic. Now, nobody knows Arabic except the noble souls of the clergy. What could I do? I racked my brains and finally decided to take it to a learned and reverend shaykh with whom I had long been on friendly terms. I gave it to him and asked, Sir, would you please transcribe[140] this into Persian for me?

He replied that he was at present involved in a discussion but would translate it that afternoon and bring it to the office. And so he did.

As some of my readers are aware, I have a smattering of basic literacy. I skimmed the paper he handed me and couldn't make any sense of it. I put on my glasses and still couldn't make sense of it. I took it out into the light and looked at it properly—and still couldn't make head or tail of it. However I tried, I couldn't understand a word.

Mashhadi Owyār-qoli was there. The shaykh suggested that if I couldn't read it I should give it to Mashhadi to read. Mashhadi took it and looked at it for a while, then said to the shaykh, Sir, you're pulling my leg! It's hard enough for me to read Persian—and you're giving me Hebrew to read?

The shaykh protested: Muslim! Where is the Hebrew? The original was in Arabic, Kablā'i Dakhow gave it me to translate into Persian, and I did!

140. The original newspaper column has *tajrobeh*, "experience," an apparent misprint for *tarjomeh*, "translation." Both the Ketāb-e Jibi edition (Dehkhodā, *Charand-o Parand*, p. 51) and Dabirsiāqi (Dehkhodā, *Maqālāt-e Dehkhodā*, p. 83) correct it without comment. However, Rezā Barāheni sees it rather as a deliberate malapropism by which Dehkhodā points to the comparative illiteracy of his editor character, as he will subsequently ridicule the educational shortcomings of Owyār-qoli and the shaykh (*"Tanz-e Dehkhodā,"* p. 520).

Owyār-qoli stared at the shaykh nonplussed, then replied, Sir, excuse me, it's true that I'm just a working stiff, but I wasn't born yesterday. When I was young I learned a bit of Hebrew, and this is Hebrew.

Believer! said the shaykh. How could this be Hebrew? It's Persian!

I swear, rejoined Owyār-qoli, it's Hebrew!

No, said the shaykh, it is Persian.

I'll wager my two ears on it, declared Owyār-qoli. It is Hebrew!

No, persisted the shaykh. You don't understand; it is Persian.

I could see that now Owyār-qoli was going to tell the shaykh that it was he who didn't understand, and then the fight would really start. I interrupted: Mashhadi! You and I are laymen; what do we know about it? The shaykh is far more learned than us; he understands it better.

No, said Owyār-qoli, *you* don't get it! That language is Hebrew; a Jewish scholar came to our village once, and I personally took Hebrew lessons from him.

I saw the veins of the shaykh's neck suddenly bulge, and he rose on to his knees, using his walking stick as a prop. In a voice hoarse with anger he declared, Muslim! You have strayed completely off the topic! The craft of Translation is a recognized branch of the science of Prosody, and apart from the fact that Logical Inference, in the opinion of some, is dependent upon Free Will . . . And he rattled off a lot of other Arabic terms that I didn't understand. I understood this much, that the shaykh was about to brain Owyār-qoli with his stick, so, fearing lest some mishap befall, I turned to Owyār-qoli and said, Man, shame on you! Do you realize whom you're talking to? Cut it out! Modesty is a virtue; this is disgraceful. To blazes with the original of this translation. What use is it anyway? The shaykh is worth a thousand of such texts. Shame on us! What's the point of quarreling?

The shaykh turned to me and vouchsafed me a smile, saying, Kablā'i, why don't you let us continue our discussion and work it out together?

Seeing the shaykh smile, I plucked up courage somewhat and said, Sir, you scared me half to death—if this is how you discuss things, what would it be like quarreling with you?

The shaykh broke into a guffaw and asked, Muslim! Were you really afraid of discussing things with me?

Heavens, I said, I swear by the lives of my own children, I thought my last hour had come!

Very well then, allowed the shaykh, we won't have any more discussion. Just publish this translation of mine in your newspaper—there are educated people who can read it for themselves.

I agreed, on the condition that there be no more quarreling while the two of them were in the office.

## Text of the [Shaykh's] Translation

O ye scribes of *Sur-e Esrāfil*: What is it with you, that ye write not your news paper as it befits you to write it? And what is this obsession with closure of screen doors, hairless young boys [amradān], and enjoyment of nonmenopausal females whose nonmaintenance of the statutory postdivorce period of celibacy is known for sure, in the case of our observation of their exiting from an adjacent room? Whereas ye can surely write of subjects other than these!

Hence on investigation it has become manifest unto us by strong evidences that such persons who write their news papers in your manner are our foes, and our foes of a surety are foes of God.

Thus we do now inform you, verily, if ye be a continuator of opprobrium of our deeds, yea, even a broadcaster of unbelief and heresy, ye shall soon suffer our ire. Verily we do menace you firstly with menace, and verily secondly we shall strike you with a severe stroke, and verily we shall denounce you as pagans and kill you thirdly and fourthly with death of a nature canine and porcine. And verily we shall hang you from the branches of the mulberry tree, which is within our madrasa. Know ye, that Plebeians have no authority over the Learned. Farewell!

# *Sur-e Esrāfil*, Series 1, No. 17, pp. 7–8

November 21, 1907

## Literature: "O Kablāy!"

*This poem, by Dehkhodā, is a* mokhammas, *a five-hemistich strophic form generally used for popular songs. The heading "Literature" (*Adabiyāt*) for this and a few other sections of* Charand-o Parand *columns is probably tongue in cheek, since these are all examples of verse in a vernacular style. We have decided again that it is hardly possible to improve on Browne's English version, which is accordingly reproduced here (see his* Press and Poetry, *pp. 179–82: Persian text and annotated translation).*

*For the term* Kablāy, Kablā'i, *see* SE *no. 2, note 5. The Kablā'i addressed here, Browne notes, "is taken by some to refer to the poet himself, but by others to the ex-Shah, Muhammad 'Ali, who was at that time the ruler of Persia" (p. 179). It is more likely to be the poet, in character as a contributor to* Sur-e Esrāfil *(whose name, as the introduction discusses, refers to the archangel's trumpet; stanza 4), the obvious target of the various subjects of* Charand-o Parand's *satire (stanzas 2 and 6), and a frustrated advocate for popular mobilization (stanza 5). Another satirical weekly,* Hasharāt al-arz *(Insects/Reptiles of the earth) of Tabriz, expressed its solidarity with* SE *by publishing in its issue no. 8 (1908) a rejoinder in the same poetical form and with the same refrain, "O Kablāy" (see Javadi,* Satire in Persian Literature, *pp. 159–60).*

### (1)

"Rejected by men and by God the Forgiving, O Kabláy!
You're a wonderful sample of riotous living, O Kabláy!
You're a wag, you're a joker, no end to your fun,
Of living and dead you are sparing of none,
    Such a limb of the Devil and son of a gun, O Kabláy!

### (2)

"Neither wizard, diviner nor warlock you fear, O Kabláy!
Nor the dervish's prayer, nor the dreams of the Seer, O Kabláy!
Nor Shapsál's revolver,[141] nor *mujtahid's* rage:
'Tis hard to believe you will die of old age,
    You limb of the Devil and son of a gun, O Kabláy!

---

141. A reference to Shāpshāl Khan's attacking Mohaqqeq al-Dowleh with a pistol. See *MD*, p. 108, note 24.

### (3)

"Times a hundred I've told you your project will fail,
   O Kabláy!
While half of the nation are wrapped in a veil, O Kabláy!
Can Islám in you and your circle prevail?
With fresh words of folly your friends you'll regale,
    You limb of the Devil and son of a gun, O Kabláy!

### (4)

"At the heels of the dervish you bark and you bite, O Kabláy!
Break the Dominie's windows and let in the light, O Kabláy!
While this trumpet of yours doth all secrets proclaim;
Yes, blazon them forth, for what know you of shame?
    You limb of the Devil and son of a gun, O Kabláy!

### (5)

"To hell with the folk, if with hunger they pine, O Kabláy!
Devil take them, the brutes, since they cannot combine, O
   Kabláy!
Since opium hath stolen their courage away,
With your minstrels and singers be merry and gay,
    You limb of the Devil and son of a gun, O Kabláy!

### (6)

"In Persia will bribes ever go out of fashion, O Kabláy?
Will the *mullás* for justice develop a passion, O Kabláy?
From magic and *murshids* can Islám win free?
Bid the dead come to life, for 'twill easier be,
    You limb of the Devil and son of a gun, O Kabláy!"

# Personal Letter [to "Pahlavān" Amir A'zam]

*The heavily sarcastic tone of this "letter" is indicated by the overfamiliar terms of address and "spoken" Persian transcription of key words (pahlavun, jun-at); in the subsequent section, which charges officials with anticipating a less liberal press law, the tone switches to an icy formality. Prince Amir A'zam, also known as Amir Khan Sardār, was the son of Vajihollāh Mirza Sepahsālār and a nephew of Ayn al-Dowleh, the prime minister whose open hostility to the constitutional movement led to his dismissal in 1906. Amir A'zam, however, was for a time more sympathetic to constitutionalism and on several occasions took an oath in the anjomans of Tehran that he would support constitutionalism (see* MD, *p. 90, note 2; Amir A'zam is pilloried again in* SE *no. 24). A champion (*pahlavān*), since he is also a* luti—*a member of a young men's benevolent and (ideally) chivalrous association, centered on the body-building and martial rituals of the traditional Iranian gymnasium (*zurkhāneh*)—takes an oath to defend the poor and weak. Dehkhodā is therefore doubly incensed that a man with no political experience or educational qualifications had become the governor of Gilan Province and then betrayed his promise and oaths and embarked on a policy of harassment and extrajudicial punishment of constitutionalists.*

*Dehkhodā's public upbraiding of the governor of Gilan as a bully antagonized Amir A'zam's powerful Qajar patron Prince Azizollāh Mirza, aka Āqā Aziz Pāmenāri, a grandson of Fath-Ali Shah Qajar and a prominent* luti *leader. Dehkhodā is reported to have braved the lion's den incognito and before revealing his identity to have asked for a little to eat and drink—thus tricking Āqā Aziz into being unable to retaliate, by virtue of the law of hospitality (*Post-e Kayhān *no. 664, 19 Tir 1376/January 10, 1997, p. 8).*

Well done, Champ. Enjoy it! But let's be honest: you bullied the weak. Neither the mulla in chief nor Rahim the Glass Cutter nor those two sayyids—none of these people ever claimed to be lutis[142] [toughs] or champions. Why did you torture them? Now look here, dear lad—it was because of the cowardice of their neighborhood youths that you were permitted to stay in their province; if members of Abu'l-Fazl's anjoman had thrown you out bag and baggage the next day, what would you have done?[143]

All right, friend, I don't know how many oaths you swore in the Tehran anjomans that you were a diehard defender of the Majlis, a supporter of the constitution. Now, I'm a diehard defender of the Majlis myself, a supporter of the constitution. So how was it that

142. For various uses of the term see Willem Floor, "Luti," in *EIr* online (2010).

143. In Gilan the constitutional movement became far more radical as peasants and artisans called for a rent strike and the abolition of semifeudal obligations to landlords. Rahim the Glass Cutter (Shishabor) and Sayyid Jamāl the Rebel (Shahrāshub) were expelled from the Rasht Anjoman for their support of the peasants. Soon, with the help of several radical intellectuals and the support of thousands of peasants, they formed the Abu'l Fazl Anjomans (aka the Abbāsi Anjomans), with at least fourteen branches in the province. Two sayyids, namely Shahrāshub and the journalist Afsah al-Motakallemin, played key roles in this organization, hence the reference to two sayyids in Dakhow's column. The authorities in Rasht and Tehran adamantly opposed the new association. Its leaders were beaten and arrested but eventually released, thanks to public outrage. At one point the Majlis sent two hundred men of the Cossack Brigade to disperse this and other local anjomans. An active member of the Abu'l-Fazl Anjoman was Mirza Kuchek Khan, who became the principal leader of the Gilan Republic in 1920. See Janet Afary, "Contentious Historiography" and "Peasant Rebellions."

before setting foot in the province [of Gilan], like some sergeant in charge of the mule stable, you bastinadoed a journalist, a man who was an ākhund, a descendant of the Prophet?[144]

Don't tell me the youths in Tehran didn't understand what tricks you were up to. From the very day that we heard the story, we kept a sharp eye on you. It turned out that the same sayyid who took you to see Moshir al-Saltaneh, the one who appointed you governor of Rasht [Gilan], inveigled you into colluding with him.

To cut a long story short, I have no hidden agenda, Champ. I'll just tell you to your face: if a man after a few years of working in the traditional gym[145] can become a governor, by now Hajji Ma'sum and Mehdi Gāvkosh should both be Atābaks in their own right.[146] The guys from Chāleh Meydān[147] all send you their best wishes. Take it easy.

(Signature withheld)

144. This refers to Afsah al-Motakallemin, the editor of the Rasht paper *Khayr al-Kalām* and a leader and supporter of the Abu'l Fazl Anjomans. (For the bastinado see *SE*, series 2, no. 3, headnote.)

145. Persian *zurkhāneh*, "house of strength," a traditional gymnasium. See H. Chehabi, "Zur-ḵāna," in *EIr* online (2006).

146. *Atābek* was an older title revived in Qajar times for certain governors. Its supreme exemplar was the Atābak-e A'zam, the rich and powerful prime minister assassinated less than three months before (see the cryptic allusion in *SE* no. 12). Hajji Ma'sum and Mehdi Gāvkosh (the Cattle Butcher, or Bull Slayer) were well-known lutis of Tehran (Yazdāni, "Siāsat," pp. 242–43).

147. Part of Old Tehran where zurkhānehs were common. *SE* no. 20 mentions the neighborhood as one of the sources of the royalist mob.

## [On Victimization of Journalists]

Our letter is ended, but here I'd like to say a few plain and simple words—man to man, with no ulterior motive—to the minister of information[148] and the minister of justice. Such as: You who today have hauled into court some poor bread-and-butter seminarian, namely the writer of *Ruh al-Qodos*;[149] who would demonstrate the force of an unwritten law on a wretch from nowhere; who would exercise your surgical experience on the scalp of us journalists! The Press Law has not yet passed through Parliament and come into force. Nor was there among existing shari'a laws any detailed legislation concerning the press under which we could be charged. Is not punishment in the absence of a law invalid anywhere, even in a small hamlet within the Constitutional Land?

As for Islamic law, it has never condoned the beating of respectable persons, especially ulama and sayyids. One of these unfortunates, Afsah al-Motakallemin, one of the ulama of Rasht as well as being the editor of the newspaper *Khayr al-Kalām*, has been paralyzed over half his body; he was beaten until he vomited blood under the bastinado and is today at death's door. Would it not have been better if you had hauled you-know-who before a government tribunal under Islamic law, to show the people that whoever exceeds his authority, even a

148. *Vazir-e ta'lim*: literally, "minister of instruction," i.e., (to go by the context) the government censor.

149. Soltān al-Olamā Khorāsāni, the editor of the newspaper *Ruh al-Qodos* ("The holy spirit," an epithet of the Archangel Gabriel, God's messenger to mortals, echoing *Sur-e Esrāfil*, the warning blast of another archangel).

champion, will be punished in the constitutional era? And if, once the Press Law did come into force, you were to require the editor of *Ruh al-Qodos* to respect it? And applied in today's context the [shari'a] law that has been in force for thirteen hundred years?

# Sur-e Esrāfil, Series 1, No. 18, pp. 6–8

November 28, 1907

## [Servants of the Privy Chamber]

*The Persian heading is* 'Amaleh-ye Khalvat, *literally "workers of the private apartment." The English term "privy chamber" was used first for the private apartments in royal residences of the Tudors and later to translate Ottoman Turkish* khalvat, khalvat-khāneh *and to refer to analogous institutions of other Persianate rulers. In both the English and Turkish cases these rooms and their associated personnel were more for the private conduct of state business by the sovereign than for personal pleasure. Dehkhodā seems to have in mind a broader range of activities, including those of the bedchamber. Thus the description of the first type of court intimate fits an* amrad *(ephebe), an adolescent boy who was kept as a sexual partner. An* amrad *was usually younger than sixteen, after which he became an adult and was deemed (ethically) inappropriate for such relations. The second type, the intimidating older male bodyguard, calls to mind the figure of the* nowkar *(a word of Mongol origin). Dehkhodā's mock-reverent tone evokes the archaic and sinister ethos of this early twentieth-century survival of an* Arabian Nights *institution. The essence of such splendid privacy is, of course, that it has to be advertised; thus, as we are shown here, when carriages carrying members of the royal family moved through town, guards accompanying them ordered pedestrians to turn their backs to the procession so as not to see anyone in the carriages. The servants of the American plenipotentiary in Tehran once dared to view a cavalcade of Qajar women as they passed by and paid the penalty: "a savage beating from the eunuchs and guards" (Abbas Amanat, introduction to Taj al-Saltana,* Crowning Anguish, *p. 15).*

O Knower of Secrets and All Things Hidden! Canst thou hear what the Servants of the Privy Chamber are saying? See what manner of things are these Servants of the Privy Chamber? Are they creatures like us? Or, God save us, of the race of fairies? Dost thou see what they are?

Who knows them, except God, who alone is the Knower of Secrets and All Things Hidden? What right have I to pry into the works of the Almighty? He alone knows what he will do, whom he will take or condemn or pardon, and how he creates mortals. These are all his works—nobody has the right to question how or why; what kind of a dog am I to utter a word, what sort of creature am I to venture a criticism of God's works? I have only one thing to say, and that is: God forgive me, God forgive me! The Lord, blessed and exalted, has created every creature all of one sort and kind. Thus he created humankind all of one sort and kind, chickens all of one sort and kind, doves all of one sort and kind, even (excuse the analogy) camels and horses and donkeys too, all of one sort and kind. By which I mean that despite individual differences in aspect or size, we can see that they are basically all of one sort and kind.

But see by what rationale the Lord most blessed and exalted created the Servants of the Privy Chamber, so different, individual by individual, so they don't match. Aha! This is where one is flummoxed by the work of God, where one knows not what to say, where—to risk being flippant—man's vaunted intellect seems to move on all fours, weighed down like a donkey under the burden of a human body. Yes, the four limbs of the human brain get weighed down by the body, just like a donkey. Because sometimes when one sees a Servant of the Privy Chamber (a rare enough occurrence) one is blown away: a disk of a face like the moon, a pistachio-shaped mouth, straight nose, stature straight as a boxwood bough, almond eyes, eyebrows extending all the way to the temples, neck slender as a rose stem . . . why go on? It says to the sun, "You stay out, I go in." Age? Ten, twelve, thirteen—OK, fifteen. By this time, the beholder is dazzled by a veritable sermon on the works of God. This is one kind of Servant of the Privy Chamber.

Another time, the sight of a Servant of the Privy Chamber makes one go weak at the knees: a giant big as an oak, a chest broad as a bazaar buttress, arms thick as elms, glowering eyes and brows, long moustaches that curl beyond the ears; thirty or thirty-five, forty at the outside. Well, yes, a case of

The expert can see the same good points in the camel

As [the layman] in the beauties of China and Turkistan[150]

—yet another sermon to illustrate a sample of the wondrous works of God.

So far, so good; even if these two persons are not all that much the same sort and kind, fine, they are at least both members of the human species. But sometimes one will see a type of Servant of the Privy Chamber that will *really* freak him out: his mouth will go dry, his hand will fly to his mouth[151] . . . how shall I describe it? Let's say someone is walking along Eshratābād.[152] Suddenly his eye meets one thousand soldiers of the guard, five hundred attendants bearing silver maces, twenty liveried footmen, and fifty or sixty high officials and dignitaries on horseback escorting an eight-horse carriage—all with a din of shouts and commands to the onlookers to move off, lower your eyes, turn away.

What's up? What is it? Who is it?

Babri Khan!—Babri Khan?—Yes, Babri Khan. Oh my lord, Babri Khan! By all that's wonderful, Babri Khan![153]

150. From Saʻdi's *Bustān*, ch. 7. See also *MD*, p. 98, note 8.

151. Literally "his finger will stay in the mouth of astonishment"—biting the index finger being the classic posture of surprise or admiration in Persian literary convention.

152. A scenic location northeast of Tehran, known for its famous palace built in the era of Nāser al-Din Shah.

153. "Babri Khan" has the aura of a legendary name, redolent of martial fame; *babr* means "tiger" or "leopard," and the legendary hero Rostam wore a tigerskin cloak called the *babr-e bayān*. See, however, note 155—but not yet!

Babri Khan must be one of the great-grandsons of Nāder Shah Afshār who wants to regain his hereditary kingship.[154] Or is Babri Khan one of the great commanders just back from the conquest of Herat, on whom the nation has bestowed the honor of parading today with the retinue of an emperor of China? Or perhaps Babri Khan is a shrewd ambassador of Iran who has skillfully concluded a treaty with friendly states that guarantees Iran's survival, and today a grateful nation is according him this splendid and extravagant jubilee.

Impossible, out of the question, but *somehow* we must pay our respects in person; by whatever means, just once, we must at least see Babri Khan's face. Then one shins with alacrity up a tree, or climbs some hill, and fixes his gaze on the carriage. Now, my fortunate friends, what does one see in the carriage? I'd like some fine youth to tell me just what there is to see in the carriage. Go on, tell us what you see! No volunteers?

Then I'll tell you myself. One's eye lights immediately upon a cat with long, soft, shiny fur and a jeweled collar and chain, splendid garments dripping with jewels, regal jewels hanging from it head to tail . . . Oh my god! What a sight! Wow! Pure ecstasy! God save them! . . .[155]

154. Nāder Shah Afshār (r. 1736–47) expelled the Ghilzay Afghans, who had defeated the Safavid dynasty and occupied Iran for a decade, and briefly restored the Persian Empire. His successors ruled little more than the city of Mashhad; Āghā Mohammad Khan Qājār dethroned and killed the last one, Nāder's grandson Shāhrokh Shah, in 1796.

155. Babri Khan was indeed the name of Nāser al-Din Shah's pet cat. According to one of the monarch's daughters, it was waited upon by the palace servants like one of the royal family and had its own personal nanny, the overseer of the royal concubines, Amina Aqdas—a Kurdish peasant

At this point people will say that Dakhow has run out of actual instances and has resorted to making this up. No, I swear by the study circle of Āqā Shaykh Abu'l-Qāsem—by the religious fervor of Āqā Sayyid Ali Āqā—by the constitutionalist convictions of Qavām al-Molk and Amir Bahādor [Jang]! I swear by Prince Arfaʻ al-Dowleh's loyalty to the government—by the honesty and integrity of the unique weekly *Nedā-ye Vatan* [Call of the motherland]—by the socialist spirit of the [Qajar] prince Nosrat al-Dowleh—by the pious poverty of His Royal Highness Zell al-Soltān—by the good intentions of the Anjoman-e Fotovvat.[156] May I leave the world dumb struck, I swear by the lives of my children that most people of Tehran fully appreciate the time of the late and pious Babri Khan and are mindful of all those kindnesses, benefits, and favors lavished on them, and all that power, authority, magnificence, and might.

---

woman who owed her advancement, and that of her family, to Babri Khan (Taj al-Saltaneh, *Crowning Anguish*, pp. 125–26, 127–28; Willem Floor, "Note on Persian Cats," pp. 40–41). Among other pertinent tales of cats at the Qajar court retold in Floor's article are these (pp. 39–41): A baggage horse was kept for one such pet, complete with a specially constructed cage with velvet-covered wire. Petitions of all sorts had only to be hung round Babri Khan's neck to be ensured of a favorable answer (as Dehkhodā approvingly notes below), and when the cat fell ill on vacation, an eight-horse carriage was prepared and conveyed Babri Khan in state back to the palace in Tehran, accompanied by the *hakim al-mamālek* (royal physician) and the shah's personal French physician, Dr. Tholozan.

156. A tongue-in-cheek series of sarcastic statements. Amir Bahādor Jang, for example, was the commander of the royal bodyguard under Mohammad-Ali Shah and a staunch anticonstitutionalist. Zell al-Soltān, the eldest son of Nāser al-Din Shah, was the governor of Isfahan in this period and was known for his vast fortune. The Anjoman-e Fotovvat was dominated by conservative royalists who only pretended to support the Majlis. The rest may readily be inferred.

Ask these gentlemen of the law the following questions: Wasn't the majority of the stipend that you have accumulated—the one that the fiscal commission of the Majlis is currently auditing, filling notebooks from top to bottom in black, like the paintings of the Mas'udiyyeh Palace,[157] fearing neither God nor his Prophet—wasn't all this wealth due to the magnanimous charity of this same Babri Khan and his successors? Was it or was it not? And didn't most of the provincial governors have to pay their respects to Babri Khan in order to receive their posts, or did they not?

Yes, let alone our old men, even our young men remember the days when the people would hang their petitions round Babri Khan's neck and send their tribute offerings through him. And it took no longer than two days before a draft for a stipend or an order for a government or civil service appointment would be issued.

Wow, what splendor! What glory! What power and magnificence! Ah, fortune, how fleeting you are! Pages, how quickly you are turned! World, how easily you are overturned! Just imagine, it was only the day before yesterday that an illiterate villager pointed to Babri Khan's carriage and was punished on the spot. Those were the days, indeed; what a time that was!

However, let's not lose sight of the topic. That was one sort of Servant of the Privy Chamber, duly recorded. And while I remember, let me mention that our correspondent writes from Qom that the reverend chief superintendent of shrines, after performing his ablutions in the water of bribery, set out on pilgrimage to Qom, and as soon as he arrived, armed one thousand each of

157. The Tehran residence of Mas'ud Mirza Zell al-Soltān, located in Bahārestān (Parliament) Square. See *MD*, p. 99, note 16.

sayyids, ākhunds, shrine superintendents, and tradesmen of the city, while he himself festooned his person with two swords, four shields, eight revolvers, and twelve rifles, and set up his own seat of government every morning in the sacred courtyard;[158] there he orders a trumpet blown for assembly, whereupon the four thousand aforementioned troops all assemble and, having kissed the reverend's head and tail and the head and tail of his mule, cry out in unison, Long live the glorious Qur'an! Down with the new law! Long live God's Qur'an! Down with European laws!

Barely literate as I am, even with my imperfect wit I can gather from the chief superintendent's enunciations that this Majlis is in favor of the newfangled European law and that the deeds of Babri Khan's days were in accordance with the glorious Qur'an. O Muslims! If this is so, why do you sit in silence? Why do you not erupt in pious indignation? Why not join hands with the chief superintendent of shrines and Āqā Sayyid Ali Āqā-ye Yazdi[159] and revive God's religion? Heaven forbid, have you tired of Islam? Or do you approve of European law? Or are you minded to introduce heresies into the faith? If so, by God, you shall not prosper and will not succeed in your purpose. I have said my say; it is up to you.

However, let's get back to our topic. Babri Khan was one type of Servant of the Privy Chamber. Even though Babri Khan was not a member of the human race, he was nevertheless a partner with other Servants of the Privy Chamber in benefiting people. He was kind, generous, and helpful to others. He facilitated stipends and

158. Referring to stories about anticonstitutionalist clerics forming armies of clerical students and other supporters and beginning to campaign against the constitutional order.

159. Perhaps a reference to Sayyid Kāzem Yazdi, one of the grand mojtaheds of Najaf, who opposed the constitutional order.

salaries, got people into government posts and offices . . . so he was somewhat of one kind with the other Servants of the Privy Chamber.

But there is one other kind of Servant of the Privy Chamber, which resembles none of the others but is in all characteristics and every aspect totally sui generis. No doubt you wish to know who this outstanding individual is and what his name is. If so, wait one week; there is no space left in this issue, and the information will be found in the next one.

# Sur-e Esrāfil, Series 1, No. 19, pp. 6–8

December 5, 1907

## [Letter to the Russian Diplomat Shāpshāl Khan]

*The Russian diplomat Shāpshāl (Szapszal) Seraya Ben Mordechai (1873–1961) had studied briefly in the Oriental Department at Saint Petersburg University and was acquainted with Muslim Iranian culture before becoming a personal tutor of the future Mohammad-Ali Shah Qajar. After the shah's coronation, Shāpshāl became his court minister and close adviser and supported the shah in his efforts to crush the Constitutional Revolution. For this he earned the nickname Bloody Shāpshāl. As a member of the Crimean Karaite Jewish community, he was despised by many Iranian and Russian Jews for his role during the Constitutional Revolution. He went on to become an influential Jewish leader and a proponent of the theory that the first Karaite Jews were Khazars who had converted to Judaism in the ninth century CE. In 1941, as the* hākhām *(Torah scholar and rabbi) of Karaites in Poland and Lithuania, Shāpshāl joined Nazi-sponsored disputations against the Jewish historian Zelig Kalmanovich and argued for the non-Jewish racial origin of the Karaites.*[160] *The incident from his earlier career that earned him this acidly polite open letter from Dehkhodā is described by the writer (after considerable digression) in the body of the letter below.*

Gather round! Hear all about it! I just know that now all of Dakhow's subscribers are on tenterhooks to see—as promised in the previous issue—how he is going to handle the remaining Servants of the Privy Chamber. Doubtless everyone is waiting, all ears, to learn how Dakhow will cope with his embarrassment before Babri Khan's successors. Of course they must all be on tenterhooks and all ears; why shouldn't they be? Where will they ever meet a crazier coot than Dakhow? Where would they find a more stupid rogue, whom they can blithely and with impunity egg on and toss into the ring like a fighting cock to torment poor, innocent creatures to death? And then when—perish the thought, God forbid, bite your tongue, let me never see the day, don't even dream of such a thing![161] —Dakhow gets to pay with his hide for his temerity, they can stand back and laugh at him for his stupidity!

160. See "Shapshal (Szapszał) Seraya Ben Mordechai." See also Browne, *Persian Revolution*, pp. 418–20, for a photograph of Shāpshāl and a caustic open letter to him by a contemporary, strikingly evocative of this piece by Dehkhodā.

161. The author here interjects five consecutive Persian idioms to ward off evil consequences.

Bravo, well done, how terribly smart! Never better! I don't believe the old Dakhow was ever as stupid as this. No, no—I swear it couldn't happen again, for them to have Dakhow jumping through hoops once more while the kids applaud and the adults laugh their heads off. After this, you'll think that if the world were washed away in a flood, Dakhow would not wake up, that he would stay asleep oblivious to all that was happening around him.

What an old stick-in-the-mud I am to be writing that until our ministers get their own offices properly "organized" our constitution can be demolished by a puff of wind! What business have I to claim that anyone who blocks our lawful anjomans and associations is aiming to have the Majlis suspended? Am I a blockhead for writing that the reason why the quota of parliamentary deputies has not yet been filled is a fear that four honest persons without private agendas might somehow enter the Majlis and an actual "disinterested party" gain power? Do I have so little sense of shame as to dare to write that the preachers at the Shrine of Fatima Maʿsum,[162] on orders from the chief superintendent, cry from the minbar [pulpit]: Do not associate with constitutionalists! Send a second, louder blessing upon the Prophet and his family to ward off this evil!

Am I so tired of life that I write, By heaven, the punishment of the twelve murders of respectable persons that were perpetrated in the square of Kerman by the eighteen-year-old son of Mr. Farmānfarmā[163] will rank with that of the son of [the brigand]

162. The popular Shrine of Fatima Maʿsum ("the Impeccable") is in Qom. It was built during the reign of Shah Abbās I (d. 1629) and named after Fatima (d. 816), the sister of the eighth Shiʿi imam, Ali b. Musā Rezā.

163. Residents of Kerman complained to the Majlis about actions committed by the son of their governor, who was also the nation's minister of justice. See "Criticism and Objection [to *Habl al-Matin*]," *SE* no. 6.

Rahim Khan and Eqbāl al-Saltaneh [of Maku] and be equivalent to the restitution of the captive girls of Quchān.[164]

Why should I write these things? Everything that I have written up to now is quite enough for me and my own seventyfold posterity. These are the sorts of things that can be written for a restricted readership in those newspapers that are available fresh every month from the foreign embassies.

All this aside, I recently ran this problem by a student of Shaykh Abu'l-Qāsem in the mosque. He said, Calumny is a worse sin than [eating] dog meat. That is, if someone says, for instance, that Amir Bahādor Jang has grown so powerful that he now wishes to put on trial two of our country's top-ranking preachers,[165] that is like preparing *qormeh sabzi*[166] with dog meat. Next I started to quiz the shaykh's student right there in the mosque about the matter of bribery. He sort of looked this way and that and said, The master's people are coming; this is not a good place—go outside the mosque, I'll come out and tell you.

Yes, it's a lost cause for me to write about such things again or to get involved in these matters. Why? Because I will then become one of those hypocrites who are "losers in this world and the next."[167]

Still, there's no harm in broaching the subject just to gripe about one's personal woes. However unpleasant one's topic, nobody can

164. See *SE* no. 4.

165. Perhaps a reference to Malek al-Motakallemin and Sayyid Jamāl al-Din Vā'ez, the prominent constitutionalist preachers with close ties to Azali Bābi communities, whom the shah tragically ordered murdered in June 1908.

166. A popular beef stew made with kidney beans, finely chopped spinach, parsley, and fenugreek and served with steamed rice.

167. See *SE* no. 13, note 123.

complain or take issue with you if you frame it as a personal complaint. So, in this issue I would like to bellyache with Mr. Shāpshāl Khan. This is no cause for blame or shame; bellyaching is surely nothing new for me! Until one gets it off his chest, his pains and woes will never heal. Unloading one's woes is good for one: just as a stomach pain will get better only when one takes medicine for it, so worry or grief will ease only when one tells others about it. So no blame or shame attaches to it. Even the great, when something is worrying them, get it off their chests.

As, for instance, his Highness Prince Arfa' al-Dowleh, whenever he is worried about unrest on the Iranian-Ottoman border, shares his unease with some of the officials of the Sublime Porte in Istanbul. Or when some of our ulama feel aggrieved, they share their sorrows with certain ambassadors. Or whenever His Royal Highness the crown prince is upset, he shares his displeasure with the competent authorities.

Likewise, I would like now to share a few words of distress with Mr. Shāpshāl Khan. But I fear this might still give cause for complaint. I'm afraid my enemies might seize on something I said to take out of context and translate my remarks in a bad light for Shāpshāl Khan. And there are a lot of other things I'm afraid of too.

So, do you think it would be wiser not to say my piece? Well? What do *you* say? Yes? You'd rather not say? All right, I won't.

But in that case I'm afraid of the opposite consequence: I'm afraid lest all and sundry say that Dakhow, for all his noise and bravado, was too scared.

Very well, God's will be done! As our gambling hajjis say, "Fear is death." But above all, I will put it politely, and stick to the point.

In the name of God the Merciful, the Forgiving!

Dear Mr. Shāpshāl Khan:

First of all, I should like to ask you a few questions. You see, there are some things I have heard about you and found credible; if any of them strike you as contrary to fact, please refute them at once.

First, I have heard, sir, that you graduated from the School of Oriental Studies at Saint Petersburg, i.e., you studied the learning, customs, culture, ethics, and religion of us Orientals. Is this so, or not?

Second, I was told that you lived for eight or nine years in Tabriz and Tehran among Muslims, i.e., you put into practice the knowledge that you had learned in that school by way of day-to-day interaction with us. Correct?

Third, I have been told that during this time you were in contact with the top-ranking elite of our country.

Fourth, I have heard that you are desirous that friendship and cordial relations between the two countries of Iran and Russia should ever endure, in accordance with the wishes of us all.

Fifth, you must, I am sure, have seen the self-mortification[168] and self-slaughter, i.e., the instances of our religious fanaticism, in Tabriz and Tehran.

Sixth, I am certain you know the story of the Russian ambassador Griboyedov in Tehran, and that unwarranted outbreak of

---

168. Persian *qameh-zani*, slashing one's own head with short swords, a rite of self-mortification that sometimes accompanied flagellation in the annual Moharram mourning processions in Iran and the Caucasus.

hatred and violence which for a time severed relations between our two states, and that you know moreover that it was obviously rooted in that same religious fanaticism of ours.[169]

Seventh, I know that through your earlier studies and your subsequent association with us you have realized that of all the nights in the world, the Night of the Decree, according to our Qur'an, is to be revered above all others, that night being one of three disputed nights during the month of Ramadan.[170]

Eighth, I have heard, and I suppose you will not deny it, that you are of the Jewish faith and a Russian subject.

Ninth, you are aware to what extent, according to international law, it is incumbent on a foreign subject to respect the religious sensitivities of any faith or sect of the country in which he resides.

Now, after all this information that you have, for all your obligation to preserve the harmony between our two countries,

---

169. Alexander Sergeyevich Griboyedov (d. 1829) was a Russian playwright and diplomat who was appointed ambassador to Iran soon after the humiliating 1828 Treaty of Turkomanchai. By this treaty, Iran lost vast territories in the Caucasus, and the public was visibly angered. Additionally, this agreement allowed Armenians who had lived in Iran to return to eastern Armenia. Shortly after Griboyedov's arrival in Iran, an Armenian eunuch and two Armenian women from the royal harem took refuge at the Russian compound, hoping to take advantage of the treaty. But the Iranian public was outraged. The women were deemed Muslim converts, and the idea that they would return to their native land (and religion) was blasphemous. Fath-Ali Shah demanded their release, but Griboyedov refused to comply. Soon a mob descended on the Russian compound and murdered the ambassador and his entourage.

170. *Laylat al-qadr*, "Night of power" or "Night of the decree," generally celebrated toward the end of the month of Ramadan and on one of the odd nights of the month—i.e., the twenty-first, twenty-third, twenty-fifth, twenty-seventh, or twenty-ninth (the exact night is disputed)—is supposedly when the Qur'an was revealed to the Prophet (see Qur'an 95).

for all your being Jewish, and for having read the history of Griboyedov—what are we to make of the fact that on the night of the twenty-third of Ramadan, i.e., on the Islamic Night of the Decree, you enter the most important mosque in the Shi'i capital, i.e., the Sepahsālār Mosque, and, not content with just entering it, stay there for several hours?

Should one say that you intended to provoke a major riot, or what?

Should one say that you intended to cause a breach in the friendship and unanimity of Iran and Russia, or not?

Should one say that in accordance with Islam and with Russian law you deserve to be punished, or not?

Mr. Shāpshāl Khan! By my mentor Mohammad (on whom be peace) and by the God of both of us, I swear that Dakhow is not all that fanatical and bigoted, and maybe you too have heard of the occasions when *Sur-e Esrāfil* has been condemned as irreligious. Not everyone is Dakhow, and not everyone would censure you. Maybe in the dawn of Islam the People of the Book were considered [ritually] pure, though now they are "preferably to be avoided." Not everyone will say that the place you visited is the courtyard of a madrasa and not a mosque. Maybe that night if Dakhow or another Muslim had introduced you to his coreligionists, would there have been an immediate uproar and riot, or not? Would your life have been in danger, or not? Would this incident have caused, at the least, a temporary state of hostility between our two states, or not?

I address these questions not to you but to the states of Iran and Russia: that they should determine in accordance with the principles of international law what responsibility such a person bears and how they ought to deal with him. The matter of the use of a sidearm is also relevant here,[171] and, if it is shown to be true, you know how much antipathy this has aroused between Iranians and their dear neighbors.

Well, my intention was to unload a personal gripe. If it stays just between us without any leaks, then I submit that you must have known all of this and already have been made aware of these issues. However, when we were kids we used to have a game and a rhyme or phrase that went with it. If you'll permit, I'll recite this rigmarole and close the article with an invocation to the blessed one:

I went to the city of the blind; I saw that everyone was blind; and I was just as blind.

That's all.

171. This is a reference to Shāpshāl Khan's attacking Mohaqqeq al-Dowleh with a pistol. See *MD*, p. 108, note 24.

# Sur-e Esrāfil, Series 1, No. 20, pp. 5-8

January 16, 1908

## [Events at Tupkhāneh Square]

*This column is devoted to the attempted coup against the Majlis in De-cember 1907. On December 13 the Majlis demanded that Mohammad-Ali Shah dismiss his anticonstitutionalist advisers Amir Bahādor Jang and Sa'd al-Dowleh. In response the shah arrested Minister Nāser al-Molk and dignitaries whom the Majlis sent to intercede. Then, on December 15, luti roughs instigated by the court occupied Tupkhāneh (Artillery) Square, immediately to the north of the palace. In response, young activists affiliated with anjomans came to the aid of the parlia-ment with four thousand armed supporters. Mirza Jahāngir Khan, the editor of* SE, *and several other journalists were also on the grounds defending the Majlis. The Tehran Bazaar went on strike in support of the constitutionalists. Shaykh Fazlollāh Nuri and his armed supporters set up tents in Tupkhāneh Square. They harassed passersby and approached the Jewish community to demand that it side with the royalists or face loss of life and property. The mojāhedin of the Tabriz Anjoman marched on Tehran. Soon even the moderate anjomans tried to end the stalemate with the royalists. A delegation of French, Austrian, and Turkish diplomats pressured the shah to negotiate, then the Russian and British ministers too pressed him to reach a compromise. Faced with this popular solidarity and pressure from foreign powers, Mohammad-Ali Shah backed down a few days later and once again pledged on the Qur'an to uphold the constitutional order.*

Yesterday from early morning until noon I was thinking about what to write, and what not to write, in this issue that would be pleasing to God and the expectant purchasers of *Sur-e Esrāfil*.

I'm in a rather odd bind; at the onset of old age I've fallen into the clutches of contentious people who won't let a matter drop, who just won't stop pestering me. Lord above, what have I done in the twilight of my life to deserve this?[172] Then suddenly the door opened, and the head of Mr. Meddler, accompanied by some stranger, came into view. After the conventional courtesies I said to Meddler, I don't know this gentleman.

He whispered in my ear, so that his companion couldn't hear, It's very odd that you haven't met anyone like this before. This

172. Dehkhodā was not yet thirty; evidently Dakhow was conceived as a member of the previous generation who was nevertheless coming to terms with new ideas. The picture of an older, more traditional person (with a henna-dyed beard) is made more explicit in *SE* no. 31.

morning you must have looked at someone who brought you the good fortune of having the honor of visiting such a person. However much I try to describe his talents, I can never manage more than one in a thousand: this much I'll tell you—I swear by the lives of our children, I swear by your moustache,[173] that this fellow has no equal under the sun. He is a paragon, a sea of knowledge, a world of perfection. He has read every book in Arabic, Persian, Turkish, French, German, English, and Russian—even languages like Sanskrit, Chinese, Japanese, and Hebrew; for all I know, in every language spoken on earth. There's nowhere in the world he hasn't been. You see how his ears are swollen? He got frostbite on an expedition to the North Pole with . . . ! Anyone you can think of who is someone and knows something, he's seen them all and studied with them; he's visited every guru and Sufi and holy man in Iran and India and had his horoscope cast by them. And for the past year and a half, no, two full years, he has been working for the Society of Humanity,[174] and the night that the president of the society and his twelve trustees saw our friend here, and took a fee of one thousand mesqāls in gold and made him a member and

173. *Sabilhā-t-rā pā zakhm kafan karde-am*: one of a variety of elaborate formulae swearing by the moustache, as the visible symbol of a man's personal honor, that the speaker is telling the absolute truth. See Abu'l-Hasan Najafi, *Farhang-e Fārsi-e 'ammiyāneh*, vol. 2, p. 853.

174. The Jāme'-e Ādamiyat was virtually a political party, whose moderate views occasionally conflicted with those of the social democrats. But members of the Jāme'-e Ādamiyat were far from united in their views. Several had been attracted to Freemason lodges while living in Europe. The radical Qajar brothers Yahyā and Soleymān Eskandari, moderate politicians such as Ehteshām al-Saltaneh, and Premier Amin al-Soltān were all members of the organization at some point. Even Mohammad-Ali Shah briefly belonged to the organization in late 1907, when it became an intermediary between the Majlis and the shah.

his certificate of membership in the society was signed, I swear that if his seal hadn't been at the bottom of that paper it wouldn't have been worth a farthing, and of the ten tumans and one qerān that the president of the society takes from people to make them into members, he pockets 10 percent, and the petition that . . . wrote on blue-tinted paper to Malkom Khan was in this person's own hand, and when the president of the society left to take that petition to Europe he appointed Rokn al-Saltaneh and Mokhtār al-Dowleh and Mo'tamed al-Dowleh and Bāser al-Saltaneh[175] as representatives of the society during his absence and Yamin-e Nezām (by reason of the service he had performed for his country and government a few years before in Sistan, as a member of the Iran-Afghanistan Boundary Commission[176]—for which no one had as yet offered him so much as a thank-you) to have the title of "ambassador of humanity" during this same period. And I've heard that he wants to give Prince Arfa' al-Dowleh the title Lover of Iran [Mohebb-e Irān], and they say he has also conferred

175. Rokn al-Saltaneh (Bulwark of the realm) was the title of Prince Mohammad-Reza Mirza, one of the sons of Nāser al-Din Shah; Mirza Abu Torāb Khan Kāshi Mokhtār al-Dowleh was the private secretary and confidant of Mohammad-Ali Shah in Tabriz and Tehran and accompanied him in his European exile (Bāmdād, *Sharh-e hāl-e rejāl-e Irān*, vol. 3, p. 443); Prince Mo'tamed al-Dowleh was the fifteenth son of Abbās Mirza, the governor of Kerman; Bāser al-Saltaneh worked for Amin al-Soltān and later for Mohammad-Ali Shah and was known for anticonstitutionalist sympathies.

176. Throughout most of the nineteenth century, Iran and Afghanistan hotly disputed their precise areas of jurisdiction in Baluchistan and Sistan (with British-ruled India, sharing a frontier with each country, as a generally neutral but interested neighbor). The group mentioned here would have been the Second Sistan Arbitration Commission, of 1903–5, established when a change in the course of the Helmand River necessitated a new demarcation of the frontier (see P. M. Sykes, *History of Persia*, p. 469).

the title Trustee of the Nation [Amin-e Mellat] on Hajji Malek al-Tojjār.[177]

To cut a long story short, make no bones about it, he's been burning the midnight oil to reach this stage. I might add that he has amassed such goodwill that he has access to every community in this city, whether Muslims, Zoroastrians, Europeans, Armenians, Jews, Bābis, despots, or constitutionalists, and is friends with absolutely everybody, and everyone knows him, from shah to beggar. He has the heart of a lion; in all this turmoil, when heaven itself dare not stir out of doors, he went about everywhere night and day, on his own, without packing so much as a knife, and saw everybody. At nightfall, under the tents pitched at Tupkhāneh Square he would carouse with Hajji Ma'sum, Sani' Hazrat, and Moqtader-e Nezām,[178] and at dinnertime he'd eat rice and *tah-chin*[179] and grilled chicken in the upper rooms of Tupkhāneh Square or the citadel or the Madraseh-ye Marvi with Shaykh Fazlollāh [Nuri], Sayyid Ali Āqā [Yazdi], and Sayyid Mohammad Yazdi. At bedtime he would sleep on the same bed with Mojallal al-Soltān. During the day, as you yourself have seen, he would lunch in the Bahārestān.

Now, you will know better than I—I'm not such a bright spark, not too quick on the uptake, but I knew that one doesn't go just anywhere during that kind of civil unrest. I kept telling him,

177. Note that these novel honorifics are Persian in form, not the conventional Arabic.

178. These three men gathered the ruffians who joined the royalist faction during the December 1907 coup (see Kasravi, *Tārikh-e Mashruteh-ye Irān*, p. 528).

179. A large cake of rice, yogurt, and eggs, layered with pieces of chicken and flavored with saffron, served usually at festive gatherings.

Friend, for the next few days go easy on visiting people around town—it's not wise for your health or your safety's sake. He would reply, You are young, and you don't know everything. Haven't you heard what the poet said?

Alike treat good and bad, 'Orfi,
    That when you die the Muslims wash
Your corpse in Zamzam water, and
    The Hindus lay it on the pyre.[180]

Mercifully, Mr. Meddler finished his peroration. I asked him, So, what might be the purpose of your visit?

He replied, Though it isn't my place to say it, you might as well know: these past few days that your newspaper hasn't been published, people are saying that you are out of ideas, that you haven't a topic to write about. I begged to differ, for I knew that the events of these past ten or twenty days in Iran have furnished a year's worth of material for you.

Don't worry, I assured him. Let them say what they will. But do ask the gentleman who has just arrived to be so good as to address some of his own words to me, unless my looks are forbidding or I appear unworthy of his attention.

He turned to the gentleman and said, Since my friend here has been present in the Bahārestān during this period and has no news

180. The Persian poet Mohammad 'Orfi (1556–91) was born in Shiraz and migrated to India, where he gained the patronage of the Mughal emperor Akbar. The original metaphors in his qasidas inspired poets in India and Turkey. Zamzam is the name of a well in the precinct of the Great Mosque of Mecca, popularly held to be especially sacred and to have healing properties.

of the wider world, it would be most appropriate if you would apprise him of what you know.

He answered, These days evil is raining upon unfortunate humankind from all quarters. I myself, who am unlucky by nature, am afraid that if I say a word and my name is leaked [to the wrong people], those who have recently been charged to kill certain persons will finish me off and send me to join my late father. Do you think I've been befuddled or smoking hashish, given up hope, or I'm an idiot? Do you want to get me killed?

Wasn't it just a few nights ago that two peasants and a sayyid—whom you know!—split open the skull of Bahā' al-Vā'ezin with a machete, so that he almost died? Do you want them to come one night and slit open my belly, as they did to Fereydun Zardoshti,[181] and leave my poor children orphaned and alone? Am I more eminent than Nāser al-Molk, the chief minister of Iran, who on the night of the tenth of Dhu'l-Qaʿda [1325] was imprisoned in a dark cell in Golestān [Palace]—and had it not been for the medal of honor around his neck, conferred on him by Churchill, would by now have been wrapped in seven shrouds?[182]

181. Fereydun Zardoshti (or Zartoshti), a prominent Zoroastrian banker and constitutionalist, was murdered in January 1908 by anticonstitutionalists connected with the royal court. The prosecution of his murderers became an opportunity to test Article 8 of the Supplementary Constitutional Laws, which called for the equality of all Iranians before state law. Constitutionalists were enraged and called for execution, while inside the Majlis clerics maintained that the execution of several Muslims for the death of a Zoroastrian was against the principles of Islam. In the end, after British intervention, the perpetrators were flogged and sentenced to fifteen years in prison. "Letter from Yazd [Hajjis in the Bath]," *SE* no. 23, also alludes to this incident.

182. On December 15, 1907, the shah summoned the cabinet and arrested Abu'l-Qāsem Khan Nāser al-Molk, the premier and finance minister, who was

Am I more respectable than the foreign minister whose house they broke into in the middle of the night with a ladder? If his sentry was not awake, heaven knows what would have happened to him! Do I have soldiers? Cavalry to stand guard over my house at night? I have only my two ears for company. Do you want me not to stay at home at night? Not to get any sleep? I should talk to a journalist! Are you out of your mind? These people have their own sources everywhere, i.e., do you think they don't know whether this ploy was hatched by the heir apparent, by Sa'd al-Dowleh, Mojallal al-Soltān, Eqbāl al-Dowleh, Mokhtār al-Dowleh, Amir Bahādor, Soltān Ali Khan and his son Mohammad-Hasan Khan—who, if he dipped his finger in the sea, would turn it to blood—and Mafākher al-Dowleh? And that they had Moqtader-e Nezām, Hajji Ma'sum, and Sani' Hazrat swear a ruffians' oath, on the honor of that person whom you yourself know, to collect funds and strive with might and money for the downfall of the Majlis and to assassinate constitutionalists? They themselves were there in Gaslights Avenue on Saturday the ninth of Dhu'l-Qa'da and saw Sani'-Hazrat and Moqtader-e Nezām, marching like Kuropatkin and Stessel[183] at the head of the lads of Chāleh

rescued by the "energetic intervention" of George Churchill, the Oriental secretary at the British legation (Browne, *Persian Revolution*, pp. 162–63).

183. General Alexei Nikolayevich Kuropatkin (1848–1925) was the Russian imperial minister of war (1898–1904). Anatoly Mikhaylovich Stessel (or Stoessel; 1848–1915) was the Russian general whose ineptitude was responsible for the fall of Port Arthur to the Japanese on January 2, 1905 (see SE no. 22, note 206). The Tajik qadi Sadr-e Ziyā (1867–1931) wrote a detailed account of this war (from a Muslim Asian viewpoint), including the actions of Kuropatkin and Stessel (Edward A. Allworth, ed., *Personal History*, pp. 225–37).

Meydān and Sanglākh and Shaghālābād[184] and so forth, converging from two directions on the Majlis, and had it not been in full view of a crowd of constitutionalist sympathizers, they would have gone to work that very day!

On Sunday, did they not see with their own eyes how the Tehran bad lads attacked the Majlis and got off a few potshots at the façade and portico of the Bahārestān? And when a few constitutionalists armed with pistols and rifles chased them off, they made straight for the Elmiyeh School and threatened to kill the teachers and the little children of the Muslims. And then they congregated in Tupkhāneh Square and, with the cry of "No to the constitution!," brought in Sayyid Mohammad Yazdi, Sayyid Mohammad Āqā, Shaykh Fazlollāh, Āmeli, Rostam Ābādi, Sayyid Mohammad Tafreshi, Hajji Mirza Abu Tāleb Zanjāni, Naqib al-Sādāt the prelate of the sayyids and his son, Akbar Shah and Hajji Mirza Lotfollāh the rowzeh-khwān, Soltān al-Olamā, and a bunch of other sayyids and mullas whom they had cast in advance as the dramatis personae of this farce, under the tents and into the upper rooms of Tupkhāneh Square, and stuffed them with a hash of Russian banknotes and spicy rice stews and flagons of locally made spirits,[185] and determined in those few days, in their own words, to lay waste the ground on which the Majlis stood.

Had they not seen the donkey drivers, ostlers, camel drivers, armorers, gunners, and gunner's mates of Hamadan, and every gallows bird, jailbait, and gambler from the slums and bazaar and

184. These were poor neighborhoods in southern Tehran known for their many ruffians.

185. These spirits were seized from the Jewish Quarter. See *MD*, p. 121, note 15.

caravansary rooftops of Tehran, who by force of the new *varandal* rifles[186] and revolvers that had been given to them [from the army reserve] left no one in possession of his hat, coat, money, or watch, plundered the poor storekeepers, and slashed and stabbed every Muslim they saw in a Western-style hat and overcoat for the presumed sin of being a supporter of the Majlis? And how poor Mirza Enāyat was killed for saying that the constitutionalists were Muslims and sought justice, and his body, missing ears and nose, was hung like a sheep's carcass for a day and a night from the tree in the drill square?[187]

Didn't these people know that the men of Varāmin whom Eqbāl al-Dowleh had called in to help him marched and rode into Tupkhāneh Square together with Shaykh Mahmud, Hajji Hoseyn Khan, Āqā Mohammad Sādeq Dolābi, and Hajji Mohammad Ali Khan Kalāntar? And hadn't they heard Hajji Hasan Khan bellowing that he would demolish the Majlis and give away its carpets to be made into packsaddles for the Varāmin donkeys?

Haven't they heard that Shaykh Mahmud had been presented with a jeweled mace?[188] Don't they know that Sayyid Hāshem Semsār, Ali Cherāgh, Big Akbar, Ali Khodādād, Ali Hajj Ma'sum, Abbās Kachal, Āqā Khan the deputy royal groom, Sayyid Ābedin the Arab, Hajji Mohammad-Ali the Butcher, Nād-Ali the Butcher,

---

186. *Varandal* or *barandal*: popular bolt-action rifle, a copy of the German Mauser 98 made in Brno, Moravia (Czechoslovakia), and sold worldwide in the early 1900s (cf. "Bren," as machine guns from Brno were later called in English). These guns can be seen in photographs of Sattār Khan, Bāqer Khan, and other constitutionalist fighters in Iran at this time.

187. The noses and ears were cut off the bodies of executed criminals as a warning to others. See the third stanza of the verse in *SE* no. 23.

188. Mohammad Ali Shah made this gift. Thus, Dehkhodā is directly implicating the king as the head of the opposition (Yazdāni, "Siāsat," p. 227).

Hajji Safar the Butcher, and the sayyid who runs the coffeehouse frequented by the Westernized dandies—all were ringleaders and facilitators at Tupkhāneh Square who stirred the pot?

Didn't these people themselves have informants in the Madraseh-ye Marvi to report on the saffron rice and stews there? The very madrasa cats were drunk with delicacies, and the huge dinners and luncheons kept the poultry bazaar flowing red, but in order to fool the simpleminded, thirty or forty women and girls with green head scarves, under the direction of the famous Gowhar Khomāri (who had served a lifetime among the troops) and a certain Āsiyeh, were instructed to lay out food upon printed sheets of the Qur'an and to bring it into the madrasa, in sight of the onlookers, weeping because of their empty stomachs.

Are these people not Tehran natives, and have they not seen the water reservoir next to the Madraseh-ye Marvi, with a capacity so huge that it holds as much as Lake Sāveh, but on the express instructions of the water engineers from outside who wanted to pipe the water into the madrasa, one or two soldiers had orders to cut open the water carriers' skins?

One shouldn't reveal everything, but you didn't personally accompany me daily to the mosque, and you didn't see their graces quaffing Kazan lemonade and soda water instead of plain water!

Can we really believe that the Tehran populace was so foolish as not to realize that, after all the killing and looting that took place by the order of the authorities, these same authorities would seek to assume the role of victims by means of these blatant and transparent subterfuges? If the Tehranis are really as uninformed and credulous as this, we will have to recite a requiem over the lot of them and give up all further hopes. But the more I think about it, the more I see that things are not quite so hopeless.

To an extent, these people examine every action from all angles so as not to make any blunders; out of an excess of cunning, they pluck hairs from the yogurt[189] and know their friends and enemies, and so far have not put a foot wrong. They are aware of all the matters I mentioned, except two, about which I will now tell you.

One is that in those first days of Tupkhāneh Square, I saw the well-known Baqqāl-oghli ["the Grocer's son"], naked saber in hand, chasing down everyone he recognized as a constitutionalist and nearly wounding one or two.

The other is that on one of those same days I saw a gang of the Tupkhāneh neighborhood toughs coming back from Nāseri Street, with "Big Akbar" carrying Āqā Sayyid Bāqer the rowzeh-khwān on his shoulders, like a little child, and together with their sons and relatives they all went into the tents. Surreptitiously I asked his son, Hey, man, what's the game?

God's truth, I swear it's not our fault, he replied. We were about to head for the Majlis, but we ran into these gentlemen who insisted on taking us to Tupkhāneh Square, and however hard my father begged, they wouldn't let go of us. Finally my father said, I'm feeling sick; I can't walk. They forced a passing hajji to give us his donkey and seated my father on it, with the donkey's owner shouting behind them, Give me back my ass! My dad got off the donkey, then this Big Akbar carried him piggyback. Since this same Big Akbar plays the lion in the *ta'zieh* [passion play], the toughs nicknamed my father Āqā Sayyid Bāqer "the Lion-Rider."

These people have heard everything I've said, except these last two things. And since they have not yet come to know me and don't know the extent of my knowledge and information, we need

189. An old expression alluding to excessive attention to detail.

to have some dealings with each other for them to realize that I am not a person of no account. Now that I've caused them some inconvenience, if they have time let's talk a few minutes more, then take leave of each other. I said, Please continue.

He said, These days we hear the people who thump their chests as champions of Iran and consider themselves nationalists claiming we should make peace [with our internal enemies]. I say, Gentlemen! This is the wrong thing to say. Is the state of Iran at odds with some other country, that you would have them make peace and conclude yet another agreement like the Treaty of Turkomanchai, to the detriment of the nation? No, they agreed. Well, said I, what's the matter? They said, Are you not a citizen of this city? I said, Of course! They said, It's obvious that during this period you have been either asleep or lounging under a quilt in a drugged stupor. Not so, I replied. I have been a part of this unfortunate and oppressed people which has risen purely in opposition to the [changes to the] constitution and refused to allow its rights to be trampled underfoot; there has been no quarrel and no military campaigning. For two whole years the people endured losses by the hundreds of thousands and casualties by the thousands until this constitution, which is a treaty between fifteen million citizens and the monarchs of the age, was signed. And the ink was barely dry before it was actively opposed.

After agreements, whose forms all the people of Iran, even old women and young children, have committed to memory, and oaths exchanged upon the Qur'an, now they want to make peace all over again. My interlocutors waxed so indignant at these words that they left without saying good-bye and told each other on the way, He's another of these rioters for riot's sake and troublemakers who destroy cities.

I have troubled you considerably. I will say this last word and leave you. Is there a single one of the constitutionally governed states where the ministers plenipotentiary and ambassadors of friendly states, representatives of their countries and nations, have the right to meet privately with the sovereign of the host country, as for the past several days even the dragomans [court interpreters] and the diplomatic advisers of Germany, Austria, Ottoman Turkey, and the rest of the ministers plenipotentiary and diplomatic counselors have been meeting privately with His Imperial Majesty? Do we not know that this activity is contrary to the constitution and the dignity and status of the Kingdom of Iran? Do we not know that, except for the ambassador himself, none of the foreign envoys is entitled to huddle in private with a monarch? Do we not know that on rare occasions an envoy or minister plenipotentiary from the person of a monarch may see a sovereign for a conversation of a nondiplomatic nature only? Can we any longer tell people that these matters are none of their business? If what I have said is really contrary to international regulations I will say no more and keep my lips sealed.

Hardly had this discourse ended when Mr. Meddler stood up and said, Before I forget, let me tell you the news that on the night of Tuesday the ninth of this month, first they arrested the principal commander of Tupkhāneh Square, namely Sani' Hazrat. He was hauled from the quilts of the *korsi* in the home of his father-in-law Hajji Ali-Naqi the tile maker by police and regular army troops, dressed in a veil and a lady's petticoat, and kept in prison for several days in the army headquarters' guardhouse.

With that, they both made to leave, despite my pressing them to stay a while. We have to go, they insisted. We'll see you again if we live long enough.

I said, I didn't catch the name of this gentleman.

Meddler replied, If it remains confidential and isn't noised abroad, I'll tell you.

Rest assured, I told him.

And he whispered in my ear: Piefinger.[190]

190. Persian *nokhud-e hameh āsh*, literally "the pea [found] in every stew." An allegedly (or tiresomely) ubiquitous and well-connected self-promoter and busybody; one who (in the English idiom) has a finger in every pie. The metaphor is found in Dehkhodā's *Amsāl va hekam* and is used at the beginning of Jamālzādeh's short story "Veylān al-Dowleh" to characterize the protagonist (see Balaÿ and Cuypers, *Nouvelle persane*, p. 201).

# *Sur-e Esrāfil*, Series 1, No. 21, pp. 7–8

January 23, 1908

## ["Watch Out—Sayyid Ali!"]

*Fascinated by popular proverbs, aphorisms, and catchphrases, Deh-khodā never tired of milking them dry to help put his point across. In this "saga of a saying" the sociolinguist in him has a field day (one of many). Perhaps looking forward to his discussion of "proverbializa-tion" in "Meanings of a Phrase [Amān az dugh-e Leyli]," SE no. 24, he may here have stepped beyond the bounds of disinterested scholarship and launched an experiment to create a catchphrase. For according to Amir-qoli Amini in* Farhang-e ʿavām *(pp. 367–68), the saying* Sayyed Ali-rā bepā, *"Watch out—Sayyid Ali," with the contexts given in this*

*column, first appeared at the beginning of the constitutional period—in*
SE. *It is also recorded in Dehkhodā's* Amsāl va hekam, *begun in about*
*1915; however, as you relish the documented history of this useful idiom*
*below,* caveat lector—*or, to coin a phrase,* Dakhow-rā bepā!

O humankind! How sunk in the sleep of ignorance you are,
how crass and dim witted! You never get the sense of anything
said, never grasp the intent of an utterance, never learn from the
advice of the ancients, never pay attention to the adages and lore
of your predecessors. Despite this, you deem yourself the acme of
creation and are full from top to toe of pride, hauteur, arrogance,
and conceit.

But I've strayed from the point.

One day nine thousand nine hundred and ninety-nine years
ago, one of the mystics of the era of the ancient kings of Iran
donned the ragged robe of spiritual guidance and, through the
power of his devotional exercises, entered one hour later into the
world of revelation. When he was in that abstract, transparent
world, the thick curtains of time and space were drawn back from
before his eyes, and there on the last spot of the line stretching into
the future—that is, nine thousand nine hundred and ninety-nine
years later—he beheld a desert ghoul, exactly as tall as 'Owj ebn-e
'Onoq,[191] with a Qashqā'i kilim weighing 298 royal man [1,788 ki-
lograms] hanging from his chin like a beard, wearing on his head a
circular dome composed of 892 cloaks, caftans, and padded jerkins
of the Abbasid [i.e., black] livery, all tumbled and in disarray, and

191. A mythological giant supposedly born in the time of Adam and Eve.
He used to catch fish in the sea, then hold them up in front of the sun to roast
them. He lived until the time of Moses, who struck him down with his rod. See
*MD*, p. 128, note 7; and Sādeq Hedāyat, *Neyrangestān*, p. 224.

on his feet a pair of Chahārju[192] watermelon rinds, each of which according to expert assessment was as broad as a camel. He was advancing with long strides from the Unseen World into the Visible World.

Our mystic, on seeing this terrifying monster, shut his eyes tight in fear, then, just to size up this apparition of a desert ghoul for the last time, opened them. This time he saw a big avenging angel kneading a portion of the smoke from the ovens of hell into a bowl of tobacco and, dipping a reed pen into this paste, writing something on the brow of this desert ghoul. The mystic waited until the angel finished writing. There, inscribed upon the ghoul's forehead in large, clear lettering, he read, Watch out—Sayyid Ali!

At the sight of this terrifying tableau and these mysterious and unknown worlds our shaykh was overcome with terror. With a shudder he flung the dervish robe aside and, as it were, turned back from an ascending to a descending arc, from the celestial to the terrestrial sphere, from the world of ecstasy to the world of rational discourse, his head and beard dripping sweat from the stress of his trance, repeating to himself, Watch out—Sayyid Ali!

The pure and devoted servants of God, disciples of the inner circle of the master—that is to say, the shaykh's "six-*dāng* devotees,"[193] who had been attentive all along to the shaykh's altered states— heard these three words of his and took them to be the significant

192. Now written *Charjev*; in Turkmenistan, on the Amu Darya, southwest of Bukhara. The Oxus basin was long famous for the variety and succulence of its melons.

193. An allusion to the saying "One stupid disciple is more profitable than a complete village." For the purpose of grants of revenue, a village is divided into six equal portions called *dāng*.

nonsense of one in a trance,[194] so, purely in order to emulate their perfect model, they said, "Watch out—Sayyid Ali!" On this occasion they chorused this together with the shaykh, but thereafter at every communal gathering and every musical session, with each nighttime *dhikr*[195] and each dawn prayer, they themselves would say these three words.

If the human race were not sunk in the sleep of obliviousness and if the children of Adam were not crass and dim witted, if humankind gave due heed and consideration to the words of great persons, those disciples ought at that time to have understood the meaning of this froth on the surface of the caldron of gnosis. But alas, they understood not one atom of the sense of these three plain and simple words, which like all mystical enigmas remained unsolved and unsolvable.

After them too, throughout the next nine thousand nine hundred and ninety-nine years, whenever a thief, a trickster, or—so to speak—someone known to have sticky fingers passed a row of stalls in the bazaar, all the stallkeepers in that row would say to one another, "Watch out—Sayyid Ali!" And every time a shopper-turned-shoplifter walked through the door of a grocer's to buy yogurt, the grocer would straight away tip off his assistant: "Watch out—Sayyid Ali!" In every coffeehouse, in the arena of every zurkhāneh, and at every neighborhood hangout where friends,

194. *Shaṭḥiyāt*, seemingly antinomian or blasphemous words uttered by a Sufi master in an altered state of consciousness.

195. *Dhikr* (*zikr*, *zekr*), "remembrance (of God), repetition (of the divine name)," in Sufism is a litany of religious or mystical formulas repeated communally in a gathering of a brotherhood, sometimes accompanied by ritual bodily movements and breathing, or music.

neighbors, or colleagues met to socialize, if some of the fellowship saw someone there who didn't belong, they would nudge one another and say, "Watch out—Sayyid Ali."

Nine years ago too, when Mirza Mohammad-Ali Khan Parvaresh, delirious in a fever brought on by tuberculosis, was uttering nonsensical phrases, an item appeared in the newspaper *Sorayyā*[196] under the heading "Letter from Tabriz," containing the remark "This person is not from Tabriz; he is a sayyid from Yazd" and concluding, "Watch out—Sayyid Ali!"

Again, the newspaper *Hekmat*[197] in its issue no. 4 of 1317 [1899], under the heading [in verse] "A lion's cub resembles a lion—in what way do you resemble the Prophet?," gave an account of the misdeeds of Hajji Sayyid Mohammad Yazdi,[198] the nephew of this same "Sayyid Ali," and by way of allusion warned us, "Watch out—Sayyid Ali."

And then only this past Ramadan, during the quarrels between Sa'id al-Saltaneh, Āqā Sayyid Jamāl, and Malek al-Motakallemin in the Masjed-e Shāh, the Masjed-e Sadr, the Azerbaijan Anjoman, and the Sepahsālār Mosque, in the course of myriad brilliant speeches we were told straight, "Watch out—Sayyid Ali."

196. A Persian-language weekly that began publication in Cairo in 1898, edited by Mirza Mohammad-Ali Khan Kāshāni. From 1905 to 1908 it was published in Tehran. See Browne, *Press and Poetry*, pp. 61–62, 67 (under its Arabic transliteration, *Thurayyâ*); and *MD*, p. 130, note 28.

197. A Persian-language weekly published in Cairo from 1893 to 1913, edited by Mirza Mahdi Khan Za'im al-Dowleh. See Browne, *Press and Poetry*, pp. 78–79; and *MD*, p. 130, note 29.

198. The notorious anticonstitutionalist, known as Tāleb al-Haq, who is remembered for his many attacks on the constitutionalist cause.

We unjust and ignorant humans,[199] we dim-witted and stupid people, dolts and idiots that we are, have understood not one iota of anything more of the purport and intent of this catchphrase, whether from the revelation of that enlightened mystic or from the esoteric pronouncements of his disciples or from the observations of the bazaar stallkeepers or from the grocer's admonition or from the carping of the lads of Tehran or from the turns of phrase in *Sorayyā* and *Hekmat* or from the pronouncements by Āqā Sayyid Jamāl and Malek al-Motakallemin. Absolutely nothing.

Centuries, years, months, days, hours, and minutes have elapsed since the date of that revelation; this phrase has rolled millions of times off the tips of the tongues of big and small, commoners and nobles, scholar and unschooled, and I had never happened upon the significance of the threat and warning implicit in these three words—until when? Until I caught sight of this very Sayyid Ali, after fully nine thousand nine hundred and ninety-nine years from the date of that revelation, in Tupkhāneh Square:

| | |
|---|---|
| His cauldron boiling, | The cannon bestriding, |
| His slogan is "One Lord," | Islam his watchword. |
| With the sect of the lutis | He sleeps and keeps counsel, |
| While right there | They're lynching some |
| before him | Muslim. |
| At times busy tippling | At other times gambling |

199. An allusion to the last verse of sura 33 of the Qur'an (The Confederates), which characterizes humankind as *zalum*, "unjust, tyrannical," and *jahul*, "ignorant, uncouth," for not measuring up to the trust it accepted from God.

| With that ass Nuri[200] | And Hasan Daburi,[201] |
| Now true to the faith, | Now fond of the fair. |

Once again, things didn't turn out the way I'd hoped.

Dakhow

## Letter from the City [from Piefinger]

*This would appear to be nothing more than a minor editorial name correction of the first Piefinger column ("[Events at Tupkhāneh Square],"
SE no. 20); however, Dehkhodā carefully maintains the make-believe.*

That day when I came and saw you, I was so harassed and out of sorts that instead of "Allāh-qoli Khan Kangarlu-ye Varāmini" I said "Hajji Mohammad Khan Kalāntar." You must excuse me; it has to do with my old age and a host of legitimate excuses. Apart from this, you know yourself that I have only one head and a thousand headaches. And it was Ali Tizeh, not Big Akbar, who carried Āqā Sayyid Bāqer the rowzeh-khwān on his back and ran away from "them" in the bazaar to the Masjed-e Shāh and together with his children and relatives fled to the Anjoman-e Hoseyni at the Bahārestān, but after all they couldn't carry him to Tupkhāneh Square.

Piefinger

200. A reference to Shaykh Fazlollāh Nuri.

201. Daburi is the clown, whose name is also a colloquial all-purpose pejorative (see Jamālzādeh, *Farhang-e loghāt-e āmmiyāneh*); it appears again (and with the same rhyme) in the context of Tupkhāneh Square in the poem in *SE* no. 23.

# *Sur-e Esrāfil*, Series 1, No. 22, pp. 6–8

February 4, 1908

## Letter [Distrust of "Vakils"]

*Once again Dehkhodā draws a parallel between private and public abuses of trust. He shows that women and children suffer most from the former, while the latter targets all ordinary citizens, yet with a similar deceptive and authoritarian process. In the curtain opener, a fictional domestic drama (in itself another illustration of the hazards of womanhood), Dehkhodā pursues a misunderstanding of an ambiguity in usage to unwarranted, but revealing, conclusions. (Not for the first time: see "Letter from the City [Looking for Religion]," SE no. 6.) Va-kil designates a proxy, trustee, or delegate, anyone who acts for another in a commercial or legal matter. Hence the term initially used for a parliamentary delegate in the early Majlis was likewise* vakil, *the same as the word commonly used to refer to an attorney at law; it was not changed to* namāyandeh, *"representative," until 1925. Dehkhodā's play on the two connotations of* vakil *cannot be directly reproduced in English, which distinguishes lexically between the two senses. The column evolves into an implied criticism of the Majlis president Ehteshām al-Saltaneh, whom the text does not name. Dehkhodā paints him as a hypocrite who, despite his supposed liberal convictions, is colluding with the royalists and the conservatives. He is the man for whom the parliamentary seal is "a mere decoration on a fob-watch chain," the legislator who shows up in parliament whenever he wants and keeps the deputies waiting for him, who ignores the procedural regulations of the Majlis, and who promises in private sessions to stop the formation of a national force (Yazdāni, "Siāsat," p. 226).*

One night I just couldn't stand it. "Mom?" I asked.

"Hmm?"

"There are lots of other married couples. How come they don't fight all the time like cat and dog, the way you and Dad do?"

"Damn you and your smartass questions! Why don't you ask your wretched father? Go away and sit over there."

"All right, but just answer me," I replied.

"No reason," she said. "We were just fated not to get along from the start."

"Fated how?"

"Simply because I was forced to marry your father against my will."

"Mom, were people forced to get married?"

"Oh yes," she said. "When my father died, I was already engaged to my first cousin.[202] My father had quite a bit of property and no heir except me. His coproprietor wanted to cut me out of the inheritance, so I sent word to this miserable specimen of a local mulla, who also acted as a vakil, a lawyer, to sue my father's coproprietor. Somehow or other this no-good obtained power of attorney over me and a week later informed me that he'd drawn up a marriage contract between us! However much I yelled and cried, jumped up and down, beat my breast and raged, he swore it was all settled and I was his wife.

"In short, after a whole year of petitions and countersuits, he cast me into a hellfire that there's no escape from. By God, may he end in hell, be disgraced before the Prophet—may his livelihood pass him by on horseback while he limps after it—may he never have a happy day in his life—may the executioner pluck out his baleful green eyes!"[203] And she burst into a torrent of bitter tears.

Ever since that night I felt truly sorry for my mother, because I was also betrothed to my first cousin, and I too believed that a first-cousin marriage was a match consecrated in heaven and knew what a great injustice it was to part a betrothed couple. Yes, I felt truly sorry for my mother, and from that night on I could never

202. A popular form of marriage was between first cousins whose fathers were brothers. Cousin marriages kept land and property within the family and offered some protection to women through the tight web of family relationships. A popular saying was that cousin marriage was consecrated in heaven.

203. The Persian phrase is literally "May the executioner pluck out his eyes, which are like Azraq-e Shāmi's [green eyes]." This personage (Azraq the Syrian) fought on the side of Shemr and Yazid in the Battle of Karbalā, in which he lost four sons and his own life. He is particularly known for his blond hair and greenish-blue eyes. See *MD*, p. 137, note 3.

forgive my father. Every time our eyes met, I was afraid, because I could actually see, as my mother had said, how baleful his eyes were. Not only was I afraid of my father's eyes, but later I grew to fear the look of anyone who was a vakil, even the name of anyone who was a vakil.

But it isn't my intention to pursue this here. Those people have died and gone to the just world, God forgive their trespasses one and all; we are left here in the unjust world. My purpose here is to ensure that you, at least—if no one else—will know that from the beginning I was the most ardent of constitutionalists. From day one I joined the protesters at the British legation, joined protest pilgrimages to the shrine of Abd al-Azim, went on foot along with the clerics to Qom—because I realized from the outset that a constitution meant justice, meant the end of oppression; that a constitution meant relief for the rank and file of subjects and prosperity for the country.[204] These things I understood. By which I mean that the gentlemen and the Westernized intellectuals had explained these matters to me, but from the day that the late monarch issued his proclamation[205] and I heard people saying that what we need to do now is to choose vakils—all of a sudden I broke into a hot sweat, as if a basin of scalding water had been poured over me; my whole body trembled, my vision darkened, my head went round and round, and I begged them, Don't do it! Please, don't hand over power of attorney with your own hands!

204. The Constitutional Revolution of 1906 began with a series of protests in the shrine of Abd al-Azim, the city of Qom, and the garden of the British legation outside Tehran (seen as places of sanctuary).

205. The royal proclamation by Mozaffar al-Din Shah (d. January 1907) issued in August 1906 allowed the formation of a majlis (assembly) and the drafting of a constitution.

Hey, they objected, from Japan to Saint Petersburg, every country has [parliamentary] deputies![206] For Pete's sake, I told them, take it from me, nothing good will come of having vakils! How about just having a simple constitution? Mind your own business, they retorted. You're illiterate; don't butt in. How can you have a constitution without representatives?! I realized they were right. Well, said I, since you're going to choose them anyway, for God's sake do so with eyes wide open and avoid the pitfalls by selecting good deputies! Very well, they said, we will.

Yes, they said they would, and indeed they did keep their eyes wide open and paid close attention to the candidates' qualities. Ah, but which qualities? The amplitude of their bellies, the thickness of their necks, the size of their turbans, the length of their beards, the opulence of their horses and carriages. The poor dupes imagined they would, as it were, be sending these deputies to a banquet without formal invitations, where the doorman would be intimidated by their bearing and not ask to see their invitation card.

Anyway, two years later they have only now come to appreciate what I said then. Only now do they realize that seventy-four parliamentary votes cast in open session have recalled a certain forty-year-old wolf from Berlin and set him loose to prey on the nation[207]—only now do they realize that sixty votes cast in some

206. Many people of the East, including Iranians, attributed the victory of Japan over Russia in the Russo-Japanese War of 1904–5 to the fact that Japan, a nonwhite nation, had a constitution, while Russia did not. Russia's defeat in turn led to the Russian Revolution of 1905, which brought a constitution to that nation as well.

207. This is probably a reference to the resignation of the liberal premier Moshir al-Dowleh in March 1907 and the appointment of Amin al-Soltān (aka the Atābak-e A'zam) to that post in April 1907. Amin al-Soltān had been the prime minister during the reigns of both Nāser al-Din and Mozaffar al-Din

secret conclaves have alienated the father and defender of the nation [the shah] from the Majlis—only now do they realize that the parliamentary seal is fast becoming a mere decoration on a fob-watch chain!

Only now do they realize that the seats of the officers of the Majlis are occupied by the fat bellies of the Right Honorable Mafākher al-Dowleh ["Pride of the state"],[208] Rahim Khan of the Chalabiānlu tribe,[209] and His Grace Mo'ayyed al-Olamā ["Buttress of the clerics"] while the four conscientious deputies we do have, poor devils, are obliged out of desperation to squat on the carpet, prey to rheumatic cramps. Only now do they realize that, like Dakhow in private, the leading deputies are quietly making a pledge not to form a national army.

---

Shah but was dismissed in 1903 after helping to negotiate a series of unpopular Russian loans for the government. In the early stages of the Constitutional Revolution he was in Europe, but his supporters were involved in the movement and hoped that as a result he would become the premier in the new order. Majlis deputies were vehemently divided over the matter, with progressive forces opposing Amin al-Soltān's appointment. In the end, the Majlis consented by seventy-four votes to his return to the country; he was appointed minister of the interior, although in fact he was the most powerful member of the cabinet (Yazdāni, "Siāsat," p. 220). Contrary to what the conservatives had feared, he did not reject the new order out of hand but chose to work within it. Nevertheless, he did not gain the trust of the radical constitutionalists and on August 31, 1907, was assassinated by a *fedā'i* (a member of the secret anjomans of the mojāhedin dedicated to acts of political terror).

208. Mafākher al-Dowleh was one of the advisers of Mohammad-Ali Shah and was known for his staunch opposition to the new order (Mahdi Malekzādeh, *Tārikh-e Enqelāb-e Mashrutiyat-e Irān*, vol. 2, p. 412).

209. Rahim Khan Chalabiānlu of Qaradāgh (see *SE* no. 5, note 40; and *SE* no. 12, note 116) secretly formed an alliance with the shah and in 1907 plundered the outskirts of Tabriz, killing many.

Only now do they realize that a legislator is actually too important to implement the law and that therefore the procedural regulations of the Majlis will fall short of due observance; that from 3 p.m. until sundown the deputies, like schoolchildren in Hemmat School, have to occupy themselves catching flies or, like the twenty-five thousand members of the hashish smokers' association, have to take a nap, until at barely a quarter of an hour before sunset the phone rings, to announce that Mr. Speaker has company today and they should convene early tomorrow since Iran is in peril.

That's what people realize now. But I had already known it for a long while, because I'd seen my mother weeping and knew that the sobriquet *vakil* would bring its character to bear on present-day Iran, and I still remembered my father's baleful green eyes. That's what I had long understood and what everybody realizes now, but there are still a few things I know now that are known only by the sixty members of that anjoman.[210]

## Editor's Reply

First, I totally disagree with your views.

Second, disrespecting the deputies today is detrimental to our national unity, because although it may not be in conformity with our religious law nor in accordance with the laws of any country in the world, everyone knows that today the person of the vakil is sacred. That is, when someone becomes a parliamentary deputy, he

210. A reference to one of several royalist anjomans in 1907.

is ipso facto as pure and immaculate as the Twelve Imams and the Fourteen Innocents.[211]

Third, how can someone be a Muslim, a sayyid, a mulla, a hajji, a holy man with a beard and stout neck, most of all swear the most solemn oaths by the Qur'an and then, as it were, dig in his heels and out of mere envy or spite—or, God forbid, merely because of a promise he had made to the chief whip in the Anjoman of Sixty—insist that these two standard-bearers of liberty and five or six honest deputies be driven from the Majlis? No, I will never go along with your fantasies, nor will any common grocer in Iran. Why? Because I cannot have it on my conscience to disavow the sacred persons of the 120 innocent deputies. Because I could not atone for 120 pious, holy, honest, and innocent creatures of God. If I were man enough to atone for my own sins, that would suffice seventy generations of my progeny. Yes, this is my opinion, and that of all virtuous Shi'ites is similar.

Yet seeing how Mohammad b. Ya'qub Kolayni in his opus *The Sufficient*, Mohammad b. Babawayh Qomi in *The Perfection of Religion and Completion of God's Bounty*, Sayyid Mortazā in his *Panacea*, Mohammad b. al-Hasan Tusi in *The Book of Occultation*, Fazl b. Hasan Tabarsi in his *Informing Humankind*, Ali b. Isā of Irbil in his *Revelation of the Occult*, Mulla Mohammad Bāqer Majlesi in volume 13 of his *Seas of Light*, Hajji Mirza Hosayn Nuri in *Saturn Rising*, and all the other [Shi'i] scholars in all their books clearly state,[212] "When the Almighty has placed 313 pious and saintly

211. The Fourteen Innocents comprise the Prophet; his daughter, Fatima; and the Twelve Imams of the Shi'a.

212. All of these men, starting with Mohammad b. Ya'qub al-Kolayni (d. 940 CE), the author of the classic hadith collection known as *Al-Kāfi*, are founding fathers of Shi'i jurisprudence.

Shi'i Muslims in the world, then the Expected One will appear"[213]
—that being the case, I am amazed that we good Shi'ites, we who
await the manifestation of our salvation, we who pray, "Hasten our
salvation and theirs," do not therefore swiftly try to add a further
193 prayer writers, professional mourners, soothsayers, and scribes
to these 120 vakils we currently have, so that merely by virtue of
entering the Majlis they will all become immaculate and honest
and innocent, and the total will match the number of those who
fought at Badr,[214] which is 313. Then *we*, yes we, might attain the
era of the heavenly kingdom and our eyes behold the glory of the
Imam of the Time! We might even experience four days of justice
in real life, apart from reading about it in a book!

But now I hear that an extra paragraph has been added to the
Fundamental Law, whereby in accordance with Qur'anic [inheri-
tance] rules two-thirds will go to a son and one-third, on the principle of *necessitas non habet legem* [necessity has no law],[215] will go
toward the entertainment expenses of the deputies.[216] God grant
it be so. Why should I object? However, the addition of those 193
persons of the type I have described is a necessity.

Dakhow

213. In the Shi'i tradition, the Mahdi (the messiah) is the twelfth imam. It is
believed that he went into a state of occultation in 874 CE and will reemerge on
Judgment Day to end injustice in the world.

214. The Battle of Badr in 624 CE, with 313 infantry and cavalrymen on the
Prophet's side, was one of the most important victories of early Islam.

215. The Arabic original means "necessity legitimizes what is prohibited."

216. According to Islamic inheritance laws, sons inherit twice the share of
daughters. This may be a tongue-in-cheek reference to the 1907 Supplementary
Constitutional Law, which called for adherence to shari'a in several articles and
gave a group of mojtaheds excessive powers in the Majlis.

# *Sur-e Esrāfil*, Series 1, No. 23, pp. 6–8

February 20, 1908

## Condolence Addressed to *Mollā Nasreddin* on the Death of the Shaykh al-Eslām

*This* masnavi, *in Azeri Turkish, is also reproduced in Dehkhodā's* Divān, *pp. 203–6 (though omitted, like all other poems, from published collections of* Charand-o Parand*). The mulla addressed here is not, directly, the legendary wise fool (Mollā Nasr al-Din) who is the vehicle of countless jokes throughout the Turco-Persian area but rather the satirical newspaper named for him (*Mollā Nasreddin*), which was published in Tiflis (now Tbilisi, in Georgia) from 1906 to 1932—and which influenced Dehkhodā in his* Charand-o Parand. *Shaykh al-*

Islam was a title conferred on the senior jurist of a city, region, or state who functioned chiefly as a mufti (one authorized to issue fatwas). This cleric was Abd-al-Salām Ākhundzādeh, who was born in Sāleyān (Salyan; south of Baku) in 1843. He moved to Tbilisi in 1864 and met Mirza Fath-Ali Ākhundzādeh (Akhundov) and others of the Azerbaijani intelligentsia. He was appointed Shaykh al-Islam of the Caucasus in 1893. He remained progressive in his outlook and was a proponent of women's education; he sent his daughters to the new girls' school (Hasan Javadi, personal communication).

The poem describes the coup of December 15, 1907, which temporarily shut down the Majlis. The constitutionalists were able to defend the parliament building, but not without some loss of life. Royalists set up multiple tents and kitchens to wine and dine their supporters, including a thousand soldiers and ruffians from Chāleh Meydān. Reportedly, large amounts of wine and arak (local vodka) were brought in from the cellars of the royal court (in some accounts, from the Jewish quarter) and distributed freely among the crowd of ruffians, who despite the presence of so many clerics drank abundantly. Sayyid Mohammad Yazdi and Sayyid Akbar Shah encouraged this behavior by shouting, "Better to commit adultery, robbery, and murder, but not come near this Majlis" (Mahdi Malekzādeh, Tārikh-e Enqelāb-e Mashrutiyat-e Irān, vol. 3, p. 568).

Our thanks to Hasan Javadi for a literal translation of this poem.


Zephyr of morn, as you pass through the Caucasus,
Tarry a while in Tbilisi, and give
My respects to the peerless *Mollā Nasreddin*.
Then tell him, Though cast down in mourning you are,
Has pitiless fate ever spared anyone?
A man sees that nobody, not slave nor king,

Stays long in this world, only almighty God.
Enough! If you think it is wise, do not mourn
Quite so much, lest you finish by dying of grief.
Though the Shaykh al-Eslām has indeed passed away,
Yet do not imagine he died without fame;
Be grateful we still have among us Shaykh Nuri,
And moreover, [that bold beggar] Hasan Daburi![217]
The tally of faith never falls below par:
The Lord will not leave us quite Mollā-less yet.
If the father is gone, may the son still be there;
Let the place of the ass be assumed by the foal.[218]

At the time when the shaykh was joyous and merry,
Mollā, you were very much missed in Tehran![219]
'Twould have freshened your faith and vibrated your soul,
If only you'd stopped by in Tupkhāneh Square,
And listened and looked at the goings-on there:
Barrels of arak ranged row upon row,
In hundreds of colanders, rice being rinsed;
One place, the fixings for hashish and opium;
Elsewhere, a display of the vine's lovely daughter;

217. Hasan Daburi is the name of a famous clown, and *daburi* refers in general to the type of the ruffian and ne'er-do-well; see *SE* no. 21, which also uses this term and alludes to the events in Tupkhāneh Square that the next stanza more extensively describes. The suggestion of the constitution's arch-enemy Shaykh Fazlollāh Nuri and Hasan Daburi as suitable successors to Shaykh al-Eslām is, of course, sarcastic.

218. This verse is in Persian. In the *Divān* it is replaced by a verse meaning "This one has gone, let the other remain."

219. In the *Divān*, the word *Tehrān* is replaced by *meydān*, referring to Tupkhāneh Square, where the shah's thugs gathered.

While our Shaykh Nuri was preaching his sermon,
Hasan Daburi was chugging the booze,
Playing the *donbak* and strumming the tār[220]—
From evening till morning he had a hangover.
Cutting a long story short: surreptitiously,
Heaven had slyly sneaked into this world.
All this is over and done; now it's history.
Only one question is plaguing me still:
Can Islam be established by means of a "party"?
Can a rabble of ruffians pull off a coup?

So many heads that were severed from bodies,
So many bodies that hung from the guns!
Thousands of households were brought into ruin,
So many families simply destroyed.
The corpse of a Muslim was hanged on the gallows;
Names of the learned were dragged in the mire.
Even Sayyid Yazdi himself became tipsy,
Mounting his ass and dismounting the while;
Holy Dhu'l-Qaʿda was shorn of taboos,
And a "Bābi," mutilated, paraded for Muslims.
In their hands, an ʿabā represented a Bābi,
Overcoat for a Shaykhi, and boots, a Wahhābi.[221]
Stores remained closed for the whole of the month,

220. The *donbak* (*tonbak*) is a goblet drum played with the fingers; the tār is a
plucked string instrument.
221. Anticonstitutionalist clerics justified their side's brutalities by calling
their opponents Bābis, Shaykhis, and Wahhābis, sects considered enemies of
the Shiʿites. The Shaykhi movement began with the teachings of the Shiʿi cleric
Shaykh Ahmad al-Ahsāʾi (d. 1826). He challenged the intercessory authority

Most of the tradesmen reduced to near-paupers.
All this is over and done; now it's history.
Only one question is plaguing me still:
Can Islam be established by means of a "party"?
Can a rabble of ruffians pull off a coup?

Minds are preoccupied; later we'll see,
When the dust settles, just what is to be.

(But forgive me, Uncle Mollā; these lines don't seem much like Turkish poetry!)

Dakhow

## Letter from Yazd [Hajjis in the Bath]

Here a crowd of hajjis formed an anjoman, declaring, Now that Moshir al-Mamālek has become a constitutionalist, God be praised, it would be a good idea for us too—just to show we are of a like mind with him—to meet one day a week to discuss national reforms. Among other things, they resolved in that conclave that henceforth, on the night before they went to the bathhouse, they would anoint their loins with [pine] pitch and egg yolk, to prevent their being enfeebled in the water of the common pool.[222] They all

---

of the mojtaheds and maintained that in each era there was only one "Perfect Shi'i," who mediated between Shi'ites and the twelfth imam.

222. The water of the *khazineh*, the large heated pool where up to ten persons could wash (and where some washed their dirty clothes), was rarely refreshed and regularly held a greasy soap scum. Nevertheless, its ritual purity had been

agreed to this and took hold of one another's beards to seal the pact—all except one hajji, who claimed that this extra expense was not in keeping with a businesslike frugality and moreover that the bathwater was *kor*[223] and did not get polluted. At any rate, to cut a long story short, he declined to go along with the consensus of the anjoman.

At this point all the other hajjis unanimously determined that he was being anticonstitutionalist. For his part, he stood his ground, saying that the members of the anjoman were unbelievers, because what they said implied that ritually pure water could become polluted before it changed color, taste, and smell. And so each party stood firm, the hajjis calling the other "anticonstitutionalist" and him calling them "Bābis." Well, the ulama took the side of the dissenting hajji, with the result that things are pretty rowdy.

Yesterday Moshir al-Mamālek said in the meeting of the anjoman, If I hear that in Tehran they have harmed one hair of the head of Fereydun Zardoshti's killer, I will order all the ulama of Yazd to issue a call for jihad: that the Muslims are to kill every Parviz, every Hajii Mohammad Taqi Māzār, and every Zardoshti on the same night![224]

---

an article of Shi'i faith since Safavid times. See W. Floor and W. Kleiss, "Bathhouses," in *EIr* (1988), also online.

223. Of sufficient quantity and quality to render anything in contact with it ritually pure: see *SE* nos. 7–8, note 83.

224. See *SE* no. 20, note 181. Yazd is a major center of Zoroastrian culture; the names of the first and third targets of the threatened pogrom are Zoroastrian. The name Hajji Mohammad Taqi "the herbalist" (*māzār*) appears to be Muslim, perhaps a spoof name for a Zoroastrian who had been forced to convert to Islam. (In the Ketāb-e Jibi edition of Dehkhodā, *Charand-o Parand*, p. 87, this name appears as "Hajji Mohammad Tafti," but the original *SE* column and all other editions unequivocally have "Taqi.")

Well, I no longer know what we are up to. May God himself manage things for the best.

## From Semnān [A Silent Parliamentary Deputy]

Here, thank God, things are cheap and plentiful; when there aren't any deaths, we have a bit of peasant bread—we manage to eat and get by. There are not too many pro-despots among us—we're all for the constitution.

You know, Mr. Dakhow, talking of the constitution reminds me—it's been a whole year since we elected 'Amid al-Hokamā as our representative, and in all that time whenever the Majlis newspaper has arrived we've looked to see what speeches our deputy has been making: none! Not once, not ten times, not a hundred. You see, there were a few supporters of 'Amid al-Hokamā, and right from the word go they persuaded us to get out the vote for him. One week, over a *chelow* kebab,[225] they bet that he would make a speech. That week, as it happened, there was no speech. Next week they bet again; still no speech. The next week, and the next, same again.

In short, they've been betting now a full six months, poor devils, watching their savings disappear. I'm afraid they'll throw away all they have and end up poor and hungry like the dispossessed peasants of Lasht-e Neshā.[226]

225. The national dish of rice and kebab.
226. In June 1907, the Gilan Anjoman sent two of its members, Jamāl Shahrāshub (the Rebel) and Rahim Shisheh-bor (the Glass Cutter), to the district of Lasht-e Neshā in the northeastern corner of the city of Rasht to form an anjoman. Faced with peasant hunger and severe public discontent,

Well now, Kablā'i! *Please*, if you are at all acquainted with this gentleman in Tehran, ask him for God's sake, and for the sake of these poor wretches too, could he just say a few words, however brief, stereotypical, and nonsensical? (God forbid, it looks like once again I'm saying something at odds with the opinions of the grocers of Tehran!) You know, by God, I felt so sorry for these poor devils that I was ready to come to Tehran myself and meet with him. But God forgive Amin al-Zarb, for he has some grievance or other against us Semnānis: he's paid fifty thousand tumans and another two thousand Amin al-Soltānis[227] to the Russians and Greeks to descend on us with picks and shovels and dig up our road! For heaven's sake, up until now horses, donkeys, carts, carriages, droshkies used to ply this road winter and summer, and now even an elephant couldn't get through this morass!

Well, when winter is over I hope to come to Tehran, if only to see Sayyid Ali in person. But now it's winter, and though in summer too there are a lot of hills and dales, pits and ditches, there's just no comparison.

---

Shahrāshub broke with the anjoman and issued a series of radical edicts, which gained him enthusiastic support among the peasants of Lasht-e Neshā. He distributed four thousand boxes of rice from the landlord's granaries among the villagers and canceled seven years of back taxes and rent owned by the community. He gained a mass following of two to three thousand peasants, who virtually worshiped him and recognized him as the de facto leader of their community. Both men were arrested and beaten by local authorities but eventually released thanks to mass peasant protests. *SE* no. 17 recounts this story.

227. The *pul-e Amin al-Soltāni* was a silver coin struck when Amin al-Soltān was in charge of the state mint in the late 1870s: see Rudolph P. Matthee, Willem M. Floor, and Patrick Clawson, *Monetary History of Iran*, p. 190, note 54, and p. 227; and Shireen Mahdavi, "All About Money."

# Reply from the Office [Drawbacks of a Quick Tongue]

My dear fellow, what use is idle chatter? As the Tehranis say, to talk one's head off is truly fun, but one who does loses face and friends; he is on everyone's lips and is heading for notoriety. And if, God forbid, something untoward happens, then as the poet of blessed memory says, "A red tongue brings a green head to ruin."

What about Hajji Ali the Shawl Seller, Āqā Shaykh Hoseyn-Ali, Mashdi Abbās-qoli the Baker, Hajji Hoseyn-Ali, and Arbāb Jamshid—are they not parliamentary deputies? And have they so far said a word? If ever any of them speaks, then I'll bet the Honorable 'Amid al-Hokamā too will break his silence!

And another thing to consider: what benefit have you gained from others' speaking, that you miss his contribution? Suppose he were to speak too; one time, God save us, he might present himself as a partisan of Qavām,[228] another time a supporter of Jahānshāh Khan, yet another he might turn the department of Rasht into a whole province.[229] Let God himself puts things to rights; let him solve everyone's problems; let God himself spare a little help from

228. Qavām al-Saltaneh wrote the 1906 royal proclamation signed by Mozaffar al-Din Shah that authorized the formation of a parliament and the writing of a constitution.

229. The electoral laws of 1906, following an older classification, divided the nation into provinces (*eyālat*) and departments (*velāyat*). Each of a province's main cities could have an anjoman. However, departments were limited to one central anjoman, in their capital city. This became a source of great resentment in states that were classified as departments but had several large cities. For example, Gilan was classified as a department and therefore could have only one anjoman, in its capital, Rasht. But Lahijan was also a large city in Gilan and demanded to have its own anjoman. It pressed the Majlis to recognize Gilan as a province rather than a department so that its anjoman could also be recognized.

his unseen treasury, otherwise what use would humankind's humble efforts be? What good comes of us weak creatures talking?

## From Tabriz [Feuds among the Mojāhedin]

For three weeks the mojāhedin were dug in opposite each other, fighting it out.[230] Initially what happened was that Shaykh Salim's fighters took the head of the sacrificial camel on the holiday[231] to give to Shaykh Salim, at which Mir Hāshem and his fighters were annoyed that it hadn't been given to Mir Hāshem, so for two or three weeks the stores were closed and a dozen to a score of men from both sides were killed. But, thank heaven, it all ended well.

Now the [Russian] consul says that if this happened in his country they'd cast a gold statue in memory of the fallen, and since you don't have any gold, you should cast one in bronze, since they are Martyrs of the Constitution!!! Some people were even ready to start up a collection for this purpose, but others declined to join

230. The mojāhedin were a volunteer army of men of all ages directed by the Tabriz revolutionary society, the Secret Center (Markaz-e Ghaybi). For details see Afary, *Iranian Constitutional Revolution*, pp. 82–83.

231. Eyd-e Qorbān (Feast of sacrifice) is an important Muslim holiday, celebrated on the tenth day of Dhu'l-Hijja, the last month of the year. It commemorates the prophet Abraham's willingness to sacrifice his son to God, before God intervened and provided him with a sacrificial ram. Eyd-e Qorbān is marked by family and communal animal sacrifices; some of the meat is distributed to the poor and the rest enjoyed by the participants. Urban communities in Iran traditionally slaughtered a camel, which thus assumed greater ceremonial importance. Mir Hāshem, who had been a member of the mojāhedin, eventually left the organization and joined the anticonstitutionalists.

in, fearing that this money too would find its way into the coffers of the Anjoman-e Golestān.[232]

Anyhow, everywhere here is secure. There is not a single supporter of despotism to be found in Tabriz—thank God, they are all fighters for the constitution.

## From Rasht [Civil Servants on Strike]

By virtue of the good stewardship of his gracious and noble highness the prince governor, matters are going well, praise God, and all is calm and peaceful. Everywhere is secure, but these days the members of the government have gone on strike and stopped work, demanding the clothes that Sani' Hazrat[233] was wearing on his last night, at the moment of his arrest: because, they claim, these were a luti's rags, and they didn't want them falling into the hands of some coward. Well, if they've put their lives on the line for this, what would they have done if the clothes in question had been on the order of a tailored jacket of furry velvet, a chiffon shawl, and a full-length chador of shot silk?!

As for that deputy who went to Tehran and helped write the constitution, he came twice to Rasht and broke the constitution.

232. There is only one reference to such an anjoman in the periodicals of the time. According to the newspaper *Nedā-ye Vatan*, the Golestān Anjoman of Tehran met at the house of a Qajar prince, Mohammad Ja'far Mirza, and included highly educated members, many of whom had attended European universities or worked for the Foreign Ministry. See Fāruq Khārābi, *Anjomanhā-ye 'asr-e Mashruteh*, p. 474.

233. Sani' Hazrat was the superintendent of the Tehran arsenal who participated in the failed December 1907 coup against the Majlis in Tehran.

He promised to go back to Tehran for two or three days and fix the constitution again, telling the strikers, I will repossess those clothes of yours officially from the military or else send a receipt from Hajji Ma'sum or mail you the items themselves; what more do you need—just be worthy of your own rags!

# *Sur-e Esrāfil*, Series 1, No. 24, pp. 6–8

February 27, 1908

## The Leaders and the Nation [Verse]

*The language of this short* masnavi *is very colloquial, being replete with mother's baby talk. The metaphor of the sickly child who expires in the arms of its wretched and incompetent parent could hardly be clearer. Browne gives a literal translation, with notes, in* Press and Poetry, *pp. 248–49.*

Oh, bother! The child has woken up!
    Go to sleep, pet—the boogeyman's coming!
Don't cry, or the ogre will come and eat you up!
    The cat will take away your bunny!

Boohoo, boohoo—What is it, sweetie?—I'm hungry!
May you burst! All that food you ate isn't enough?
Get out, dog! Nice kitty, here, kitty, kitty!
Hushaby, darling, my flower, hush, hush!
Mommy, I'm dying of hunger!
Don't cry; tomorrow I'll give you bread.
Oh help, Mommy, my soul is leaving me!
Don't cry; the pot's just coming to a boil.
But see, my hand is as cold as ice!
Tsk, tsk, pet; my milk is all gone.
Why is my head spinning so?
The lice are digging holes in your scalp.
Akh-kh-kh . . . Darling, what's the matter with you?—
(convulsive sobs).
God help me! Why are his eyes rolled up toward the
ceiling?
Oh come and look, his body is cold as well!
Why, oh woe, has he gone so pale?
Oh, woe! My child has slipped away! Alas, alas!
And I am left with only sighs and sorrow.

## Meanings of a Phrase [*Amān az dugh-e Leyli*]

*As children we trust everything written in a book, but as adults we
learn that the printed word might not be true. It is the same with government authorities, politicians, and even some radical constitutionalists. One cannot trust their lofty promises, no matter how sincere they
seem. Power corrupts, people can be bought with money, and even the
most seemingly earnest might change course under new circumstances.*

*Dehkhodā illustrates these old truths with copious examples from the Constitutional Revolution, barely disguising his obvious intent under the familiar mask of the scholarly philologist. The parentheses in the "telegram" are his.*

Beware, beware of Leyli's *dugh*—
    water, too much; yogurt, not enough.[234]

I'm not quite sure. Perhaps it was in the *Key to the Sciences*, or the *Epitome of the Key*, or the *Expanded Version* [of the *Epitome*], or maybe in the *Gardens of Enchantment*[235]—I don't rightly recall—that I once read about the concept of "proverbialization" [*ersāl-e masal*]: the author defined this term as the use of a phrase in verse or prose which, by virtue of the speaker's or writer's eloquence and rhetorical ingenuity, becomes proverbial in that form, passing into universal popular parlance.

At the time that I read this, I was of the same mind as the ancients, who imagined that everything written in a book was true, but now that my eyes and ears have been opened a little more, my perceptions have become more alert, and my mind newly probes inside the minds of others, I see that most of those statements,

234. *Dugh* is a refreshing drink made from a mixture of yogurt and water. The saying is used with reference to empty promises. For the Persian, see note 236.

235. Titles of Persian and Arabic books on rhetoric, style, and poetics (*Miftāh al-ʿUlūm* of al-Sakkākī, *Talkhīs al-Miftāh* of al-Qazwīnī, *Al-Mutawwal* of al-Taftāzānī, and *Hadāʾiq al-Sihr* of the Persian Rashid al-Din Watwāt) by scholars of the twelfth to the fourteenth centuries. The second and third are respectively an abridgement of the first and a commentary on the second. The remark is an oblique allusion to postclassical scholarship, often criticized as being a succession of sterile commentaries on commentaries of classic works of the past. See also *MD*, p. 151, note 1; and *SE* no. 14, note 126.

even when written in books, are quite unreliable. Most of the claims the ancients judged to be solid and well grounded, merely because they were written in books, don't have a leg to stand on.

And that includes this "proverbialization" written about in books, as the use of a phrase in verse or prose in so artful and eloquent a way that it becomes imprinted in popular usage. Let me take as an instance this well-known saying that we hear a thousand times every day: "Beware, beware of Leyli's dugh—water, too much; yogurt, not enough." When one examines this "verse," one sees that, apart from having neither meter nor rhyme,[236] it does not yield a complete meaning. Additionally, it may fit into any enunciation and crop up in any conversation, i.e., it is what lexicographers call a catchphrase.

Suppose, for example, Amir Bahādor Jang[237] four months ago attends the Majlis and after one hour gives a brilliant speech and even takes a Qur'an from his pocket and, before an audience of two thousand, swears on it to uphold the national assembly. In confirmation he pronounces three times, in classical Arabic, I undertake a pact with God, in good conscience. And one month after this pact and oath taking, one sees this same Bahādor Jang's men in Tupkhāneh Square, bent on subverting the foundation of the

236. *Amān az dugh-e Leyli—māstesh kam bud, ābesh kheyli*: Certainly the couplet does not meet the demands of poetical meter. Superficially, the two parts rhyme at least enough for "rhymed prose" (*mosajja'*), but the name Leyli would ordinarily take final stress (*leylí*), while the adverb or adjective *khéyli* is always accented on the first syllable. Such assonance is not enough to satisfy the stricter rules of Persian prosody.

237. The minister of court and military commander Hasan Pasha Khan Amir Bahādor Jang was a staunch loyalist in the service of Mohammad-Ali Shah. He was part of the shah's close circle of confidants, who plotted against the new order with the help of Russian diplomats and advisers.

Majlis, haranguing the conscripts in complicated Turkish at the guardhouse and the men from Varāmin in Persian. At this point, when one recalls the amir's brilliant speech in support of the Majlis and those emphatic oaths of his in the Khedmat Anjoman, one involuntarily exclaims, Beware, beware of Leyli's dugh—water, too much; yogurt, not enough!

Or let's say Amir A'zam for three months straight gathers people around him in the Bahārestān and, with all the fire of the Athenian orator Demosthenes and the French speaker Mirabeau, addresses them on the benefits of liberty, then two months later sends this telegram from Rasht to Tehran:

> Humblest of homage to the Most Precious Anointed Sovereign: All the telegrams your servant sends you on behalf of the nation are a formality (i.e., may be ignored). Gilan completely in order, bazaars open, people calm and in their place (i.e., I have given a speech in the government building saying, Look here! The Majlis has collapsed and will never rise again; go about your business, get on with your lives, and earn your bread. Nothing will come of this constitution tomfoolery). Let the Resplendent Royal Mind—may our souls be its sacrifice!—rest perfectly easy on this score. Your household slave knows his housekeeping duties (i.e., whatsoever challenge comes from whatever corner I will squash)—signed: Military Commander.

Here too, when one recalls these heroic deeds of Amir A'zam's in the cause of the nation,[238] what immediately occurs to one is:

238. See "Personal Letter [to 'Pahlavān' Amir A'zam]," *SE* no. 17.

Beware, beware of Leyli's dugh—water, too much; yogurt, not enough!

Or, for instance, His Highness Prince Farmānfarmā standing before the parliament chamber, facing the nation, with tears in his eyes and a lump in his throat, addressing the nation sadly as follows: O people! I am about to go to Sāvojbolāgh and risk my life for you. Then three weeks later one sees in the jurisdiction of this same prince his worthy son and heir Nosrat al-Dowleh shoot down a dozen poor, naked, hungry wretches of Kerman.[239] Here too when one contemplates those sincere sentiments of His Highness Prince Farmānfarmā, this couplet immediately comes to mind: Beware, beware of Leyli's dugh—water, too much; yogurt, not enough.

Or let's say one beholds the father of the nation, Mr. Sa'd al-Dowleh,[240] in the Iranian Parliament, declaring with consummate patriotism, Why should I fear they might kill Sa'd al-Dowleh, when from every drop of my blood there will spring forth a thousand Sa'd al-Dowlehs!

God grant success to Shaykh Ali-Akbar the faqih,[241] who said, Whenever Satan rubs his legs together, a thousand devil's eggs are laid.

239. Nosrat al-Dowleh ruled the province of Kerman on behalf of his father, who was also the minister of justice. See "Criticism and Objection [to *Habl al-Matin*]," *SE* no. 6.

240. Sa'd al-Dowleh, initially dubbed "the father of the nation," was the principal architect of the 1906 constitution and the leader of the liberal-radical faction in the Majlis before joining the royalist faction after losing his leadership role to Hasan Taqizādeh.

241. Persian *mas'aleh-gu*: a cleric who from the pulpit (*minbar*)—or, nowadays, on radio or television—answers listeners' questions on religion and interprets difficult points of doctrine in everyday application.

Well, let's not lose the thread. Four or five months later, this same Sa'd al-Dowleh could be seen voting against the constitutional government altogether. At that point, recalling those pure drops of blood, one just has to repeat: Beware, beware of Leyli's dugh—water, too much; yogurt, not enough!

Or one sees Sayyid Jamāl Shahrāshub once in Amin al-Dowleh's Lasht-e Neshā[242] standing up for the rights of hungry peasants, and for forty-five days in Amir A'zam's jail, frying lice for the crime of constitutionalism, and even ten days after his release, having climbed on top of the Bahārestān's pillared porch, showing the manacles and fetters on his legs and neck to the crowd and calling on the Muslims of the world to help him obtain justice from Amir A'zam. Then, barely a couple of days after this prelude, one night he is closeted in private with this same Amir A'zam (as he was with Dakhow).

At this point too when one remembers the gentleman's heart-rending appeals and the heat and vehemence of his call for vengeance, this couplet comes unbidden to mind: Beware, beware of Leyli's dugh—water, too much; yogurt, not enough.

Likewise, at one time one sees Sadr al-Anām Shirāzi and Mirza Javād Tabrizi crushed by distress for the nation, crying "Woe for the people" at every street corner, in every mosque, and in every anjoman, then a short while later sees one of them, with the help of five hundred tumans, as the founder of the Society of Chivalry[243] and the Progressives (i.e., the atheists), and the other with

242. See *SE* no. 17 for details of Shahrāshub's adventures.

243. Sadr al-Anām Shirāzi and Mirza Javād Tabrizi were two well-known constitutionalist orators. Following the assassination of Amin al-Soltān, royalists and members of the elite began to join popular councils, including the conservative Anjoman-e Fotovvat (Society of chivalry). The Central Anjoman

twenty tumans per month, pimping for the sons of Qavām al-Molk, on his way to becoming the toast of Fars Province. Here too when one thinks back to all the weeping and wailing of Sadr al-Anām Shirāzi and Mirza Javād Tabrizi and all their showy deeds and patriotic, nationalistic boasts, the thought that comes to mind is: Beware, beware of Leyli's dugh—water, too much; yogurt, not enough.

But this is not the point. The point is that, in all these situations, this saying is a cliché that may be used in the many contexts I have cited and in many others, with which you are more familiar than I. It has no eloquence or rhetorical ingenuity, nor any proper rhyme or meter, to justify the scholars' claim of proverbialization—namely, that an expression by virtue of the speaker's eloquence may become a catchphrase and pass into universal popular parlance.

Dakhow

---

of Tehran did not accredit the Fotovvat and accused it of harboring anticonstitutional sympathies.

# *Sur-e Esrāfil*, Series 1, No. 25, pp. 6–8

March 12, 1908

## Object Lesson [Inquisitive Child]

Mom?
Uh-huh.
What does the earth stand on?
The horns of an ox.
What does the ox stand on?
A fish.
What's the fish on?
The water.

What's the water on?

Ay, ay! God gut you! How you do talk! I've had enough.

## Six Place Settings and No Food

*A more literal gloss of the title phrase speaks of six (or, in a variant, a hundred) water pitchers and bowls (for guests to wash their hands) but no lunch or dinner. The purport is plain: the peripherals are available, but the one item essential for the activity is missing (see Amini,* Farhang-e 'avām, *pp. 25–26, incorporated below). Dehkhodā, in his* Amsāl va hekam *(under* āftābeh va lagan*), glosses it as an abundance of outward ostentation and lack of anything of value to offer. In this column he has recourse to a variety of scenarios, similes, and metaphors to refine his point—that the country suffers from too many political, civil, and religious officials, who bask in their own importance and are incapable of cooperation with mere subjects. Therefore nothing meaningful is accomplished, and the needs of the people are ignored.*

Six place settings and no food. She said, Don't eat it. Honey doesn't go with honeydew melon. He didn't listen and ate it; an hour later, she saw the guy doubled up and writhing like a snake. She said, Didn't I tell you not to eat it, that those two things don't mix? He replied, Actually, they mix quite well, to do me in.

I shall compare the government officials with honey and the nationalist leaders with honeydew melon. If the Ministry of Information[244]

244. *Vezārat-e 'olum,* ostensibly "Ministry of Sciences." However, in a similar context (of government interest in subversive writing; see "[On Victimization of

calls this an insult, I am prepared to produce in testimony 250 stories about the virtues of the honeydew and 140 tales about the virtues of honey.

People who write this sort of fantasy are called "anarchists" by Westerners and "Kharijites" by Muslims.[245] But I beg you, do not lay a bloodthirsty hand on my collar; Lord bless you, whatever I may be, I am not an anarchist or a Kharijite! I'm not saying that we don't need a ruler; among the dumb animals, the lion is the king of the predators, and Shaykh Sa'di explicitly names the lynx as the chief minister and the ass as the captain of the royal guard. In the vegetable kingdom the pear is the king of fruits, and the cabbage is perhaps something of note, and if the constitutional order has also influenced the plants, then undoubtedly the potato must be . . . (how can I put it politely)?[246] But let's return to the topic.

I'm not saying that the Noblest of Creation is lower than the animals and plants. I'm not saying that asses and cattle should have a ruler or that beets and carrots should have a chairman and a senior cleric and a representative while we the Noblest of Creation should be left to fend for ourselves. Right now I am reminded how, after my father died, whenever we kids ran riot as if we ruled the roost, my Aunt Fātim would say, Lord, let no household be without a head!

---

Journalists]," *SE* no. 17) Dehkhodā uses *Vezārat-e ta'lim*, "Ministry of Education," in a way evocative of the office of censorship.

245. Kharijites were those Muslims who initially supported the leadership of Ali b. Abi Tālib, the cousin and son-in-law of the Prophet, only to turn their backs on him later. The term is thus highly pejorative in predominantly Shi'i Iran.

246. The potato is traditionally thought of as passive and spineless.

We need a boss, a chief, an elder; we need a national leader too, and a head of state, and we need unity and accord between these two classes—that is, they need to work together, so long as the alliance is not meant to do us in. No one can deny this: we in Iran, out of a population of 10,000,000, have 2,857,000 viziers, amirs, field marshals, generals, brigadiers, colonels, ministers plenipotentiary, chargés d'affaires, aldermen, lieutenants, sergeants, and corporals. Apart from these, among our population of 10,000,000 (God be praised), there are 3,452,642 ayatollahs, *hojjat al-eslām*s [mid-ranking clerics], mojtaheds [clerics competent to interpret shari'a], *mojāz*es [licensed instructors], emām-jom'ehs [leaders of Friday prayer], *shaykh al-eslām*s [high judges], sayyids [descendants of the Prophet], *sanad*s [transmitters of traditions of the Prophet], shaykhs [elder leaders], mullas, ākhunds, *qotb*s [pivots of the religion], morsheds [spiritual guides], *khalifeh*s [assistants to the spiritual guide], *pir*s [leaders of Sufi sects], *dalil*s [guides], and *pishnamāz*es [prayer leaders]. On top of these, in our population of ten million, we have two million princes, lords, landed gentry, khans, tribal chiefs, tribal subchiefs, and clan chieftains. Finally, in addition to these (God permitting), we have two or three thousand parliamentary deputies, anjoman representatives, municipal representatives, secretaries, archivists, and so on.

All the classes enumerated above fall into just two categories: one group, heads of the people, and the other group, heads of government. And each of these has but a single objective. They tell us, You people, toil and labor, endure heat and cold, go naked, hungry, and thirsty, and give us what you earn to eat, and we will guard and protect you.

What can we say? We accept their solicitude, God grant them success; it's perfectly true that but for them, stone would not stand on stone, humans would devour humans, civilization and education, distinctions of rank, would disappear. Of course these people's existence is more or less essential for us—but for how long? In my opinion, as long as they do not collude to do us in.

I'm not saying the Iranian people was once the first nation in the world and today, thanks to the ministrations of these same leaders, it is the disgrace of contemporary civilization. I'm not saying that the frontiers of Iran once extended from beyond the Great Wall of China to the banks of the river Danube and today, by reason of the efforts of these leaders, if in the length and breadth of Iran two mice have a quarrel, one of them will bump its head against the wall.[247]

I'm not saying that with all these chiefs and bosses all looking after us, only the other day eighteen cities of ours in the Caucasus were bagged by the Russians, and that a few days hence the rest of them will be carved up like sacrificial meat.

I'm not saying that for many years Europe has not had to suffer plague or pestilence, while every other year we must bury with our own hands half a million of the working population—that is, of our own young men and women.

I'm not saying that in these past few centuries every state has pulled itself up by its bootstraps, extended its sway over its own territory, established colonies, while we, for all our chiefs and superiors with their protection of our country, have not even been able to protect our own nation.

247. A saying commenting on cramped quarters. See Dehkhodā, *Amsāl va hekam*, s.v. "Do mush . . .".

No, I'm not saying any of this. Because I know that it all goes back to fate and chance. All this was our destiny, all decreed as the fate of us Iranians.

But hear me, have some decency! By God, I'm near to ripping my shirt collar,[248] ready to renounce my faith, about to close my eyes and open my mouth and say, If fate is to fix everything for us, if our affairs are to be improved by the inner sense of shari'a, our actions to be ordered by the hand of the invisible—then what do you millions of chiefs, bosses, and superiors want from us poor wretches? Why are you hundreds of thousands of generals and field marshals and khans barbecuing us under the sun? Why have you latched on to our bodies like leeches, so shamelessly sucking our blood?

OK, granted, you don't have the money to stop the floodgates of Ahwaz, nor the power to dispatch armies to defend the borders; you cannot build roads across the country. But by God, by all thirty books of the word of God,[249] you surely have enough power to summon Shaykh Mahmud of Emāmzādeh Ja'fari from Varāmin to Tehran. You have sufficient power to dispatch a hundred soldiers to Yazd, to preserve order in the city, to exact revenge on the murderer of Sayyid Rezā the police superintendent, and to recover seven hundred tumans' compensation for what Adl al-Dowleh's men had lost in gambling to Hojjat al-Eslām and Malāz al-Anām Mirza Ali-Rezā Sadr al-Olamā Yazdi, may God prolong the days of his teaching. And with five hundred cavalry you can remove Mir Hāshem from the rulership of the province of Azerbaijan.

248. The traditional way of expressing grief or frustration.
249. The Qur'an is divided into thirty joz', "parts," of approximately equal length, for convenience of nightly recitation over the course of the holy month of Ramadan.

Since you are not doing so, I may justly claim that you two groups, like honey and honeydew melon, are collaborating to do away with us, this wretched nation. And the minister of information can complain all he likes. I have 250 stories of the virtues of the honeydew and 149 stories of the benefits of honey ready to recite. I'll provide witnesses in any ministry. If you decline, then here is the ball, here is the field—let the game begin!

## A Riddle

Please don't be afraid, don't be afraid! O God, pray for Mohammad and Mohammad's kin![250]

250. Dakhow is asking readers to decipher this Turkish phrase. According to Dabirsiāqi it is a reference to Crown Prince Mozaffar al-Din Shah, who was afraid of thunderstorms when he was a young child and even in early adulthood. He sought protection in the lap of a Turkish male nanny, who calmed the young prince with these words (see *MD*, p. 159, note 15).

# *Sur-e Esrāfil*, Series 1, No. 26, pp. 6-8

April 23, 1908

## The Year in Review

*This column and its continuation (in* SE *no. 27), after a mock-superstitious apology, are couched in the style of Qajar chronicles, those dynastic histories (such as* Fārsnāmeh-ye Nāseri *and* Montazem-e Nāseri*) that record events in strict chronological order, year by year and even month by month. They are characterized by the sometimes incongruous juxtaposition of affairs of state, court trivia, and snippets of news from abroad. Particularly in the second part, with its catalogue of assorted murders, the style is even more evocative of a modern television news program. Dehkhodā improves on this by linking front-page stories* *with satirical fictitious anecdotes from the everyday: thus the report of an international balloon race in the United States (true) is followed by a hapless dervish's ascent to heaven (as it turns out, in a daydream). The stories involving Iranian notables are based on actual events but redacted and skewed for satirical effect.*

All over the world it is the custom, when the year comes to its end, to write down some of the main events of that year and publish it in a book. We too wanted to write a detailed account of the main events of the past year for publication. But somehow we didn't get around to it. Probably we were fated not to. So now I'm going to write up those events in brief, and if it contravenes the law, it isn't our fault. Because we consulted our horoscopes and performed the usual divinations.[251] If the result had been "inauspicious," we would not have written this; likewise if it had come out "wait." So since it came up neither of these, it appears that we must write it.

Well then, we'll proceed. Last year was the Year of the Ram,[252] and as all the members of the court, some of the parliamentary deputies, and eight of the ministers are aware, it wasn't a bad year for sheep: fodder, shelter, grazing, and the rest of their basic necessities were plentiful (God grant that it be always thus—we're not envious). This year too an Islamic truce was announced from the Ottoman government by Fariq Pasha, throughout the regions of Sāuj Bolāgh, Urmiyeh, Miāndoāb,[253] Saqqez, and Bāneh;[254] the king of the na-

251. Normally performed by counting the beads of a rosary.
252. According to the Turco-Mongol twelve-year zodiacal cycle, derived from the Chinese system, which the chroniclers typically cited (concurrently with other calendars).
253. Cities in western Azerbaijan.
254. Cities in Kurdistan.

tion of Azerbaijan, His Highness Mir Hāshem Āqā, also ratified the declaration.[255] And on 21 Ramadan the [Middle] Eastern Marshal Oyama, the minister of war,[256] while eating oranges between prayer times in the Sepahsālār Mosque, heard a terrifying noise: "Aargh! Where am I hit?" he cried, and fainted. After some strenuous massaging, he recovered consciousness just before dawn, to learn that the door of the mosque had slammed in the wind and there had been no gunshot. (But thank heavens the oranges were not sour, or else with a fright and a start like that, he could have had a stroke.)

Also in this year there was concluded the Anglo-Russian treaty, actually intended to preserve the independence of the Kingdom of Iran though seemingly aimed at partitioning it, and in the Parliament of the Sublime Realm there were lengthy debates about taxes on ice-cream street vendors.

In the same year, the Hejaz Railroad made great progress, the Germans presenting themselves as supporters of the Islamic world. And at Yuzbāshi Chāy, a wheel of Abbās Ganjei's carriage broke, and Abbās picked up a stick and viciously attacked his traveling companion, the merchant Hajji Mohammad Āqā, and beat him mercilessly. Hajji Āqā asked him why he beat him unjustly, and Abbās replied, Simply because, if my fellow-traveler were pure, why did the carriage wheel break? (After which the unfortunate hajji, despite being certain of his purity, went to bathe in the stream and performed the ritual ablutions.)

255. This sarcastic remark points to the extraordinary authority of Mir Hāshem in Azerbaijan by April of 1908.

256. This is a mocking reference comparing the cowardice of the Persian minister of war, Mostowfi al-Mamālek, to the bravery of the Japanese military leader Field Marshal Oyama Iwao, who commanded the Japanese army in Manchuria in the Russo-Japanese War.

Likewise in this year, an apprentice cook in the [Persian] consulate at Istanbul, who later took up selling oil and went broke several times, first went to Istanbul, then to Tehran, then back to Istanbul, back again to Tehran, returned to Istanbul, and finally turned up in Tabriz (though I don't know what happened next).

Toward the end of this year, Mirza Āqā Esfahāni was elected from Tabriz, or not elected (some Tabrizis say he was not). He is determined to refute whatever [the Tabriz deputy] Āqā Sayyid Hasan Taqizādeh says in the Majlis, even if Taqizādeh recites the Qur'an instead of giving a speech. (Our betters say [in Arabic], "If you want to make a name for yourself, become a contrarian"; if it doesn't work one way, try the other.)

During this year, one day Nāser al-Molk sorely missed his fellow student Lord Curzon, the viceroy of India, and asked the Government, Give me leave to go and see Lord Curzon. The Government did not reply. Again, Nāser al-Molk said, If you permit me to leave, I will come back right away. The Government made no reply. Once again, Nāser al-Molk said, You know, I really miss him! Still the Government said nothing. Nāser al-Molk placed the tip of his thumbnail against the tip of his index finger and held it out in front of the Government's face, saying, By God, I miss Lord Curzon *sooo-o-o* much![257] The Government finally lost pa-

---

257. The Persian idiom is *delam barāye Lārd Corzon in qada [tang] shodeh*, "my heart has become this much [tight] for Lord Curzon"—the gesture suiting the metaphor better than can be conveyed in translation. Nāser al-Molk, by some accounts the only Iranian graduate of Oxford University at the time, had known Lord Curzon in England. In December 1907, as the prime minister of Iran, he was sent by the Majlis to the royal palace to negotiate with the king but was arrested. Through the intervention of the British Legation, he was released on condition that he leave the country, and he went to England (Yazdāni, "Siāsat,"

tience and snapped, Hey, get off my back! Go, then, go! I'm going, he said. Get a move on! said the Government. I'm going, he said. For heaven's sake, be off with you! said the Government. I'm going, he said. The Government suddenly rose to its feet, seeing red. It grabbed Nāser al-Molk by the waist and shoved him through the sliding window and out into the yard. Get the hell out of here, it said, and don't let me see you again! Nāser al-Molk retorted, You'll see me again when you see the backs of your ears!

Also in this year, women in England renewed their agitation for political rights. They formed large societies and filled most of the press and the public speeches with their activities and wrote numerous articles and books advocating their rights. And one night, the wife of Mulla Mohammad the rowzeh-khwān in Qazvin saw that it was two o'clock in the morning and the children were hungry and wanted their supper, and she was getting sleepy, and that fellow visiting her husband was sticking like tar to the roadbed and simply would not leave. So she put one of the children's heads on her knee, hunted out a louse as big as a split pea, tiptoed up to the doorway of the men's drawing room, and tossed it into one of the visitor's shoes. The visitor instantly shot up like wild rue seeds sprinkled on the fire, and however much the mulla insisted he stay and smoke a hookah, he wouldn't. The guest left, and in two minutes the wife emptied the cooking pot.

Then again, Boyuk Āqā the viceroy of Astārā on the third night after the death of his maternal nephew asked his wife to sew on a button that had come off his shirt. The woman replied that it would not be a good omen; the family would be destroyed. Boyuk

---

p. 232). Dehkhodā is reminding readers of the close ties between the anglophile prime minister and the British government.

Āqā asked her how that could happen. She answered that death would befall them as well. The man told her, What nonsense is this—God decides all this! I tell you, just sew my button on. What a fuss! The woman kept refusing, the man kept insisting; at last she sewed it on. And from that day forth, there has been a series of deaths in the family.[258]

In this year too His Highness Ashraf Prince of Peace, Ambassador, PhD, and LLD, Mirza Rezā Khan Dānesh Arfa' al-Dowleh (God bless his long title, which stretches like the manifold tripe of a sheep), on the pretext of a general regulation issued by Amin-e Shojā', went underground on one of the Aegean islands. He then had the Ottoman authorities detain all Iranian travelers in Istanbul on the grounds that they had orders to kill him.[259] And Mirza Ali-Mohammad Khan Ghaffāri, the consul at Baku—who is of the same ilk as those poorly glazed tiles—simply to go along with

258. Dehkhodā suggests that while British women were fighting for suffrage, Iranian women had very limited rights, even in their own households, and were mired in superstition.

259. About April 1907 it was reported that Prince Arfa' al-Dowleh, the Persian ambassador in Constantinople, had expelled two Iranian merchants from the city for no cause. He was further known to be hostile to the constitutional cause, and the Persian press had accused him of a lack of patriotism (*RMM* 2, p. 543). The following year, after the shah's coup and bombardment of the Majlis, the ambassador exhibited a complete volte-face: to an anguished letter from Iranians resident in Smyrna (now Izmir), he replied that he had already sent a telegram to Tehran, reminding the shah that a failure to convene the parliament and recall the troops sent against the rebels in Tabriz would result in a fatwa from the mojtaheds of Najaf declaring the monarch an infidel and calling for a jihad against the throne—and in his own resignation as ambassador. When the shah backed down, Arfa' al-Dowleh sent another telegram to the Smyrna consulate, to notify its staff and congratulate all his compatriots (*RMM* 6, pp. 683–84).

his townsman,[260] played possum and infiltrated the Iranian anjo-man of the mojāhedin of the Caucasus, identified several persons, reported them to the Russian governor, and had them all arrested. (Unfortunately the secret societies are composed of cells comprising a limited number of members, none of whom can know more than a few others, so the consul remained ignorant of thousands of other branches of the anjoman.)

Also in this year, 150,000 tumans of the royal budget was expended on pipes of tobacco for the hoodlums of the public squares (though the latter themselves claim that a third of this money was not spent on them: most of it went into the purses of Amir Bahādor [Jang], Sayyid Ali Yazdi, Mojallal [al-Soltān], and Shaykh Fazlollāh [Nuri]. Let them tally up their accounts, and I will give you the correct figure later).

In this year too Amir Bahādor and the *qullar āqāsi bāshi* [commander of the palace guard] were at loggerheads over something and couldn't come to terms. Though I doubt that the qullar āqāsi could get along with his boyfriend.[261] As the poet says,

I am old, and he is young—it's a tale of camel and cat;
Cold and cool is the amorous exchange between old and young.


Dakhow


260. The Ghaffāri clan was from the city of Kashan. Dehkhodā is indulging in a pun, since *kāshāni/Kāshi* means both a person from the city of Kashan and a glazed tile.

261. Apparently a well-known falling-out between lovers (Yazdāni, "*Siāsat*," p. 233).

# *Sur-e Esrāfil*, Series 1, No. 27, pp. 6–8

April 29, 1908

## The Year in Review—*continued*

Last year too that distinguished scholar of celestialia, terrestria-
lia, subterrania, and interalia Āqā Sayyid Abu Tāleb Zanjāni, who
several times in the past had declared Shaykh Fazlollāh [Nuri]
an infidel, became reconciled to the correctness of the shaykh's
views and in regard to the riotous occupation of Tupkhāneh
Square delivered the verdict [in Arabic] "Everything that the
mufti has ruled on this in his fatwa is God's judgment, so far as
I am concerned," thus imitating the shaykh just like an Indian
monkey.

Also in this year, with the adoption of the constitution, all the human rights to life, property, residence, and dignity were accorded to all the inhabitants of the kingdom. Two hundred and twenty people in Azerbaijan were dispatched to the hereafter by the son of Rahim Khan Chalabiānlu and twice as many in Kargāneh Rud by Arfaʿ al-Saltaneh of Tālesh; twelve people in Kerman by the pick of the bunch of the noble Qajar tribe, the eighteen-year-old son of Farmānfarmā, and several persons such as Hajji Moham-mad Taqi Māzār and his brother, Sayyid Rezā Dārugheh in Yazd, on the instigation of the Moshir al-Mamālek and Sadr al-Olamā; ten to fifteen people in Kermanshah by Aʿzam al-Dowleh the son of Zahir al-Molk, and two to three hundred of the Qashqāʾi tribe, among them a sayyid and a mojtahed and others, by the sons of the exalted Qavām of Shiraz; fifteen people in Tabriz (kicked to death by the sacrificial camel, a miracle of Āqā Mir Hāshem Āqā); Enāyat with several others in the raid on Tupkhāneh Square by the mojāhedin for the sake of a smoke; seventeen people attending [the play] *The Wedding of Bilqis* at the State Theater;[262] and twelve on the day of the shrapnel bomb blast at the arsenal set off by the servants of Nowkar Haydar, an associate of Qanbar, Abuʾl-Fath, and Ebn al-Zafar. A devoted mourner at the shrines of the blessed Imam Hoseyn and his son Ali Akbar, viz., Lord of the Scimitar and Wielder of the Musket Mowlānā al-Qoldur [the Thug] Amir

262. The Tekyeh-ye Dowlat, built by Nāser al-Din Shah in the 1870s, was a central stage for the performance of passion plays (taʿzieh) during the month of Moharram in Tehran (see Peter Chelkowski, "Taʿzia," in *EIr* online [2009]). Bilqis is the name in Islamic tradition of the queen of Sheba, who married King Solomon; she appears in a number of plays in the taʿzieh cycle, some with titles such as *The Wedding of Solomon [and Bilqis]* (see Ettore Rossi and Alessio Bombaci, eds., *Elenco di drammi religiosi persiani*, nos. 73, 421/I, 527, 679, 1014).

Bahādor Jang, died by God's decree [Arabic motto]: "God causes people to die at their allotted time."

This year, military balloons were virtually perfected in Europe. In Saint Louis, the grand prize for the balloon race was won by the German balloon *Pommern*, which covered 880 miles in 40 hours.[263] And one night in the Anjoman of the Poor, Mr. Khorus Ali-shāh[264] all of a sudden, for no reason, felt light headed and saw before him a cloud of black fog, which little by little enveloped his whole person; the heaviness of the air and lightness of the fog gradually lifted him off the ground, and light as a bird he floated heavenward. Leaving the atmosphere and stratosphere, he continued on to the outer bounds. He said, Since I've come so far, why not take a look at the heavens? No sooner had he begged strength for this endeavor from his Sufi mentor than in the twinkling of an eye he shot through the heavens and entered heaven itself. At this point he noticed that a spring of pure water was flowing beneath his feet; he reached out to cup a handful of water to cool himself, when all of a sudden his friend Tāus-Ali shouted, Uncouth lout! What are you doing? Has the space between your ears gotten completely vacant, that right here in the *khānqāh* you're p . . .

The poor man opened his eyes and saw—disaster: the sweat, or something, was pouring from his pants legs like water from

263. In October 1907, the James Gordon Bennett Cup International Balloon Race, held in Saint Louis, was won by Germany's *Pommern*, which traveled a distance of 867.4 miles. See "German Aeronauts Win Balloon Race: The Pommern Descends at Asbury Park, After a Flight of 880 Miles," *New York Times*, October 24, 1907. In the Persian text here the name of the balloon appears garbled, as *Bumāri*.

264. Khorus Ali-shāh, "King [of Humankind] Ali's Rooster": another mock-Ne'matollāhi dervish name, like Tāus-Ali, "Ali's Peacock," below; cf. "Reply to Letter," *SE* no. 11, note 98.

a jug. Quickly he collected himself and said, Faqir! I've just had a strange trip. Tāus-Ali asked, *Darvish*! What kind of trip? He replied, The kind of trip where Shams threw Mowlānā's books[265] in the water and not one page got wet, and when Shaykh Najm al-Din in Balkh urinated, his repudiated disciple in Khuzistan was drowned.

Last year too, freedom of assembly was passed by the consultative assembly and ratified by the royal hand. The Anjoman of Members of the Customs Office brought in from the torn purses of the Belgians and Messrs. Expectant-of-an-Ambassadorship and Mostashār al-Soltān and others one hundred tumans annually from the levying of fines, increasing the state and national revenues (though for the life of me I can't figure out why [Minister of Commerce] Mr. Mo'tamen al-Molk, the head of customs, still so hates the term *anjoman*).[266] However, let's get back to the topic at hand.

This last year too (if my fellow citizens can credit it) a Dr. Giorgio in the United States invented a machine by means of which those who have drowned or frozen to death or have been poisoned may be revived, i.e., it actually brings people who have died in those ways back to life. And in Kashan, the neighbor woman in the house on the right called down from the rooftop: Naneh Hasani!

265. The collected poems of the mystic Mowlānā Jalāl al-Din Rumi, known as the *Divān-e Shams-e Tabrizi*, are dedicated to his beloved Shams of Tabriz, who died mysteriously.

266. Mo'tamen al-Molk was ostensibly a constitutionalist (see Yazdāni, "Siāsat," p. 225). Here Dehkhodā aims his attacks at supposed constitutionalists who after assuming office supported the policies of the conservative governing elite.

Naneh Hasan answered, What?

—How's your uncle Hoseyn?

I'm frantic; he's croaked!

—What do you mean, croaked?

Clenched his teeth, and staring at the ceiling.

—Pour a drop of tincture-of-tomb-water down his throat.

But he's finished, I tell you!

—Don't say it, don't say it! Is life or death in our hands? No, it's in the hands of the innocent martyred [Imam] Hoseyn![267]

## Gum [The Story of Hajji Abbās]

*As the introduction (in "The Style and Structure of* Charand-o Parand*") notes, this column—continued in the next issue of* SE *but lacking the promised third episode in subsequent issues—differs substantially from all other* Charand-o Parand *items in being less diffuse and more focused and having in every way the makings of a serialized short story or novella (cf. Balaÿ and Cuypers,* Nouvelle persane, *pp. 95–97). Social criticism—of the ulama and the situation of women—is still firmly lodged in the subtext, and the authorial voice-over begins and punctuates the tale at intervals. The life of Hajji Abbās to date is seen in flashback, a retrospective reverie triggered at the end of the first episode by the sight of the hajji's attractive neighbor Roqiyeh.*

267. Dust collected from the tomb of Imam Hoseyn at Karbalā was popularly considered especially holy and endowed with curative properties. It could be mixed in water and drunk.

Everybody knows that among us, calling a woman by her own name is wrong. Not just a little wrong, but egregiously wrong. Actually, what's the point of a man calling his wife by her name? Until she has children, he says, Hey! And when she has children, he uses the child's name to call her, as for example: Abul! Fāti! Abu! Roqi! and so on. The wife answers, Uh-huh! Then the man says his piece, and that's it. Otherwise, to call a wife by name is plain wrong.

In the month of the sacrifice [Dhu'l-Hijja] last year, on a Thursday, Hajji Mulla Abbās came home around noon after several nights spent away. At the doorway he coughed twice, said once, Yā Allāh, and called, Sādeq![268]

His wife came bustling from the brazier, on which she was roasting indigo leaves for eyeliner, toward the hallway, and the neighbor women in the courtyard, two of whom were applying eyeliner in their indoor clothes [a pleated overskirt over pantaloons] while a third combed her hair in the sun, ran into their rooms. But one of them, at the moment when Hajji Mulla Abbās entered, tripped and fell flat on the ground, and her short jacket (as all Muslims have seen happen) was forced over the top of her skirt and rode up as far as her shoulder blades. She cried out, Woe! Shame on me! A strange man has seen me undressed! Woe! Oh God, I want to die! And as fast as she could she got up and, clutching a corner of her head scarf tightly over her face, rushed into her room. The hajji's wife meanwhile laughed out loud and said, It doesn't matter, Roqiyeh! Hajji is your brother, in this world and the next.

268. Sādeq is a boy's name, presumably that of their first child.

Hajji Mulla Abbās gave his wife the two loaves that he held in his right arm and the piece of sesame halva wrapped in blue paper clutched in his left hand. They both went into their room, though Hajji Mulla Abbās's eyes were still fixed on Roqiyeh's room.

# *Sur-e Esrāfil*, Series 1, No. 28, pp. 7–8

May 5, 1908

## Gum—*continued*

Hajji Mulla Abbās was originally from Kand,[269] a landless peasant. Up until the year of the last glanders outbreak he had eked
out a living with his late father as a donkey driver, hiring out the
few donkeys they owned to the villagers. When his father caught
glanders and died, that was the end of them as a family; he sold
the donkeys and came to Tehran to work as a tradesman. For a
few days in Tehran he sold sieves from Istanbul, fans for keeping

269. A small town northeast of Tehran in the Alborz foothills.

braziers alight, and pajama drawstrings and at night went to the mosque of the Yunos Khan madrasa to sleep. His merchandizing did not prosper, what with the high cost of living in Tehran and his own profligate leanings. For instance, somehow or other he had to have a chelow kebab once a week, and on the other days two *sangak* loaves[270] and a one-*abbāsi*[271] pot of soup hardly sufficed him.

Finally, one Friday afternoon he went into the courtyard of the madrasa to take a nap and happened to see some unexpected things that set him thinking. So he went to see one of the ākhunds and got him to spill the beans by asking, That woman who was just here—was she your wife?

The ākhund said, Muslim, what would I want with a wife? With all these women hanging around Tehran, what would I need a wife for?

Abbās understood all that he needed to and without any shyness asked about the rates. The cleric told him, Five shāhis, ten shāhis, and if she's very young, one qerān tops.

Abbās heaved a sigh and said, You ākhunds have it made.

The cleric asked, What's the matter, don't you have a place to live?

No, Abbās told him.

Do you have any money? asked the cleric.

Yeah, said Abbās hesitantly.

OK, said the cleric. Since you're a stranger here, my cell is your home. Friday and Saturday are my days off, when some postmenopausal women hoping for marriage, sometimes widows, and young virgins too, come around; you can come—I am at your disposal.

---

270. Flat wheat bread baked on a bed of pebbles (from *sang*, "stone").
271. A small-denomination coin, worth about four shāhis.

Abbās thanked the cleric and thereafter did more or less as he was told,[272] and bit by bit the money from the sale of his donkeys was running out.

One day he asked the ākhund, I wish I could become a theology student.

No problem, the latter replied. You can read, can't you?

Of course, replied Abbās. I learned a little bit of reading in the village because my father forced me to. I can read *Yā Sin* and *Al-Rahmān* and *Yusabbah* very well.[273]

Very good, that's enough, said the cleric. Immediately he brought out an old outfit of his own and a tattered turban, saying, The cost of these is two tumans—I'll give them to you on credit; pay me when you have the money.

And indeed, in a few minutes Abbās was a full-fledged ākhund, quite delighted at the way he looked. Starting the next day, he attended the course on exegesis[274] taught by the madrasa's mojtahed and was allocated a half cell and a one-tuman monthly stipend plus two qerāns and five shāhis for lamp oil. Six months later, Ākhund Mulla Abbās was participating everywhere in the commemorative prayer gatherings held at annual and forty-day intervals, banquets, and rowzeh-khwānis. He also read the prayers at funerals and performed, on commission, proxy fasts and prayers and the recitation of the whole Qur'an during special periods. From his contact with

272. "More or less": i.e., he took advantage of the sexual opportunities, but kept his options open.

273. The names of three suras (36, 55, and 64) of the Qur'an. Usually "reading" such Arabic texts meant the ability to recognize the extract and recite it aloud, mostly from memory, without necessarily understanding it.

274. Using the textbook *Lom'at al-Tafsir*, a basic commentary on the whole Qur'an for beginners.

the other students he learned to thicken the Arabic consonants, overdoing it so as to pronounce even *h* like *ḥ* and *alef* like *'ayn*, *s* like *ṣ*, and *z* like *ẓ*; then he presided as Qur'an reader in the [major] mourning rituals.

But the real rise of Āqā Shaykh began when he heard that the mojtahed of the madrasa was appropriating half of the waqf revenues for himself, contrary to the will of the donor and indeed in contravention of the regulations governing pious endowments. So he gradually started to mutter insinuations and then openly to defy the teacher, and one by one the other students joined in. The mojtahed realized he would have to buy off the ringleader of the rebellion, who was Mr. Mulla Abbās. Accordingly he gave the ākhund a three-hundred-tuman stipend out of the tithe paid by one of the neighborhood magnates, in order to make the hajj; Mulla Abbās took the cash and set off for Mecca. He made sure, of course, to beg at least two-thirds of his expenses for the journey from his fellow-pilgrims.

When the ākhund retuned from Mecca, with just those liras he had earned by conducting rowzeh-khwānis for Iranian merchants resident in Istanbul and Egypt, he had left, all expenses paid, 225 tumans. He went straight to his old madrasa, but the mojtahed—ostensibly to comply with the waqf regulations; in reality to get rid of that nuisance Hajji Mulla Abbās—had given his half cell to somebody else. He made a fuss and expostulated, and might have been able to get his room back somehow, but his heart wasn't in it. Because now Hajji Mulla Abbās was rich, a man of some consequence. It was time for Hajji Āqā to get married and settle down in a house of his own with a life of his own. How long was he supposed to squat in a corner of a madrasa waiting for Thursdays and Fridays? Hajji Āqā decided to get married and asked all his friends and acquaintances, if they came upon an attractive and well-to-do virgin, to let him know.

One day a local grocer informed Hajji Āqā that there was an orphan girl on his street whose father had been a merchant, and though young, she was of a noble family and, so far as he had heard, pretty; it seemed to be not a bad match. Hajji Āqā followed up on this, and he brought home a girl of eleven, with a dowry of five hundred tumans. This was that same Sādeq whose maiden name was Fātemeh and who was now known by the name of the son she had borne to Hajji Āqā.

But Hajji Shaykh's youthful ardor, his seven or eight hundred tumans, which included his personal wealth and his wife's dowry, were not enough for a Hajji Āqā to rest content. Two or three weeks later he secretly contracted a temporary marriage [*sigheh*],[275] and a few months after that he married a second wife. At the turn of the year, after making the ablution of repentance,[276] he took another [presumably a former prostitute] in a sigheh.

At present, as he brought home the bread and sesame halva, Hajji Āqā has four lawful wives, besides the adventures he enjoys in his friends' cells.

275. Temporary marriage (Arabic *mut'a*, called *sigheh*, "contract," in Persian) is an arrangement whereby a woman enters into a contract for exclusive sex with a man (on her part) for a definite period of time and for a stipulated sum. The woman in a sigheh union is also called a sigheh. The caliph Umar (r. 634–44) outlawed mut'a marriage as a form of fornication. Shi'i scholars have upheld the custom, viewing it as a legitimate form of marriage, though without the social status of *nekāh* (formal marriage).

276. A ritual of purifying a prostitute, by pouring sacred water collected at a shrine over her head. Such a woman could then enter a marriage and was (grudgingly) accepted by the community. For more discussion of women's issues in the pages of *SE* see Afary, *Iranian Constitutional Revolution*, ch. 7.

It must be said, however, that Hajji did not have his former stamina. He had lost his old waggishness, now that his money was nearing its end. Little by little he had spent the girl's dowry, and four or five days earlier, when he had left the house, to much yelling and cursing, he had taken his wife's bathing bowl and sold it. He ignored her protests that she still had the honor of her late father's family to uphold and this bowl was the last of the worldly possessions she had inherited. Not only did he not care about her lamentations; he had cursed her dead parents severalfold. And now, as I said, he had been away four whole days without news from home.

(To be continued)[277]

277. The story "Gum" ("Qandarun") appeared in only these two install-ments, and despite this promise no further episode was published. Persian *qandarān* (colloquially *qandarun*) is the juice of certain plants, notably salsify, which on exposure to the air coagulates into a gum that may be chewed (Najafi, *Farhang-e Fārsi-e ʿāmmiyāneh*). Popular wisdom holds that chewing this makes a man thin bearded and that if you swallow it you will have difficulty urinating (Hedāyat, *Neyrangestān*, p. 138). Its significance here remains unexplained.

# *Sur-e Esrāfil*, Series 1, No. 29, pp. 7–8

May 13, 1908

## [Sani' al-Dowleh's Dream]

*Mortazā-qoli Sani' al-Dowleh ("Artisan of the state"), married to a daughter of Mozaffar al-Din Shah and the first president of the Majlis, had studied mineralogy in Berlin and Brussels and reportedly had been interested in building a railroad system in Iran from an early age. After his return to Iran, he made a series of unsuccessful investments in various industries, including iron mills, to help achieve his lifelong dream. In 1910, Sani' al-Dowleh began negotiating with the German Deutsche Orient Bank in Iran to raise funds for the railroad project, much to the consternation of the British and Russian govern-*

*ments. On February 6, 1911, he was assassinated by two of his Georgian employees in Tehran. The public blamed the Russian government, and anti-Russian sentiment dramatically increased, whereupon the Russian legation arranged for the transfer of the assassins to Transcaucasia. (See Ahmad Kasravi,* Tārikh-e Hejdah-sāleh-ye Āzarbāyjān, *pp. 152–53). The anonymous author of this piece includes a prologue arguing tongue in cheek for an idealistic view of progress and spins a fanciful alternative explanation for the debacle, in which international humanitarian motives trump the hero's initiative. (Dakhow will use the same ploy of a naïve and counterintuitive explanation in discussing the shah's mobilization against the Majlis in* SE *no. 32.)*

All nations expect that one day, whether through the traditions of their prophets or the foresight of their philosophers, the earth will become a model of the Garden of Eden. We Iranians too used to say in ancient times, Let the light conquer the darkness, and today we say, Let the earth be filled with justice and righteousness after it has been filled with tyranny and oppression.[278] Although I am an Iranian and a Muslim, sometimes when I saw the Mahmadovs in Azerbaijan, or the Mortazavis in Zonuz [in eastern Azerbaijan], or the Sadr al-Olamās in Yazd, or the Shari'atmadārs in Rasht, or the Eqbāl al-Dowlehs in Mohammadābād, or the Hajji Malek al-Tojjārs in the gymnasium arena, or the Majd al-Eslāms in the embassies,[279] an idea contrary to religious belief would flit across my mind like a mosquito's wing, and I would say, Maybe—just maybe, Lord forgive me—maybe these traditions

278. Alluding to a prophetic hadith used by Shi'is in reference to the twelfth imam, of whom it is believed that he has gone into occultation and will reappear on Judgment Day.

279. These were all elite families of Iran at the time.

about the betterment of the world, as about many other matters, are intended for the guidance of the common people and based on some rationale. But I soon realized that this thought was a temptation of the devil to weaken my faith; then I would twice ask forgiveness of God, bite my hand once between thumb and index finger, and spit two or three times, to escape the snares of the cursed Satan.

Now I understand without a shadow of a doubt that the world really, really *is* progressing and that humankind is day by day becoming more desirous of loving his neighbor and spreading absolute justice throughout the world, and it is thus certain that the world will one day actually be filled with universal love, goodwill, equality, and justice, and the Golden Age of the poets will return.

In support of this claim I must adduce for you a parable to make the matter somewhat clearer.

During his childhood in Berlin, Saniʿ al-Dowleh came out of school one holiday and went for a walk on the outskirts of the city. It was very cold; the snow lay eight inches deep, and despite his warm clothing Saniʿ al-Dowleh keenly felt the chill. Suddenly he heard a whistle and the sound of some machine, and behind him there appeared the head of a steam locomotive pulling 255 carriages and 7,591 passengers. Apart from his pleasure at seeing this strange sight, Saniʿ al-Dowleh was plunged into a deep reverie. In his child's mind he wondered whence these passengers might be coming: from China? Māchin? Jābolqā or Jābolsā? The region of Mt. Kāf?[280] God knows. But see how warm their rooms are in this

---

280. Māchin (cf. Sanskrit *Maha-China*, "Great China") is eastern Turkistan and Mongolia, the lands of the Kara Khitay Turks (hence the English "Cathay"); Jābolqā and Jābolsā are two legendary cities at each end of the earth (see Hedāyat, *Neyrangestān*, pp. 217–18); (Kuh-e) Kāf is a legendary emerald

cold weather; they have lunch and dinner on call, bed and washing facilities right there, books and newspapers at hand, just as if they were in their own homes!

On the heels of these thoughts, he said, By God, I swear that if I get a favorable letter from Tehran this week, granting me the two marks' raise in my pocket money that I asked for, when I grow up and return to Tehran I'll build one of these railroads in Iran!

He stored these ideas in his young memory as the train gradually disappeared into the distance, then he went back to school to nurture these novel ideas to fruition.

Childhood plans such as these usually last a few minutes or hours, or at most two or three days, before being forgotten. But on the contrary, as Sani' al-Dowleh grew older, so this idea of his matured. As time went by he no longer slept at night nor relaxed during the day; he was constantly writing, rewriting, calculating, drafting plans, until some thirty or forty years later he became the finance minister of Iran. Now was the time to put his forty-year-old plan into practice. Now was the moment to link every city in Iran by rail.

But this required money.

He looked into the state treasury and saw that it was as empty as the heads of those who would not lend to it. He looked at the purses of the merchants and princes of Iran and saw that they were sewn shut with twine made of goat's hair. Finally he figured out that an indirect tax would need to be levied on some imports, and by means of this revenue his dream project would secure a life of its own. And in fact he nearly pulled it off, when all of a sudden—O

---

mountain, or mountain range, that encircles the terrestrial landmass (ibid., pp. 220–21).

my fortunate brothers who have never suffered misfortune!—all over England, all throughout Russia, an unbelievable tumult and uproar erupted, and a hue and cry, a quarreling and yelling filled the world.

Whence came this almighty uproar? From the animal protection society [Société protectrice des animaux].[281] Perhaps some of our citizens have never heard the name of this society and are unaware of its goals. You see, the Europeans in general, and our neighbors in particular, as the prophets foretold and philosophers predicted, have expanded the struggle for justice, equity, and humanity to the point where, besides being the supporters of all the peoples of the East and enacting treaties to guarantee the independence and survival of the weaker Asiatic nations, besides spending billions for the liberation of the black peoples, they now state that they will no longer tolerate cruelty to animals and will prevent anyone's harming even insects and predators. Accordingly they have set up large associations, societies, institutions, and committees for this purpose.

Now you are undoubtedly going to ask, What connection have these societies with Iran's railroad?

Aha! This is where I tell you that you are on the wrong track. Listen well and you'll see; if these two things have no connection with each other, I'll change my name and instead of "Dakhow" I will henceforth call myself "Deputy [Vakil]."

281. Corrected from Dehkhodā's transcription, which would correspond to an ungrammatical "Société protecteur d'animaux." The SPA, founded by Dr. Etienne Pariset in 1845, is France's national organization for the prevention of cruelty to animals. The first such animal welfare charity was the Royal Society for the Prevention of Cruelty to Animals (RSPCA), established in Britain in 1824.

Good. So, we said that many societies have been founded in Europe with the aim of protecting animals. And Sani' al-Dowleh, for his part, wants to build a railroad across Iran, right? Very well: what will be the result? The result of this will be nothing other than four hundred million donkeys, packhorses, camels, and mules sitting idle, forelegs folded, staring at one another, like the Anjoman of Sixty after the arrival of Ehteshām al-Saltaneh and Mirza Āqā Esfahāni.[282] These creatures have no tongue like Mr. Sa'd al-Dowleh to go and print a newspaper[283] and declaim, Unjust humans! Why have you deprived us of our work? Why do you leave us idle at home? Have the justice and humanity of the Europeans had no effect? The pure idealism of those activists for universal welfare is surely still alive!

282. Following the assassination of Premier Amin al-Soltān on August 31, 1907, a number of conservative elites cautiously joined the Adamiyat and other conservative anjomans. The new Majlis president Ehteshām al-Saltaneh was a leading member of the Adamiyat Society, and he worked to bring moderate and liberal deputies and the conservative anjomans closer. As a result, on October 1907, the first anniversary of the Majlis, members of conservative anjomans came to the Majlis and paid their respects. Mirza Āqā Esfahāni was the representative from Tabriz, whose claim to have been elected a deputy from Azerbaijan was seriously questioned (Yazdāni, "Siāsat," p. 234).

283. Sa'd al-Dowleh's father jointly owned a printing press and in 1850 was instrumental in launching the first newspaper in Iran, the court-sponsored *Ruznāmeh-ye vaqāye'-e ettefāqiyeh* (Journal of current events). The son, who was a merchant and industrialist with years of experience in European countries, became the leader of the liberal-radical faction of the Majlis in 1907, gained notoriety for duplicity and support of repression, and eventually became a royalist. After the 1908 coup he briefly became the prime minister but was exiled from the country when the constitutionalists took over Tehran. See Browne, *Press and Poetry*, pp. 99, 146; Abu'l-Hasan Alavi, *Rejāl-e 'asr-e Mashrutiyat*. See also *SE* no. 24, note 240.

Thus it was that the Europeans started telegraphing orders to their embassies to tell these Iranian savages, If you build this railroad and render the pack animals idle and homeless, we, in accordance with the international laws of rights, will legitimately invade and swallow you one by one like santal and copaiba capsules![284]

Of course, they wouldn't *really* have come and swallowed us. But by the steps they took they did give us Iranians (and indeed all Orientals) to understand that the Golden Age was back, that the time of revelation of the messages of the prophets and sages was drawing nigh, that an absolute benevolence had enveloped the whole world, from the fish of the sea to the fowl of the air, and finally that our humanitarian neighbors have outstripped us in this regard.

Well, I had a lot to say and would have kept you even longer. But somehow my attention wandered to the treaties signed between the sovereign state of Iran and the friendly states, and then I was put in mind of this Arabic verse of Imru' ul-Qays:

Ask your own eye who is killing us,
Dearest; what sin is it of fate, what fault of destiny?[285]

284. "Santal" refers to sandalwood extract, intended to strengthen the body. Copaiba (or *copahu*, as given here, a related product) is an oil extract from a tree in the South American rain forest with various medicinal and commercial uses. See *MD*, p. 187, notes 16 and 17; and *Wikipedia* entries.

285. The writer (the artless Dakhow, though unsigned) claims to be quoting a pre-Islamic Arab poet. However, the verse is in Persian and is recognizable as coming from a ghazal by Hafiz (". . . jorm-e setāreh nist": pp. 50–51 in the Foroughi and Qāsem Ghani edition of his *Divān*; cf. *MD*, p. 187, note 19). The Persian is even misremembered: Hafiz's original translates as " . . . it is not the sin of fate, nor the fault of destiny."

# *Sur-e Esrāfil*, Series 1, No. 30, pp. 7–8

May 25, 1908

## [The World Order]

*At first this column reads like a philosophical treatise on the existence of good and evil in the world. We enjoy happy moments in life because we know there can also be sad moments. Without darkness, light would be meaningless. Without bitterness, we cannot appreciate sweetness. On closer inspection, it is a social democratic critique of religious thought, a secular analysis of economic and social injustice in Iranian society. One man has all the comforts of life, while another suffers from cold, hunger, and poverty. One family lives in total security, while another*

*is devastated by the revenge of anticonstitutionalists. In the end there is
no justice in this world.*

O Kablā'i! Last night, may it happen to your young men
and all Muslims, was the wedding of my Roqi. The men had a
male musician, and the women had a female dancer for themselves. At times we swapped over—that is, the female musicians came to the men's party and we sent the male musicians
to the women's party. Wish you'd been here; they twisted my
arm, old man that I am, to join the party. But, sorry to tell you
this, Kablā'i, may it never happen to any family, suddenly at four
o'clock in the morning a screaming and ruckus came from our
next-door neighbor's house: Mashdi Rezā-Ali's wife had passed
away. I felt very sorry for him, since she was young and had
several small children.

To avoid a bad omen among the women, I lied about this business and said, It's no big deal; Mashdi Rezā-Ali knocks his wife
about, and his children are crying. But you can imagine how hard
it was to endure this tragedy. Here's one household throwing a
wedding party, with dancing and all, and the house next door is
in mourning. Anyway, when I was sitting in the party—maybe
because of my age or just because I ate dinner late, or hadn't slept,
or because of this shock I got—somehow when I was just sitting, I was gradually overcome by a weakness as if I had forgotten everything around me, and my thoughts went to the thread
of world affairs. You see, the world works in this way too: in one
place there is a wound, in another a poultice; one place there is joy,
another mourning; here there is poison, there honey. The poet put
it really well:

Stings and sweets, roses and thorns,
    sorrow and joy belong together.[286]

Then I thought, Why must it be so? God was surely capable of creating the world comfortable, of making the whole of creation sweet and enjoyable, filling the world with roses and sweets and joy instead of these thorns and stings, grief and sorrows. Then, I swear, I must have been inspired by that line of Shaykh Saʿdi's where he says that if every night were the Night of the Decree, the Night of the Decree would be like any other night.[287] I asked God's forgiveness several times and said, O God, greatness befits thee only; truly, if there were no darkness, who would know light? If there were no bitterness, who would appreciate the taste of sweetness? These things, then, must be so.

Kablā'i, I don't have much of an education, but our philosophers and mystics must have a good grasp of this matter, and I think they also believe that the world must function in this way and the basis of the world order rests on this.

Anyway, while I was immersed in such thoughts, I gradually began to take a nuanced look at major affairs of state. I imagined, for instance, the house of Aʿzam al-Dowleh the governor of Ker-

286. Apparently an alteration of a line by Saʿdi: "Treasure and serpents, roses and thorns, sorrow and joy belong together."

287. Saʿdi not so much misremembered as paraphrased in a prose form that preserves the meaning but obscures a clever poetical conceit. The original couplet (from *Golestān*, ch. 8, which the writer cites below just before his last quotation from Saʿdi) puns on the polysemous word *qadar*, "power; decree; value, worth," and translates best as "If all nights were [the Night of] Power/Decree, the Night of Power/Decree would be worthless." This especially holy night is an issue in "[Letter to the Russian Diplomat Shāpshāl Khan]," *SE* no. 19.

manshah at four in the morning: he himself sprawled half asleep on a velvet cushion in the middle of the main hall, three personal servants with silver waistbands waiting at his beck and call, on one side a seductive beauty teasing and caressing him, on the other a charming boy singing and dancing for him, high-grade oil lamps turning the gloom of night into bright daylight, the scent of violets and roses making the air as life-giving as the breaths of that Christlike odalisque,[288] wines from Khollar and Sheverin[289] rising to the head as light as a spirit, and, excuse the language, short pleated skirts slung a good span below navels with protruding bellies like the corpulent bodies of the religiously observant reclining on the banks of the irrigation canals of Tehran[290]—in short, all the requisites of luxury and sensual pleasure supplied to order, with not one detail missing.

Now, if it were the norm for all houses to be like this and for all people to have these means of enjoyment available, then what delight would these facilities afford, and how would a person tell pleasure from pain or render thanks to the true benefactor? It is for this reason that the Lord, blessed and glorious, has provided something else to contrast with this luxury and indulgence, so that humankind will not forget God, will appreciate his bounty and realize that God has power over all eventualities.

For example: In this same city of Kermanshah, in contrast to all that luxury and indulgence, one finds a good-looking young

288. The salient quality of Jesus in the Islamic tradition is his power to breathe life into the dead.

289. Obscure villages in the regions of, respectively, Shiraz and Hamadan, known for their wine grapes. See *MD*, p. 193, note 9.

290. *MD*, p. 193, note 11 represents this as licentious behavior.

man who, for the theft of three qerāns, so as to preserve order in the state, in front of the government building, in the middle of the day, on the orders of His Highness A'zam al-Dowleh and before the eyes of the boy's own mother, had his throat slit from ear to ear. Then the mother of this young man, once her baby, now kisses him, now licks him, now dyes her hair with her son's blood, embraces him, repeats, Mother, mother! Then her state of mind suddenly changes; like a madwoman she utters a shuddering cry, lays her head on her son's throat, and, as if very thirsty, drinks her son's blood as it flows. Then she picks up her son's body and, like a person who doesn't recognize this young man, stares at his face with terrified eyes, and calmly, without a sound, like a new bride relaxing in the arms of a beloved husband, embraces her child and lies down in the dust and blood to sleep forever.

What is all this? These things all make good sense; it all forms the basis of the world order; these things are necessary for it to be thus. Our thinkers are also of the opinion that if it were otherwise, there would no longer be a sense of competition; humankind would not be ready for progress and would not distinguish good from evil.

Then another parable occurred to me. I recalled how pure the air of Shemiran[291] is, and how fresh the parks and public gardens are, and the personal gardens of those ministers of the interior and ministers of foreign affairs and ministers of war. On one side flow rivulets like streams of tears, on another grow colorful flowers of iridescent hues; on the one hand you hear the twitter of nightingales and canaries, on the other you see vistas of mountains and waterfalls. Truly, what purity! What verdure! What freshness! Just

291. A resort village in the cool hills just north of Tehran.

like the otherworldly paradise God described in the Qur'an, and its likeness that Shaddād built in this world.[292]

Then I recalled an incident when in [the Azerbaijani village of] Bileh Savār four or five shacks and shanties in the customs area caught fire and the flames shot skyward, and in between these blazing fires a clutch of women, children, and old men, without anyone to aid or guide them, yelled for help, their screams and laments and prayers to the Prophet and imams ascending to the skies.[293] And there was no one to sprinkle a drop of water on the ruined home of these unfortunates or to spare a crust of bread for their hungry children.

What is the purpose of all this? It is so that you and I might appreciate our good fortune, so that we might gain wisdom. It is so that we become aware that "if every night were the Night of the Decree, the Night of the Decree would be worthless." And to understand that the poor poet understood something when he said,

Some day when ill befalls you, be not sad;
Give thanks for escaping something worse than bad.

Then my mind's eye wandered into the private quarters of the high-ranking ulama and hojjat al-eslāms whose veiled consorts slumber behind the curtain of chastity and immaculacy and rest protected by seven veils from the eyes of strangers, where even the sun's rays are excluded from their promenade and the moonlight

292. Shaddād was a legendary king of ancient South Arabia. The garden he built was known as the Garden of Iram (Eram) or the Paradise of Shaddād.

293. Persian *vā-ghowsāh, vā-Mohammadāh, vā-Aliāh!* For such Arabicate formulas combining prefixed *wā-*, "alas," with suffixed vocative *-ā/-āh* see W. Wright's *Grammar of the Arabic Language*, vol. I, 295D; and *MD*, p. 194, note 23.

too is a stranger. I thought of 150 women in Khalkhāl [southeastern Azerbaijan] who one night were taken captive by forty thousand tribesmen of the Fulādlu and Shāterānlu, and next morning only four of them, half-dead and naked, returned to their villages—to find, alas, only mounds of ashes where their villages had been.

Aye, Kablā'i! I was pondering these things and marveling at the works of God, when suddenly—excuse me!—I heard the children's mother shout, Shame on you, man! You always have to snore at top volume! Get up! Get up! Get up! Take this kerchief and tie it round the girl's waist!

I opened my eyes and saw that [the groom's family] had come to escort the bride home, and since they had no related males with them, it fell to me to tie the bread and cheese around the bride's waist.[294]

294. This ritual reflects a folk tradition that the bride carries blessings to the house of the groom. See *MD*, p. 194, note 28.

# *Sur-e Esrāfil*, Series 1, No. 31, pp. 7-9

June 11, 1908

## [Women's Education]

*Elite and upper-middle-class women of Tehran and several other cities became involved in the nationalist movement to secure a parliament and a constitution and later to form women's anjomans and schools. In March 1908, the Majlis debated the right of women to form anjomans and whether these were in accordance with the laws of shari'a. Initially some deputies deemed the subject inappropriate for parliamentary debate. But Sayyid Hasan Taqizādeh and Vakil al-Ra'āyā Hamadāni spoke in favor of women's anjomans, stating that there was no religious prohibition against them (the latter even proposed, audaciously, that women be given the vote). In the end, women were allowed to keep their anjomans, though without any financial or institutional support from the Majlis. In recounting this episode and criticizing the deputies for their lackluster support of women, Dehkhodā blames Iranian culture for clinging to old traditions and holding on to archaic social hierarchies of class, seniority, and gender, divisions that he believed held back both men and women. Curiously, he again affects the persona of an elderly gentleman, as he did in SE no. 20.*

Napoleon says, To bring up good sons, we must educate good mothers.

Our Prophet too says, Paradise lies under the feet of mothers.

This sentiment is undoubtedly a primary axiom: the morals, habits, and beliefs of the mother are influential throughout children's lives, that is, every scruple, habit, and belief with which a child is infected by his mother in childhood is the source and foundation of that child's actions for the whole of his or her life.

Shaykh Sa'di took cognizance of this idea and says in this chapter [of his *Bustān*],

A vice once seated in the soul will stay
And not be lost until the Judgment Day.

I've often wondered how it is that, with all the emphasis by prophets and sages and the great men of the world on the need for education of women, when our women have so often assembled and, humbly but insistently, petitioned the Majlis and the cabinet to set up a modern school for the education of women, the deputies and the government ministers have each time not merely refused to comply but actively fought against it!

I thought a great deal about this, wandered mountains and valleys, and came to the conclusion that it was all because the women of Iran—that is, our mothers—have complete trust in their seasoned earthenware cooking pots. Now, please don't laugh at me when I say this, and don't think I'm joking or baiting you. At this advanced stage of life, joking and leg-pulling doesn't befit me, nor my neatly trimmed [henna-dyed] red beard. I tell you in all seriousness that if all the scientifically minded ladies and all the progressive gentlemen in Iran reeled off one thousand reasons for the ministers' and deputies' opposition to a school and a society for women, I for one am convinced that the core reason is that same complete trust which our mothers place in their seasoned earthenware cooking pots.

I have never been ashamed to express this opinion about our own womenfolk before my fellow citizens. I've said it straight out, like it is, and I hope they too will stand up, put all hesitancy aside, and admit, man to man, that our mothers will not swap one old earthenware cooking pot for ten brand-new, unblemished ones. Why do I need them to confess to this fact? Because even if our own compatriots realize that Dakhow is telling the truth, still the foreigners will say that I'm joking. And as I've already said, joking at my age and with my neatly trimmed red beard does not befit me.

As I have already said, the opinions, ethics, and habits of mothers form the basis of all the opinions, ethics, and habits of their sons throughout their lives. One such opinion—this same faith our mothers have in their seasoned earthenware cooking pots—is the reason why we all, without exception, have complete faith in men who "have backbone."[295] Now, it goes without saying that all men have bones; what I mean by this expression is people like those seasoned earthenware pots.

Our deputies and ministers are well aware that if the women of Iran do join forces to open schools, have associations, and be educated, they will gradually realize that clean, hygienic cooking pots are better than pots with a layer of soot two fingers thick on the outside and thirty-five-year-old inches-thick grease on the inside, and undoubtedly once this idea they inherited from their mothers has been expunged, their sons for their part will no longer pin their faith on "solid citizens," and like Mr. . . . Taqizādeh will put their collective foot down and demand, How much longer must our ministers and statesmen and government officials be chosen from among a small, select coterie? If the composition of the cabinet changes a thousand times, how long must Moshir al-Saltaneh's belly, or Nezām al-Saltaneh's doleful voice, or Āsaf al-Dowleh's fursleeved topcoat still be the ornament of that body? And of course you know that in the words of that consummate stylist and accomplished scholar the future minister of censorship of Iran Hajji Sadr al-Saltaneh, "This skein has a long, long thread." Meaning that tomorrow, once this idea has won general acceptance, during the second round of parliamentary elections it will be the deputies' turn.[296]

Now I tell you frankly, and call to witness the consciences of all the ministers and deputies and officials, that the source of the

295. The Persian phrase (*ādamhā-ye bā ostokhwān*, literally "persons with bones") refers to individuals who are solid, reliable, influential, and of good family, and by implication also old and conservative.

296. That is, there will be other ramifications to such developments, such as the formation of women's societies, a less elitist pool of cabinet ministers, and eventually more democratic elections for the Second Majlis.

country's ruin and of the population's misfortune is that same complete trust our women have in their seasoned earthenware cooking pots, and undoubtedly on whatever day this conviction is removed from us, Iran will be in a state of heavenly bliss. So if the ladies and gentlemen of our country really desire reform, then as soon as possible this is what they must do. First, the gentlemen should gather up all the beards, full-girth fur-sleeved robes, buckled shoes, and all suchlike emblems and badges of the long-toothed men, load them on to a donkey, and send them out of town. Then the ladies should gather up every old earthenware pot in their kitchens, bring them out, and smash them behind that departing guest.[297]

If they do this, I will promise you faithfully that within a short time everything that is wrong will be righted. And if, God forbid, they ignore my advice and the moral of all my parables just goes in one ear and out the other, then I have no solution. Let them recite the whole of *a-man yujīb*,[298] and maybe God will make a start on reforming things.

This is the end. Yours truly,

Dakhow

297. Referring to the donkey and its load; it is a popular custom to smash crockery behind a departing visitor whom one is glad to see the back of. See *MD*, p. 199, note 13.

298. The opening of verse 62 of sura 27 (The Ant), "Or, who listens to the distressed [soul] when it calls on him," was to be read twelve thousand times by one person or a thousand times by twelve people in order to solve a problem (see *MD*, p. 199, note 15). This is part of a short litany enumerating various benefits for which humankind should thank the One God, and not other deities. In Dakhow's quotation the first word of the Arabic is deliberately misspelled, with *'ayn* instead of *alef*, reflecting a popular misunderstanding.

## Announcement

The Anjedāni sayyids, who are a charismatic community and able to work wonders, as has frequently been tested by our Karbalā'is and hajjis, are particularly efficacious at rendering hitherto barren women fertile.

In recent days they have quitted the Arab Quarter and settled I know not where. Individuals unable to have children should make their way to that [new] location, because so long as one has no doubts and truly believes, it works.

# Sur-e Esrāfil, Series 1, No. 32, pp. 7–8

June 20, 1908

## [The Shah on the Warpath]

*In this final column before he and his newspaper had to flee Iran, Dehkhodā predicts the June 1908 coup, while maintaining a sense of levity. On June 4 the shah, accompanied by the Cossack Brigade, decamped to his garden Bāgh-e Shāh, outside the city gates. People in Tehran panicked. Soon a thousand supporters of the Majlis surrounded the building, and negotiations with the royalists began. On June 13, Mohammad-Ali Shah demanded the arrest and exile of radical constitutionalists, including Mirza Jahāngir Khan and Malek al-Motakallemin. Members of more than 180 anjomans took over the adjoining Sepahsālār Mosque and hung their emblems on the doors of its rooms. Many supporters slept on the roof of the Majlis to shield it from an ambush. Sayyid Hasan Taqizādeh, a leading member of the First Majlis, continued to negotiate with the shah, who refused to back down. European powers complained that the anjomans had become too radical and were threatening the nation's stability. As a result, and as part of the negotiations with the shah, Taqizādeh and other deputies persuaded members of the anjomans to leave the premises, leaving that body defenseless.*

*On June 20, the day this column appeared, Mohammad-Ali Shah issued his conditions for ending the siege, a list that amounted to an end of the constitutional order (See Janet Afary,* Iranian Constitutional Revolution, *p. 141). On June 23 the shah's Russian troops under Colonel Liakhov indeed bombarded the Majlis, as most people (including Dehkhodā) had feared they would, and the constitution was suspended. The mojāhedin and members of several anjomans put up a fierce resistance before they were defeated. A number of constitutionalists were arrested; Mirza Jahāngir Khan and Malek al-Motakallemin were hanged the next day, while Dehkhodā took sanctuary at the British legation and eventually fled the country.*

Hey, come off it! Go get a new brain. Does one have to believe whatever someone says? If so, why was this brain installed in a person's skull? A human is supposed to be a creature that thinks. Otherwise, he's called an animal. If a reasonable man cooks twenty man [about 60 kilograms] of rice every day, he expects at the least—at the very least—to make five or ten shāhis on every ten tumans. Why is this? For nothing? Ha! You expect me to believe that? See this head? This head has lots of things in it. If at this late stage of my life I were to turn this head over to louts and thugs, I'd become just like them, wouldn't I?

This guy has a heavy growth of beard on his face, yet see what he was telling me yesterday. He was telling me that the government intends to mobilize its forces and bombard the Majlis with cannons. May God give you some brains and me a lot of money! Why would someone pitch camp from the back of the Tehran city gate to the other side of the world for the sake of a dilapidated, tumbledown building? Why would someone call up all those Tall Alis, Lance-Thrower Alis, street vendors, laborers, and porters in order to demolish a crumbling mansion from the time of the Sepahsālār? Tell me another![299] Pity the simpleminded souls of Tehran.

Someone else says, The shah wants first to occupy the whole of the Royal Garden with these troops, then to levy a force to capture Mehrabad, then Yangi Imam, and finally all of Iran.[300] I tell him, Man! If a person doesn't know something, let him say so; he doesn't have to make things up. I ask you, would any child believe that someone would spend money to levy one army after

299. Persian *Ahmaqi goft va ablahi bāvar kard* (with variants), "A fool said [it] and an idiot believed [it]"—a proverb decrying serial credulity. See Dehkhodā, *Amsāl va hekam*, vol. 1, p. 79. The Sepahsālār, or Generalissimo, Hajji Hoseyn Khan had become the chief minister in 1871, thirty-seven years before. Dehkhodā's sarcastic ridicule is of course disingenuous: the shah's target was not the old, dilapidated parliament building as such but rather the constitutionally elected national assembly within it.

300. The Royal Garden was on the west side of the old city of Tehran. Mehrabad was a village farther to the west, which later became the city's airport. Yangi Imam was a village halfway between Tehran and Qazvin. See *MD*, p. 203, notes 7–9.

another and announce to the world, I'm going to reconquer my kingdom, which I inherited from my father, who established a constitutional monarchy in the name of my family?[301] What kind of talk is that?

No, by God, these things cannot be. It's all a government ploy, a scheme, state secrets; heaven's sakes, one shouldn't broadcast everything one hears to the whole world!

Just to put some of the deputies' minds at rest, right now I'm going to tell you some of these secrets. But please, I beg of you, by my life and honor, don't tell them to any foreigners. They'll snap it up and write off home and divvy up the map of our country!

Do you know what the government really intends? It wants to mobilize these troops quietly, so nobody realizes what's afoot, just as the Ottomans, in the name of fighting the constitutionalists of Van,[302] raised an army and suddenly it came to light that they were really plotting a war with Russia. Our government likewise wants to mobilize this army quietly, in the name of destroying the Majlis and capturing Sayyid Jamāl and Malek[303] and any other constitutionalists, i.e., subversives. Listen carefully, and you'll learn what their real purpose is. Once mobilized, this force will be divided into two columns; the government will send one southward, ostensibly to pacify the Qashqā'i and Bakhtiyari tribes, and one

301. The 1906 revolution established a constitutional monarchy, with the Qajar family to reign in perpetuity.

302. Van is in eastern Turkey near the border with Iran. In the Ottoman Empire, agitation for a constitution had begun in the 1860s and succeeded in 1876. The sultan abolished the constitution in 1878, and it was not restored until the Young Turk Revolution in 1908.

303. The liberal clerics Sayyid Jamāl al-Din Vā'ez and Malek al-Motakallemin were arrested and executed after the coup.

northward, supposedly to subdue Azerbaijan. Then one dark night, the first column will board a few dozen boats in the Persian Gulf and in a surprise attack move toward England. Meanwhile, at the crack of dawn, the government will order the second column, with all their baggage, waterpots, food supplies, etc., loaded on forty or fifty donkeys, to quietly cross the border near Julfa via back roads and march into Russia. Then one morning Edward VII in London and Nicholas II in Saint Petersburg will wake up to find themselves in the hands of a score of Qarājeh-dāghi conscripts.[304]

Aye, may the Lord sharpen his sword! May he annihilate his foes! This is the plan hatched by Shāpshāl, since our Iranian brains are not up to such subtlety.

Satan tempts you: Sell all your belongings and give to these soldiers for this campaign, and they will bring you back foreign booty—carriage free, customs free. Your hundred tumans will bring you back five hundred, praise God. I've half a mind to go myself, but then I think, Wouldn't Shāpshāl be offended? Because he might think, This scoundrel has never set foot in Europe, and now he wants to establish a constitution there as well!

Anyhow, God grant them all safe passage.

Dakhow

---

304. Qarājeh-dāgh is a district in Iranian Azerbaijan, along the south bank of the river Aras, the border with Russia.

# *Sur-e Esrāfil*, Series 2, No. 1, pp. 7–8

January 23, 1909

## "The Speech of Kings Is the King of Speeches"

*Safe in Switzerland, having narrowly avoided the same fate as his murdered colleague Mirza Jahāngir Khan, and still grieving, Dehkhodā in his last three satirical columns feels no compunction about mocking the ruler and the Qajar family in frankly insulting terms. Now he freely refers to the royal family's supposed sexual indiscretions (in which category he includes rumors about socially liberated Qajar women), statements that prudence had tempered in his earlier publications.*

*As a sequel to this, again in his grammarian's role, the author humorously deconstructs the bombastic Arabic phrase of the title (*Kalām al-moluk moluk al-kalām, *recorded in his* Amsāl va hekam*). Alborz and Caspian languages such as Tāti, Gilaki, and Māzandarāni form such possessive noun phrases in the opposite direction to those of Arabic or Persian, i.e., modifier before head noun, thus* shaykh-e khar, *"the shaykh's donkey," versus Persian* khar-e shaykh, *"the donkey of the shaykh." Dakhow's pseudoexample, based on this principle, is comically tendentious: on the false analogy of a Persian appositive (not possessive) phrase, such as* shahr-e Tehrān, *"the city (of) Tehran," he coins a pseudo-Gilaki* shaykh-e khar, *"the ass (of a) shaykh, that ass the shaykh." (Thanks to Habib Borjian for clarification of the invalidity of this sleight of tongue.) Our linguist author is poking fun at Shaykh Fazlollāh Nuri and illustrating the vapidity of the title catchphrase, just after having done the same to Moshir al-Saltaneh's fatuous witticism.*

I always told myself that we the people need a king, so that if, say, we go to war with Russia, he can protect eighteen cities in the Caucasus so that the Russians don't capture them; if we have children, he will establish free schools so children are not raised illiterate and blind; if we have a parliament, he'll swear three times on the Qur'an, backed by appeals to his mother's chastity, to do his utmost to defend the parliament.[305]

Yes, we need to have a king for deeds like this. Yet I was at a loss to understand what is meant by "speech of kings," that it should be called the "king of speeches."

It is now five months, five days, five hours, and five minutes since I wrote my last *Charand-o Parand* column; that is, I had given up my one-and-a-half-year-old habit, and as every Iranian knows, giving up a habit makes one ill. For example, if the 180,000

305. Another ironic dig: cf. the reference to the Queen Mother below.

inhabitants of Rasht are not always trampled upon by fourteen or fifteen gofers, houseboys, masseurs, and bathroom attendants of the state, they become unwell; likewise the residents of Shiraz, Isfahan, Baluchistan, Khuzistan, Kermanshah, Luristan, the Zagros provinces, Kurdistan, or Yazd fall sick if they fail to provide annually several hundred virgin girls and thousands of beardless boys for the harems and bathhouses of their governors. Similarly, the late king Fath-Ali Shah Qajar, if he did not sleep two consecutive nights under the slide in the Negārestān palace,[306] felt unwell; and so did Nāser al-Din Shah if he didn't consort with his sister-in-law every day;[307] and if the Queen Mother, the mother of Nāser al-Din Shah, didn't put on chambermaid's clothes every night and consort with the guards and soldiers, she became unwell; and likewise Omm al-Khāqān, Hajji Nasir al-Saltaneh's wife, if she didn't spend some time each night in private with Mohammad-Ali Khan, she became ill.[308] Likewise Mohammad-Ali Mirza, if,

306. See *SE* no. 2, note 11 for the palace slides.

307. An allusion to the fact that Nāser al-Din Shah married two sisters, in violation of shari'a.

308. Despite her illustrious pedigree, the constitutionalist press vilified Omm al-Khāqān ("Mother of the monarch") because she was Mohammad-Ali Shah's mother. She was also a granddaughter of Nāser al-Din Shah, a daughter of Amir Kabir (ordered murdered by Nāser al-Din Shah, even though Amir Kabir was the king's son-in-law), and a wife of Mozaffar al-Din Shah. Her marriage to Mozaffar al-Din Shah unraveled because of court intrigues and especially her mother-in-law's hostility. Omm al-Khāqān was accused of sexual improprieties and machinations to avenge her father's death. After her divorce, she married several times, lastly to Nasir al-Saltaneh. Radical constitutionalists led by Mohammad-Reza Mosāvāt, the editor of the newspaper *Mosāvāt*, sent a list of her supposed improprieties to the bazaar for more signatures. Censuring this conduct, Kasravi writes about Mosāvāt, "If any of the constitutionalists deserved to be killed, it should have been him" (*Tārikh-e Mashruteh-ye Irān*, p. 594–95).

during the first year of his reign, he didn't consort with his aunt Tāj al-Saltaneh every day, became sick;[309] and Mojallal al-Soltān, the head of the royal harem employees, if he didn't eat forty to fifty egg yolks with cognac and lamb kebab each day, would become ill; or His Majesty the All-Powerful Shadow of God Mohammad-Ali Shah Qajar, if one night he wasn't closeted for a few hours with Mojallal; and finally, Mr. Moshir al-Saltaneh, if he didn't take a laxative every Friday, would be unwell; and if Amir Bahādor Jang didn't dye his beard with henna every Saturday morning, he would be ill. I was nearly sick myself. And all this time I was waiting until the newspaper could be printed again and after five months, five days, five hours, and five minutes I could enjoy the fruits of my labors on *Charand-o Parand*.

But, my dear brothers, when the facilities finally became available and I picked up my pen in breathless anticipation of resuming my habit, suddenly a letter arrived from one of my friends containing a document written in the luminous hand of His Majesty the Shadow of God in reply to telegrams from the hojjat al-eslāms of Najaf, which collided full tilt with my mood and aspirations.

On seeing this manuscript, not only did I confess myself unable to write a *Charand-o Parand*, but an important question that has

309. The title *mirzā*, "[crown] prince," is clearly obsolete if Mohammad-Ali had ascended the throne; Dehkhodā presumably retains it to characterize the new shah as too immature to recognize that his higher rank brings with it new obligations of propriety and decorum. Tāj al-Saltaneh (1884–1936) was a daughter of Nāser al-Din Shah and an aunt of Mohammad-Ali Shah. As a young feminist she broke with many social conventions of her time and became a leading member of some of the women's anjomans of the constitutional era. She was the subject of much gossip and malicious rumor because of her open lifestyle, though there is no indication that she had a liaison with her nephew. See her memoir, *Crowning Anguish*.

dogged me the whole of my life was resolved. This was the problem of "the speech of kings is the king of speeches."

God requite His Excellency Moshir al-Saltaneh, the prime minister of the victorious state of Iran; this time last year, when he bore the title of minister of the interior, he was sitting one day on the balcony overlooking his private garden, together with all the distinguished men and important notables of the state. While they were there, a herd of cattle passed in front of the building, and by chance a cow belonging to Moshir al-Saltaneh was at the head of the herd. His Excellency the Pivot of the Ministry, addressing those present, observed in regal tones, Distinguished gentlemen! The cow of the interior minister is likewise the interior minister of cattle.

Well, let's not wander from the point.

The point here is that the cow of the interior minister was likewise the interior minister of cattle, and in the Rashti [Gilaki] and Māzandarāni dialects, the Persian *khar-e Sheykh Fazlollāh*, "the donkey of Shaykh Fazlollāh," is expressed [in the reverse of the Persian word order] as *Sheykh Fazlollāh-e khar*, meaning [in Persian] "Shaykh Fazlollāh the donkey." Similarly, *harf-e pādshāh pādshāh-e harfhāst*, "the speech of kings is the king of speeches."

O literati of Iran! You have now been accustomed to Dakhow's style of balderdash for a year and a half, and you know full well the meaning of *charand-o parand*. Now read this royal missive and judge whether I have ever in all my life written such balderdash or whether you have ever read the like. Then you too, like Dakhow, will believe the saying "the speech of kings is the king of speeches," period.

# Response of Mohammad-Ali Shah to the Clerics of Najaf

*Three grand ayatollahs of Najaf, Mohammad Kāzem Khorāsāni, Abdollāh Māzandarāni, and Khalil Tehrāni, sent a petition to the Hague Tribunal and to several tribal leaders detailing the atrocities committed by the shah and asking for their support (for more on the involvement of these clerics, see Abdul-Hadi Hairi,* Shi'ism and Constitutionalism in Iran, *pp. 87–109). In addition, Khorāsāni sent a letter to the shah urging him to respect the wishes of the people and renounce his autocratic ways (see* SE, *series 2, no. 2, pp. 3–7, and no. 3, pp. 5–6). Here, after unexpectedly receiving a copy of the shah's reply to the clerics, Dehkhodā presents Mohammad-Ali Mirza's patronizing verbiage as "an unconscious self-parody" and the acme of its particular kind (see* Javadi, Satire in Persian Literature, *pp. 55–56).*

Peace be upon the esteemed triumvirate of Grand Clerics:

Through the agency of the esteemed Prime Minister, your telegram was observed, and it became evident that you do not yet have full intelligence of the original effects of that incident and of the assassination attempt which seditious sects made in regard to the Faith and the State,[310] from the evidence of their own writings which are extant and have been discovered, and that your information has actually been obtained through channels of foreign conspiracies and their domestic sympathizers.

---

310. On February 28, 1908, the secret leadership of the National Revolutionary Committee attempted to assassinate the shah with a bomb in an automobile moving ahead of his carriage. See Kasravi, *Tārikh-e Mashruteh-ye Irān*, p. 543.

Since all classes of the Iranian people, from the spiritual clergy, who are truly sympathetic toward Islam and Islamic people, to the ranks of merchants, tradesmen, village folk, and nomadic tribes, have found out about their dastardly tricks and have been generally horrified by these recent occurrences and rendered averse and hostile to the very word "constitution," they have been criticizing our manner of rendering assistance to the constitutionalists. So many petitions and complaints of oppression have poured into the court by mail and telegram from all over the Protected Realms that Iran seems in reality to have become a single wail of anguish. And if we were to continue to tolerate the heresy of these Mazdakites[311] and neglect to seek the spiritual assistance of the Grand Clerics, the suspicion is that our era will actually become the Age of Decline of the Faith and of the State of Iran both.

I swear by the pure essence of the Provider, by whose will the Kingship of Kings of the World subsists and who hath seated us firmly and victoriously on the throne of our crowned fathers (may they rest in peace), that in consequence of this event that has occurred we acknowledge ourselves before [Mohammad] the Lord of the Sacred Law to be worthy of the reward of holy warriors and strivers in the Manifest Faith, and thanks to God on High this day the Kingdom of Iran is in perfect order and the population absolutely calm, and the leading lights of the learned Grand Clerics and all the notables and celebrities in the whole of Iran daily express their gratitude by post and telegram, and the courtiers by the power of providence are all pious and observant of Islam—

311. Mazdak (d. ca. 524 or 528) was a religious leader and reformer in the late Sasanian Empire. He broke with many tenets of Zoroastrianism and established communal possession of property. Mazdakism has been called the earliest communist ideology, and it later influenced Manichaeism in Europe.

especially the Prime Minister, who over and above his competence is well known to those gentlemen for his dedication to Islam and piety.

We too, by the grace of Almighty God, are engaged with all our might in the promotion of the Sacred Law and religious practices, carrying out the precepts of Islamic law, and creating the means of justice for all, and we also previously had this sacred intention.

If a person was abused, one who according to the edict of the late Ayatollah Shirāzi had withdrawn from the [clerical] hierarchy and overstepped the bounds and revealed himself as the leader of the Corrupters on Earth, then it is his own fault. Anyone who abdicates his particular duties and oversteps the limits proper to him naturally will incur the same unpleasant consequences, whosoever he be.[312] We in our sacred purposes seriously hope that, during our auspicious reign, respect for the ulama of Iran and the hierarchy of senior mojtaheds and the propagation of the doctrine of the Family of Mohammad (God bless them every one) will surpass that of past monarchs and that the autonomy of the court of Iran, through the special favors shown by the King of the Religion of the Imam of the Age (may our souls be his sacrifice), will equal and compare with that of the great countries of the world. And we hope, please God, that through the favors vouchsafed by the Imam of the Age (God hasten his happy advent) the Lord will day by day encompass us with success so that the propagation of the Manifest Faith shall not be delayed a single minute.

Peace be upon him that followeth [God's] guidance.

312. E.g., the murdered clerics Malek al-Motakallemin and Sayyid Jamāl al-Din Vā'ez.

# Sur-e *Esrāfil*, Series 2, No. 2, pp. 7-8

February 6, 1909

## Political Economy

*Iranian social democrats had recently been introduced to the field of political economy and were busy making sense of works by Adam Smith and Karl Marx. The problem they faced was how to fit these new theoretical concepts to the reality in Iran. Socialists including Dehkhodā debated whether precapitalist Iranian society had to go through a capitalist stage of production before it could reach a utopian socialist order. While this column is another unrestrained attack on the shah and his supporters, it can also be read as a satire of Dehkhodā's cohort, young social democrats who couldn't make sense of their "scientific" understand-*

*ing of modern political economy and didn't understand why what they read in* The Wealth of the Nations, The Communist Manifesto, *and* Das Kapital *could not be applied to their Eastern nation.*

O Adam Smith, you who call yourself the father of economics! Meaning, I suppose, that no one on earth knows the science of economics better than you. If you really are the father of economics, why have you confined the prerequisites for the production of wealth to nature, labor, and capital and written at great length on the significance of these three things?

From these pronouncements of yours, it seems that unless one makes use of these three tools one is bound to starve to death. Hurrah, bravo for your intellect and acumen, bravo for your understanding and expertise! Now let's take a peek at the science of economics as practiced by the shah of Iran, and then be just a little ashamed of yourself—and reckon yourself no longer the leading scholar of economics!

My dear man: you yourself know that our sovereign does not work. Because he is the king. I mean that all over the world, wherever there is a king, he rules over everybody, so for such a person to work is simply out of the question.

Coming now to the question of nature: you have doubtless heard that ever since he picked up the habit of smoking a grain of opium every night, the shah of Iran's [digestive] nature has not functioned so well.[313]

And as for capital, you must have read in the press last year that in the month of Dhu'l-Qaʻda last he was so short of money that he pawned his wife's belongings at the Russian bank so that

313. Opium use leads to constipation.

he could wine and dine the rabble in Tupkhāneh Square for four days. So now, according to your theory, the shah will have to fold his arms and sit staring at Amir Bahādor while Amir Bahādor—as the Turks say—stares blankly back.

No, my dear Adam Smith, you are mistaken. Your science is still inadequate. You do not yet know that, besides nature, labor, and capital, wealth is produced by other means. No; in reality, neither does the shah sit staring at Amir Bahādor nor does Amir Bahādor stare blankly back. When the shah realized he was out of cash, Sattār Khan [with his army of mojāhedin] was pressing him from one side and the shah's boy concubines on the other side for their stipend. Do you know what he did? He ordered a dining cloth spread out in the royal court of Kayvān Madār. He gathered all the viziers, generals, officers, colonels, and mojtaheds around the edge of the cloth, had the crown prince sit in the middle of it, and summoned the barber. All at once, from, say, the folds of Shaykh Fazlollāh [Nuri]'s turban or the fringe of Prime Minister Moshir al-Saltaneh's shawl, out popped a sparrow and went flying around the room. The crown prince fixed his eyes on the sparrow, the barber finished his work [circumcising the crown prince], and suddenly you saw 152,000 hands reaching into pockets: shāhis, five-shāhi coins, silver ten-shāhis, and qerāns rained down on the cloth. When it was counted, God be praised, the money totaled 707 tumans and 2,011 shāhis.

Tell me now, where do you think this cash came from? Did nature help with this? Did the shah soil his hands? Or was any capital invested for the process?

Later, Ayn al-Dowleh was seen to pour this money into a large sack and, with a seemingly invincible army of forty thousand,

marched on Tabriz.[314] Sattār Khan did not hesitate and faced him
with two hundred men in battle. Naturally, this was scary enough
to make anyone drop seven hundred tumans, let alone seven thousand, and take flight. Sure enough, Ayn al-Dowleh left the re-
mainder of this cash and fled. Sattār Khan took it and distributed
it among the poor and hungry of Tabriz.

O Adam Smith! At this point, according to your theory, the
shah must simply succumb to God's grace and, as the saying goes,
lie down with his feet stretched out toward the Ka'ba [to die]. Ha,
ha! Bravo for your theory! Bravo for your intellect and acumen!

No, my dear fellow, the shah still doesn't react in this way. The
shah secretly diverted the state's rifles to the livestock market. He
lit a lantern, put it on top of the rifles, and called it a clearance sale.
He sold rifles worth a hundred tumans for fifteen each. That night
when they counted the take, the guns had brought in 345 tumans.

The very next day, the shah ascended the Keyāni throne bestowed on him by God. He summoned the Sharp Sword of Islam, the Stout Pillar of the Manifest Religion and Protector of
Islam and the Muslims, viz. our lord General Liakhov,[315] and gave
him his orders: According to a report submitted to His Sacred
and Imperial Majesty, a number of seditious troublemakers with
no other purpose than the ruin of the religion and the state and
the destruction of the foundation of Islam and the kingdom have

314. Ayn al-Dowleh's arrival at the siege of Tabriz and subsequent defeat
(August to October 1908) is briefly chronicled by Browne (*Persian Revolution*,
p. 256).

315. Colonel Vladimir Liakhov commanded the Persian Cossack Brigade
in the June 1908 coup against the Iranian Parliament. His promotion here to
*jenerāl* is a satirical touch.

stockpiled rifles in their homes to be used in rebellion and sedition. You are to search all their houses with your Russian Cossacks specifically (since Muslim Cossacks are not *mahram*,[316] and it would be sacrilegious for their eyes to light upon Muslim women and children!), confiscate every rifle found, and impose a fine of fifteen tumans for each.

So the next day, General Liakhov with his Russian Cossacks raided people's houses—that is, charged in among the Muslim women and children and took back the rifles, plus a fifteen-tuman fine and ten tumans for vodka money, in the name of the Mojāhedin-e Eslām. Thus, those 345 tumans became 690 tumans, which would now pay for another military expedition.

Now, Adam Smith, please explain to me: Has this money in its present form been produced by nature? Or labor? Or capital?

So you are still naïve, your science is not complete. You have not yet earned the title of father of political economy. The father of political economy is the Jamshidian Monarch of the Angels of the Army, Most Noble Father of us Iranians, His Supreme Highness the Omnipotent, Pride of the Firmament, of Ancient Glory and Permanent, Rustam of the Battle Charge . . . Mohammad-Ali Shah Qajar.

I rest my case.

---

316. The state of being a close family member, and thus having access to the women's quarters.

# *Sur-e Esrāfil*, Series 2, No. 3, p. 8

March 8, 1909

## Draft of a Royal Letter to the Swiss Parliament

*Unlike the shah's letter in* SE, *series 2, no. 1, this specimen is undoubt-edly attributable to Dehkhodā. The bastinado was a peculiarly Iranian form of discipline, designed to inflict severe pain without breaking a limb. The two essential implements mentioned here are the switch or cane (*chub*) and the* falak *or* falakeh *(in Central Asia,* fallāq*). In its basic form, the latter is a wooden pole with a slackened cord tied at each end to make a loop; the victim is laid on his back with his legs stretched out in front, and the cord is looped over his ankles and tight-ened by twisting the pole, which is held by two men so that his legs are* *immobilized while a third canes the soles of his feet (for a more detailed description, see* MD, *p. 222, note 10; Sadriddin Aini,* Sands of Oxus, *p. 229; and a photograph in W. P. Cresson,* Persia, *facing p. 106). The author's final potshot at the* pādshāh *(with a nod to the royal economics as illustrated in the previous column) implies that the shah's ruinous policies may have left him without even the postage to mail his gift package to Bern.*

Let the Esteemed Parliament of Switzerland know, with all good intentions from his Imperial and Proud Majesty, that:

According to a report submitted to the presence of his Supreme and August Imperial Majesty, a group of sowers of sedition in our kingdom and enemies of religion and state, who propose no less than the abolition of the sovereignty conferred upon us by the Lord Almighty in his mature wisdom and cherish hopes of the overthrow of that authority which our noble ancestors won for us by dint of the sword, have congregated in the jurisdiction of that esteemed entity [the Swiss Parliament].

Whereas the degree of competence, expertise, capability, and international goodwill of that esteemed entity has long been noted by our keen imperial eye, and continues so to be, we know that it will spare nothing in the way of expense or even life and limb to comply with the royal commands.

Accordingly, by this luminous rescript we instruct that esteemed entity, at first perusal of this definitive royal edict, to apprehend the aforesaid miscreants—who are bereft of the ornament of loyalty and, consequently, in the sight of the Lord also are void of all religion and piety—and pillory them in front of the government building, and to flog them so long as the government functionaries have strength and stamina, until their skins and bones show the effects, so that they be a lesson to the spectators and a warning to all other rebels, and so that thereafter they will know that monarchy is a divine trust vouchsafed to us by Almighty God, and nobody has the right to disobey our Imperial Majesty or to shrug off the yoke of the *yāsā* and *tozuk* of our administration.[317]

And since it has been reported to our Majesty's firmament-firm court that the proper bastinado equipment is hard to come by [over there], we have instructed the personnel of the Royal Office of Corporal Punishment to pick from the Royal Garden in Tehran, the center of our rule and of the jurisdiction of our government, a bundle of pomegranate switches, which are the very template of "fire from the green tree,"[318] and to send this together with one first-rate, decorated falakeh to your esteemed address.

That esteemed entity may rest assured in regard to customs dues and carriage fees for the items dispatched. His Excellency General Liakhov has promised within the next few days, through

317. *Yāsā* and *tozuk* are Turco-Mongolian terms for the customary laws further codified by Chengiz (Genghis) Khan and Timur (Tamerlane). The Qajars consciously revived these words, though not the full extent of their meaning, together with other Mongol terms in Persian (e.g., *khāqān*, "paramount chief," for the head of the ruling Qajar clan). The word translated here as "administration" (*siāsat*), now the usual Persian term for "policy, politics," originally in Arabic referred to horse breaking and training and in Persian by Mongol times usually meant judicial torture or execution.

318. From Qur'an 36:80, illustrating God's creative power. The tree is probably the Arabian *markh* (*Cynanchum viminale*), whose branches are leafless and were used to make fire by rubbing them against another piece of wood. It is said that when the wind tangles and rubs the branches together, they sometimes spontaneously combust (Edward W. Lane, *Arabic-English Lexicon*, part 7).

the agency of his esteemed friend Mr. Hartwig,[319] to send us a considerable sum he has acquired from his own country. And in the event that nothing arrives from there, we have issued orders that Field Marshal Ayn al-Dowleh, the commander in chief of the imperial forces and leader of the glorious Iranian army, is to raid the English post office for the fifth time and deliver the proceeds to the royal treasury.

In any case, let the mind of that esteemed entity rest completely easy on this score, that if neither of these eventualities materializes, we will arrange for His Royal Highness our most dear and august child, the Crown Prince endorsed of heaven of this axial realm, to be circumcised a second time.

Purely out of good wishes and altruism, we have sent as a gift from our royal wardrobe to that esteemed entity a rich garment of dark red cashmere with a jeweled sunburst, to be a source of pride to the wearer and the envy of all and sundry.

It is on record that the accountants and secretaries acknowledge their duties to transcribe this authoritative edict into the permanent archives and ledgers.

Written on this fourth day of Dhu'l-Hijja in the Year of the Ox of auspicious omen, 1326 [December 28, 1908].

319. Nikolai H. Hartwig was the Russian minister (ambassador) at Tehran in 1906–9. A passionate pan-Slavist, in 1913 he was in Belgrade, goading the Serbian government into confrontations with Austria.

# Bibliography

Several of the following works will be particularly useful for further reading and general reference. These include publications directly concerning the Constitutional Revolution (by Ādamiyat, Afary, Bayat, Browne, Ettehadieh, Kasravi, Kermāni, Minuchehr, Mozaffari, Nabavi, Najmabadi, Soroudi, and Vejdani) and *Sur-e Esrāfil* or *Charand-o Parand* (by Afshār, Atabaki, Barāheni, Chehabi and Martin, Dorri, Yazdāni, and Yousofi). Edward Granville Browne's *The Press and Poetry of Modern Persia* has a detailed running chronology of the revolution (December 1905–April 1912, pp. 310–36), and both this and his *Literary History of Persia* have excerpts from *Charand-o Parand* in translation. In Christophe Balaÿ and Michel Cuypers, *Aux sources de la nouvelle persane*, part 2 by Balaÿ, "'Ali Akbar Dehkhodâ et les *Čarand parand*" (pp. 51–106), has nine excerpts in translation from *Charand-o Parand* essays, together with structural analysis and commentary (pp. 65–101).

Aarne, Antti, and Stith Thompson. *The Types of the Folk-Tale: A Classification and Bibliography*. 2nd revision. FF Communications 184. Helsinki: Academia Scientiarum Fennica, 1961.

'Abduh, Muhammad. *The Theology of Unity.* Translation by Ishaq Musa'ad and Kenneth Cragg of *Risālat al-Tawhid.* London: George Allen and Unwin, 1966.

Ādamiyat, Fereydun. *Ideolozhi-e Nehzat-e Mashrutiyat-e Irān.* Vol. 1. Tehran: Payām Publications, 2535/1977.

Afary, Janet. "The Contentious Historiography of the Gilan Republic in Iran." *Iranian Studies* 28 (1995), pp. 3–24.

————. *The Iranian Constitutional Revolution: Grassroots Democracy, Social Democracy, and the Origins of Feminism, 1906–11.* New York: Columbia University Press, 1996.

————. "Peasant Rebellions of the Caspian Region During the Iranian Constitutional Revolution." *International Journal of Middle Eastern Studies* 23 (1991), pp. 137–61.

————. *Sexual Politics in Modern Iran.* Cambridge and New York: Cambridge University Press, 2009.

Afshār, Iraj. "Sur-e Esrāfil." *Āyandeh* nos. 7–9 (Mehr–Āzar 1358/1979), pp. 509–63.

Aini, Sadriddin [Sadr al-Din 'Ayni]. *The Sands of Oxus: Boyhood Reminiscences of Sadriddin Aini.* Annotated translation by John R. Perry and Rachel Lehr of part 1 of *Yoddosht'ho* and two novellas. Costa Mesa: Mazda, 1998.

Ākhundzādeh, Mirza Fath-Ali. *Maktubāt.* Ed. M. Sobhdam. [Düsseldorf]: Mard-e Emruz, 1364/1985.

Alavi, Abu'l-Hasan. *Rejāl-e 'asr-e Mashrutiyat.* Edited by Habib Yaghmā'i, further (2nd impression) by Iraj Afshār. Tehran: Asātir, 1363/1984.

Alavi, Bozorg. *Geschichte und Entwicklung der modernen persischen Literatur.* Berlin: Akademie-Verlag, 1964.

Algar, Hamid. *Religion and State in Iran, 1785–1506.* Berkeley: University of California Press, 1969.

Allworth, Edward A., ed. *The Personal History of a Bukharan Intellectual: The Diary of Muhammad-Sharif-i Sadr-i Ziyā*. Translated from the original manuscript by Rustam Shukurov; with an introductory study and commentaries by Muhammadjon Shakuri [Shukurov]; project director Shahrbanou Tadjbakhsh. Leiden and Boston: Brill, 2004.

Amanat, Abbas. *Resurrection and Renewal: The Making of the Babi Movement*. Ithaca, NY: Cornell University Press, 1989.

Amini, Amir-qoli. *Farhang-e 'avām, yā tafsir-e amsāl va estelāhāt-e zabān-e Pārsi*. Tehran: Elmi, [1960s].

Atabaki, Touraj. "Sur-e Esrāfil payāmāvar-e tajaddod-e Irāni bud." *Tārikh-e Irān*. 15 Ābān 1391 [2012]. Accessed November 4, 2012. http://tarikhirani.ir/fa/files/21/listView.

Balaÿ, Christophe, and Michel Cuypers. *Aux sources de la nouvelle persane*. Paris: Éditions Recherche sur les civilisations, 1983.

Bāmdād, Mahdi. *Sharh-e hāl-e rejāl-e Irān qorun-e 12–13–14* [Dictionary of national biography of Iran, 1700–1960]. 5 vols. Tehran: Zavvār, 1347/1968–69.

Barāheni, Rezā. "Tanz-e Dehkhodā va ta'sir-e nasr-e Dehkhodā bar ru-ye nasr-e mo'āser." In *Qesseh-nevisi*, pp. 508–21. Tehran: Sāzmān-e enteshārāt-e Ashrafi, 1348/1969.

Bayat, Mangol. *Iran's First Revolution: Shi'ism and the Constitutional Revolution of 1905–1909*. New York: Oxford University Press, 1991.

Browne, Edward Granville. *A Literary History of Persia*. Vol. 4, *Modern Times (1500–1924)*. Cambridge: Cambridge University Press, 1928; reprint, 1930, 1953, 1959.

———. *The Persian Revolution of 1905–1909*. Cambridge: Cambridge University Press, 1910; reprint, New York, 1966; Washington DC, 1995.

———. *The Press and Poetry of Modern Persia: Partly Based on the Manuscript Work of Mirzá Muhammad 'Alí Khán "Tarbiyat" of Tabriz.*

Cambridge: Cambridge University Press, 1914. Reprint, Los Angeles: Kalimát, 1983.

————. *A Year Amongst the Persians: Impressions as to the Life, Character and Thought of the People of Persia Received During Twelve Months' Residence in That Country in the Years 1887–1888*. London, 1891. 2nd ed., Cambridge: Cambridge University Press, 1926; reprint, 1927; 3rd ed., 1950; reprint, 1959, 1970.

Chehabi, H., and V. Martin, eds. *Iran's Constitutional Revolution: Popular Politics, Cultural Transformations and Transnational Connections*. London: I. B. Tauris, 2010.

Cole, Juan R. I. *Modernity and the Millennium: The Genesis of the Baha'i Faith in the Nineteenth-Century Middle East*. New York: Columbia University Press, 1998.

Cresson, W[illaim] P[enn]. *Persia: The Awakening East*. Philadelphia and London: J. R. Lippincott, 1908.

*Dakhownámeh: Hekáyát va dástánhá-ye Dakhow bá tasvir-e rangi*. Tehran: Hajji Mohammad-Ali Elmi Bookstore and Press, 1338/1959.

Dehkhodā, Ali-Akbar. *Amsál va hekam*. 4 vols. Tehran: Amir Kabir, 1339/1960.

————. *Charand-o Parand*. In *Sur-e Esráfil*, Year 1, nos. 1–32 (17 Rabi' II 1325/May 30, 1907–20 Jumādi I 1326/June 20, 1908), Tehran, weekly; Year 2, nos. 1–3 (1 Muharram 1327/January 23, 1909–15 Safar 1327/March 8, 1909), Yverdon, Switzerland, intermittent.

————. "Charand-o Parand." In Sa'id Nafisi, ed., *Shāhkārhā-ye nasr-e fársi-e mo'áser*, vol. 1, pp. 35–174. Tehran: Kānun-e Ma'refat, 1330/1951, 1336/1957.

————. *Charand-o Parand*. Tehran: Ketāb-e Jibi, 1341/1962.

————. *Charand Parand*. Ed. Sayyed Ali Shāheri-Langarudi. 4th impression. Tehran: Majid, 1391/2012.

————. *Divān-e Dehkhodā*. Ed. Mohammad Dabirsiāqi. 3rd impression. Tehran: Tirāzheh, 1362/1983.

————. "Inshallah gurbah ast: 'God Willing, It's a Cat.'" Annotated English translation by Paul Losensky. *Iranian Studies* 19 (1986), pp. 31–45.

————. *Loghatnāmeh* [Lexicon]. 136 folio fascicles in various bindings. Tehran: Majlis, University of Tehran Press, 1939–75; rev. ed. in 15 vols., 1993–94.

————. *Maqālāt-e Dehkhodā*. Ed. Mohammad Dabirsiāqī. Vol. 1. Tehran: Faridun Elmi, 1358/1980. Includes all *Charand-o Parand* columns from *Sur-e Esrāfil*, with notes, pp. 3–223, plus later columns with this heading published in *Irān-e konuni*, pp. 224–72.

————. *Nāmeh'hā-ye siyāsi-e Dehkhodā*. Ed. Iraj Afshār. Tehran: Ruzbehān, 1358/1979.

Dehkhodā, Mirza Ali Akbar Khan, and Mirza Jahāngir Khan "Sur-e Esrāfil." *Sur-e Esrāfil*. Facsimile edition of the complete run, 1325/1907–1327/1909. Tehran: Nashr-e Tārikh-e Irān, 1361/1982.

Destrée, Annette. *Les fonctionnaires belges au service de la Perse, 1898–1915*. Leiden: Brill; Tehran and Liège: Bibliothèque Pahlavi, 1976.

Dorri, Dzh[ehangir]. *Persidskaia satiricheskaia proza: Traditsiia i novatorstvo*. Moscow: Nauka, 1977.

*Encyclopaedia Iranica*. Ed. Ehsan Yarshater. Multiple vols. New York: Encyclopaedia Iranica Foundation, 1983–. Selected articles available online at www.iranicaonline.org.

*The Encyclopaedia of Islam*. New [2nd] edition. Ed. H. A. R. Gibb et al. 12 vols. and supps. Leiden: Brill; London: Luzac, 1960–2002.

Eskandari-Qajar, Manouchehr M. "Novellas as Morality Tales and Entertainment in the Newspapers of the Late Qajar Period: Yahyā Mirza Eskandari's 'Eshgh-e Doroughi' and 'Arousi-e Mehrangiz.'" *Iranian Studies* 40 (2007), pp. 511–28.

————. "*Shajarehnameh* Project: Eskandari-Qajar (Kadjar)." Accessed July 7, 2015. http://www.qajarpages.org/eskandari.html.

Ettehadieh [Nezam Mafi], Mansoureh. *Peydāyesh va tahavvol-e ahzāb-e siyāsi-e Mashrutiyat: Dowreh-ye avval va dovvom*. Tehran: Gostardeh, 1361/1982.

Floor, Willem. "Hospitals in Safavid and Qajar Iran: An Enquiry into Their Number, Growth and Importance." In Fabrizio Speziale, ed., *Hospitals in Iran and India, 1500–1950s*, pp. 37–116. Leiden and Boston: Brill, 2012.

———. "A Note on Persian Cats." *Iranian Studies* 36 (2004), pp. 27–42.

———. "Les premières règles de police urbaine à Teheran." In C. Adle and B. Hourcade, eds., *Téhéran: Capitale bicentenaire*, pp. 173–98. Paris and Tehran: Institut français de recherche en Iran, 1992.

———. *Public Health in Qajar Iran*. Washington DC: Mage, 2004.

Gheissari, Ali. *Iranian Intellectuals in the Twentieth Century*. Austin: Texas University Press, 1997.

Hāfez-i Shirāzi, Khwājeh Mohammad Shams al-Din. *Divān*. Ed. Mohammad Foroughi and Qāsem Ghani. Tehran: Sinā, n.d.

Hairi, Abdul-Hadi. *Shi'ism and Constitutionalism in Iran: A Study of the Role Played by the Persian Residents of Iraq in Iranian Politics*. Leiden: Brill, 1977.

Hedāyat, Sādeq. *Hāji Āghā: Portrait of an Iranian Confidence Man*. Translated by G. M. Wickens; introduced by Lois Beck. Texas: Center for Middle Eastern Studies, University of Texas at Austin, 1979.

———. *Hājji Āghā*. Tehran: Jāvidān, 2536/1977.

———. *Neyrangestān*. With illustrations by Ardeshir Mohassess. Irvine, CA: Iranzamin, 1365/1986.

Hegland, Mary Elaine. "Two Images of Husain: Accommodation and Revolution in an Iranian Village." In Nikki R. Keddie, ed., *Religion and Politics in Iran: Shi'ism from Quietism to Revolution*, pp. 218–63. New Haven, CT: Yale University Press, 1983.

Jamālzādeh, Sayyid Mohammad-Ali. *Farhang-e loghāt-e 'ammiyāneh*. Ed. M.-J. Mahjub. Tehran: Ebn-e Sinā, 1341/1962.

————. *Yeki bud, yeki nabud.* Winter Park, FL: Kānun-e Maʻrifat, 1363/1984.

Javadi, Hasan. *Satire in Persian Literature.* Rutherford, NJ: Fairleigh Dickinson University Press, 1988.

————. "ʻYād ār ze shamʻ-e mordeh . . .'-ye Dehkhodā." *Daftar-e Honar* 19–20, no. 21 (Farvardin 1392 / March 2013), special issue on Dehkhodā, pp. 3262–65.

Kai Kāʼūs b. Iskandar b. Qābūs b. Washmgīr. *Qābūs-nāma.* Ed. Reuben Levy. London: Luzac, 1951. Translated by Levy as *A Mirror for Princes: The Qābūs Nāma.* London: Cresset, 1951.

Kamshad, H. K. *Modern Persian Prose Literature.* Cambridge: Cambridge University Press, 1966.

Kasravi, Ahmad. *Tārikh-e Hejdah-sāleh-ye Āzarbāyjān, bāzmāndeh-ye Tārikh-e mashruteh-ye Irān.* Vol. 1. Tehran: Amir Kabir, 1333/1954.

————. *Tārikh-e Mashruteh-ye Irān.* Tehran: Amir Kabir, 1330/1951.

Kazemzadeh, F[iruz]. "The Origin and Early Development of the Persian Cossack Brigade." *American Slavic and East European Review* 15, no. 3 (October 1956), pp. 351–63.

Keddie, Nikki R. *An Islamic Response to Imperialism: Political and Religious Writings of Sayyid Jamāl ad-Dīn "al-Afghānī".* Berkeley: University of California Press, 1983.

Kermāni, Mirza Āqā Khan. *Seh Maktub.* Ed. Bahrām Chubineh. Essen: Nima Verlag, 2000.

Khārābi, Fāruq. *Anjomanhā-ye ʻasr-e Mashruteh.* Tehran: Moʼassaseh-ye Tahqiqāt va Towseʻeh-ye Olum-e Ensāni, 1385/2007.

Lakhnavi, Āftāb Rāy. *Tazkereh-ye riāz al-ʻārefin.* Ed. S. H. Rāshedi. 2 vols. Islamabad, 1977–82.

Lane, Edward W. *An Arabic-English Lexicon.* Ed. Stanley Lane Poole. 8 parts and suppl. in 8 vols. London and Edinburgh, 1863–93. Reprint, New York: F. Ungar, 1955–56; Beirut: Librairie du Liban, 1968; New Delhi: Asian Educational Services, 1985.

Mahdavi, Shireen. "All About Money: The Birth of Iran's Modern Monetary System." *The Iranian*, September 6, 2000. Accessed June 19, 2013. http://iranian.com/History/2000/September/Mint/index.html.

*Majlis* [Parliament/Assembly]. Ed. Sayyid Mohammad Sādeq. 1906–11.

Malekzādeh, Mahdi. *Tārikh-e Enqelāb-e Mashrutiyat-e Irān*. 7 vols. Tehran: Elmi, 1363/1984; reprint, 1371/1992; Tehran: Sokhan, 1383/2004.

Martin, Vanessa. *The Qajar Pact: Bargaining, Protest and the State in Nineteenth-Century Persia*. London: I. B. Tauris, 2005.

———. "Shaikh Fazlallah Nuri and the Iranian Revolution, 1905–09." *Middle Eastern Studies* 23, no. 1 (January 1987), pp. 39–53.

Matthee, Rudolph P., Willem M. Floor, and Patrick Clawson. *The Monetary History of Iran from the Safavids to the Qajars*. London and New York: I. B. Tauris, in association with the Iran Heritage Foundation, 2013.

Minuchehr, Pardis. "Writing in Tehran: The First Freedom of Press Law." In H. Chehabi and V. Martin, eds., *Iran's Constitutional Revolution: Popular Politics, Cultural Transformations and Transnational Connections*, pp. 225–38. London: I. B. Tauris, 2010.

Mojābi, Javād. "Dar bāreh-ye *Sur-e Esrafil* ke mashhurtarin ruznāmeh-ye mashruteh bud." In "*Sur-e Esrāfil* ru-ye pishkhwān-e tārikh." Special issue, *Tārikh-e Irān*. 23 Khordād 1390 [June 13, 2011]. Accessed November 25, 2013. Available at http://tarikhirani.ir/.

Mojtahedi, Mahdi. *Rejāl-e Āzarbāyjān dar 'asr-e Mashrutiyat*. Tehran: Naqsh-e Jahân, 1327/1948.

Mojtahed-Zadeh, Pirouz. *Small Players of the Great Game*. London: RoutledgeCurzon, 2004.

Momen, Moojan. *An Introduction to Shi'i Islam*. New Haven, CT: Yale University Press, 1985.

Mozaffari, Nahid Nosrat. "Crafting Constitutionalism: Ali Abkar Dehkhoda and the Iranian Constitutional Revolution." PhD diss., Harvard University, 2001.

————. "An Iranian Modernist Project: Ali Akbar Dehkhoda's Writings in the Constitutional Period." In H. Chehabi and V. Martin, eds., *Iran's Constitutional Revolution: Popular Politics, Cultural Transformations and Transnational Connections*, pp. 193–212. London: I. B. Tauris, 2010.

————. "Visions of Secularity in Constitutional Iran." In Marion Eggert and Lucian Hölscher, eds., *Religion and Secularity: Transformations and Transfers of Religious Discourses in Europe and Asia*, pp. 155–74. Leiden: Brill, 2013.

Nabavi, Negin. "Readership, the Press, and the Public Sphere in the First Constitutional Era." In H. Chehabi and V. Martin, eds., *Iran's Constitutional Revolution: Popular Politics, Cultural Transformations and Transnational Connections*, pp. 213–23. London: I. B. Tauris, 2010.

Najafi, Abu'l-Hasan. *Farhang-e Fārsi-e 'āmmiyāneh*. 2 vols. Tehran: Nilufar, 1378/1999.

Najmabadi, Afsaneh. *The Story of the Daughters of Quchan: Gender and National Memory in Iranian History*. Syracuse, NY: Syracuse University Press, 1998.

Nejāt, Amir. *Jam'iyat'hā-ye Serri va Farāmasyunari*. San Mateo, CA: Eastern Publishing Society, n.d.

Nuh, Nosratollāh. *Barrasi-ye tanz dar adabiyāt va matbu'āt-e Fārsi*. Introduction by Mohammad Ja'far Mahjub. San Jose, CA: Kāveh, 1996.

Nuri, Shaykh Fazlollāh. *Lavāyeh-e Shaykh Fazlollāh Nuri*. Ed. Homā Rezvāni. Tehran: Nashr-e Tārikh-e Irān, 1983.

Pirnazar, Jaleh. "Chehreh-ye Yahud dar āsār-e seh nevisandeh-ye motajadded-e Irāni." *Iran Nameh* 13, no. 4 (1995), pp. 483–501.

Rajaee, Farhang. *Islamism and Modernism: The Changing Discourse in Iran*. Austin: University of Texas Press, 2007.

*Revue du monde musulman*. Published by La Mission scientifique du Maroc, 1906–26. Vols. 2–7 (1907–9).

Rossi, Ettore, and Alessio Bombaci, eds. *Elenco di drammi religiosi persiani (Fondo Mss. Vaticani Cerulli)*. Vatican City: Biblioteca apostolica vaticana, 1961.

"Shapshal (Szapszał) Seraya Ben Mordechai." *Jewish Virtual Library*. Accessed September 20, 2011. www.jewishvirtuallibrary.org/jsource/judaica/ejud_0002_0018_0_18216.html.

Soroudi, Sorour. "Sur-e Esrafil, 1907–08: Social and Political Ideology." *Middle Eastern Studies* 24 (April 1988), pp. 230–48.

Steingass, Francis Joseph. *A Comprehensive Persian–English Dictionary*. London: K. Paul, Trench, Trubner, 1892; reprint, 1930.

Sykes, P[ercy] M. *A History of Persia*. Vol. 2. London: Macmillan, 1915.

Taj al-Saltana. *Crowning Anguish: Memoirs of a Persian Princess from the Harem to Modernity, 1884–1914*. Translated by Anna Vanzan and Amin Neshati; edited with an introduction and notes by Abbas Amanat. Washington DC: Mage, 2003.

Tapper, Richard. *Frontier Nomads of Iran: A Political and Social History of the Shahsevan*. Cambridge: Cambridge University Press, 1997.

Vejdani, Farzin. "Crafting Constitutional Narratives: Iranian and Young Turk Solidarity, 1907–09." In H. Chehabi and V. Martin, eds., *Iran's Constitutional Revolution: Popular Politics, Cultural Transformations and Transnational Connections*, pp. 319–40. London: I. B. Tauris, 2010.

Wright, W[illiam]. *A Grammar of the Arabic Language*. 3rd ed. Revised by W. Robertson Smith and M. J. de Goeje. 2 vols. Cambridge: Cambridge University Press, 1933; reprint, 1951, 1955.

Yazdāni, Sohrāb. "Siāsat dar 'Charand-o Parand'-e Dehkhodā." *Majalleh-ye Takhassosi-ye Goruh-e Tārikh-e Dāneshgāh-e Tehrān* 4, no. 4 (1382/2003), pp. 207–43.

Yousofi, Gholam Hoseyn. "Dehkhoda's Place in the Iranian Constitutional Movement." *Zeitschrift der Deutschen Morgenländischen Gesellschaft* 125 (1975), pp. 117–32.

# Index

Naus, Joseph (director of customs), 108, 108*n*63

non-Muslims, 12, 26, 35, 36, 37, 62, 63, 63*n*74, 103*n*57. *See also* Armenians; Bābis; Bahā'is; Christians/Christianity; Jews/Judaism; Zoroastrians

Nosrat al-Dowleh, Prince, and murders in Kerman, 105–6, 150, 156, 160, 180, 186, 186*n*163, 241, 241*n*239, 259

Nuri, Shaykh Fazlollāh, 3, 97, 105*n*60, 132, 214, 226, 226*n*217, 257, 297, 300, 306; flight from Tehran, 35–36, 83*n*25, 105, 105*n*60; at Tupkhāneh Square, 194, 197, 201, 258

Obeyd-e Zākāni, 21, 29

opium, 23, 67–72, 74, 117, 169, 226, 305

*'orf* (customary law), 14, 34

Ottoman Turkey/Turks, 11, 31, 32, 36, 53–54*n*56, 140, 141*n*118, 144–46, 145*n*123, 148, 150, 175, 188, 206, 252, 256, 294

Parliament. *See* Majlis

peasants/villagers, 12, 13, 15, 17, 22–23, 24, 58, 70, 83, 85, 94*n*39, 111–21, 150, 155, 159, 161, 171*n*143, 179*n*155, 199, 265; and Shahrāshub, 230, 230*n*226; *Sur-e Esrāfil* on, 5, 6; voting rights, 13

political economy, 304–8, 305*n*312, 307*nn*313–14, 308*n*315

politics: Jāme'-e Adamiyat (Society of Humanity), 195–96, 195*n*174; needs of the people ignored, 244–50, 245*n*244, 246*nn*245–46, 248*n*247, 249*nn*248–49, 250*n*250; promises of authorities and politicians, 237–43, 238*nn*234–35, 239*nn*236–37, 241*nn*239–41, 242*n*243. *See also* bribery/corruption/intimidation

polytheism and monotheism (*shirk* and *tawhid*), 40, 41, 54–58

press. *See* journalism/newspapers

Privy Chamber, servants of (*'amaleh-ye khalvat*). *See* Qajars: court and harem

prostitutes, 48, 159, 269, 269*n*276

proverbs, use of. *See under* Dehkhodā, Ali-Akbar

provincial and departmental *anjomans. See anjomans*

Qajars: alleged improprieties, 102*n*54, 296, 298–99, 298*n*308; atrocities of, 49*n*50, 137–42, 140*nn*115–17, 141*nn*118–19; court and harem, 175–83, 179*n*155, 185, 185–86*n*155; regime and family members, 5, 38, 75–76*n*11, 176, 190*n*169, 234*n*232, 294*n*301, 296, 311*n*310; women, 49, 49*n*50, 176, 296, 298–99